WOMEN OF COLOR AND SOUTHERN WOMEN:

A BIBLIOGRAPHY OF SOCIAL SCIENCE RESEARCH, 1975 TO 1988

Annual Supplement, 1989

Edited by

Andrea Timberlake

Lynn Weber Cannon

Rebecca F. Guy

Elizabeth Higginbotham

Library of Congress Cataloging-in-Publication Data
(Revised for volume supplement)

Women of color and southern women.

    Kept up to date by annual supplements.
    Includes indexes.
    1. Minority women--United States--Bibliography.
2. Women--Southern States--Bibliography. I. Timberlake,
Andrea.
Z7964.U49W637 1988 (HQ1421) 016.305.4'0975 89-63010
ISBN 0-9621327-0-5

ISBN 0-9621327-1-3

A publication from *The Research Clearinghouse and Curriculum Integration Project on Women of Color and Southern Women*, Lynn Weber Cannon, Project Director, Center for Research on Women, Memphis State University, Memphis, TN 38152

Supported in part by a grant from the Fund for the Improvement of Post-Secondary Education and contributions from the Office of Planning and Public Service, the College of Arts and Sciences, the Department of Sociology and Social Work, Memphis State University, Memphis, TN 38152

CONTENTS

INTRODUCTION

This 1989 bibliography supplements the original bibliography, *Women of Color and Southern Women: A Bibliography of Social Science Research 1975 to 1988,* published in 1988; both are produced by the Center for Research on Women at Memphis State University. The Center's mission is to promote, conduct and disseminate social science and historical scholarship on women of color in the United States and women of the southern United States. To that end, the Center has undertaken numerous projects in addition to these bibliographies. Projects include: curriculum integration workshops, research institutes, working papers, annotated bibliographies, a newsletter, original research, and a Research Clearinghouse.

Presented in this bibliography are approximately 900 unique citations drawn from the 1200 references entered into our Research Clearinghouse on Women of Color and Southern Women during the first six months of 1989. The Research Clearinghouse is an on-line database of 4,500 bibliographic citations to recent (published or produced since 1975) social science research on these two groups of women. Citations cover books, chapters in books, published papers, unpublished works such as PhD dissertations, working papers or papers presented at meetings. This supplement is intended to make the latest scholarship available to users of the original bibliography, as well as to introduce new users to the burgeoning research on regional and racial/ethnic diversity among women in the United States.

Citations for this supplement were obtained from many of the same sources used for the 1988 bibliography; this is but a small portion of the research on women of color and southern women readily becoming available. Center staff regularly review journals, periodicals, newsletters, books, abstracts, vitae, publishing house brochures and proceedings from pertinent research forums. Our National Advisory Board members, researchers in various disciplines, send materials to review for possible inclusion in the database. Also, approximately 200 scholars conducting research on southern women and women of color are included in our Human Resource File and submit their work for examination. In addition to alerting us to new materials, people from these two groups help in other ways, too: they distribute Center materials at professional meetings, encourage others to submit works to us, to use the Clearinghouse and to purchase the products of our labor.

The format of the supplement is the same as the original bibliography with six major subject headings: culture, education, employment, family, health and political activism/social movements. Under each of these headings, the racial ethnic categories remain the same. They are: African American, Asian American, Latina, Native American, comparative research on women of color and South. The South is defined to include Washington, DC and the following states: Alabama, Arkansas, Florida, Georgia, Kentucky, Louisiana, Maryland, Mississippi, North and South Carolina, Tennessee, Texas, Virginia and West Virginia. Both a keyword index and a first-author index again are included.

Each citation is accompanied by keywords used to describe, identify and define the content of the work. These keywords are taken from *A Women's*

Thesaurus, Mary Ellen Capek, ed. (New York: Harper and Row, 1987) and our own racial ethnic descriptor list. A sample citation section and the list of racial descriptors, both specific and general, follows this introduction.

Acknowledgements

We appreciate the ongoing efforts of our National Advisory Board. Members of the board are: Margaret Andersen, Maxine Baca Zinn, Helen Bannan, Kathleen Berkeley, Rosie Bingham, William Boone, Elsa Barkley Brown, Esther Ngan-Ling Chow, Earnstein Dukes, Joe R. Feagin, Mary Fredrickson, Cheryl Townsend Gilkes, Jacquelyn Hall, Rhoda Johnson, Jacqueline Jones, Julianne Malveaux, Vicki Mays, Sandra Morgen, Leith Mullings, Pamela Palmer, Jacqueline Pope, Clara Rodriguez, Vicki Ruiz, Sheryl Ruzek, Carol Stack, Rosalyn Terborg-Penn, Sarah Watts and Ruth Zambrana. We acknowledge the scholars of the Human Resource File for allowing us to review their work and for making themselves available for contact by users of the database.

None of the work of the Clearinghouse would have been completed without the labor of the Center's graduate assistants and work study students. The students who have most recently worked on this project are: Roy Barnes, Janet Mandanna, Shang-Bin Hsieh, Kristin Claar, Melissa Connelly, Weyni Ajanaku, Tanya Allison, Dinah Dickerson, Lori Bondon, Mary Beth Snapp, Hong-Xiang Sun and David Blackard. They now know more about proofreading, library reference rooms, page formatting and/or data entry than they ever wanted to know. Pat Jackson and Jo Ann Ammons, Center secretaries, have helped us keep track of forms, budgets, dates, people and loose ends.

Thanks y'all.

Andrea Timberlake

Lynn Weber Cannon

Rebecca F. Guy

Elizabeth Higginbotham

Memphis, Tennessee

1990

SAMPLE CITATIONS

BOOK: single author

citation number ——— 0006 Bethal, Elizabeth R.

author ———

keywords ———

(1981) Promiseland: A Century of Life in a Negro Community. Philadelphia, PA: Temple University. pp. 318.

History/ People of Color/ Social Environment/ Cultural Heritage/ Coping Strategies/ South Carolina/ Resistance

BOOK: two or more authors

publication date

0183 Rodriguez, Clara E.

second & third authors ———

Korrol, Virginia S. and Alers, Jose O. (1984) The Puerto Rican Struggle: Essays on Survival in the U.S. (2nd edition). Waterfront Press, Maplewood, NJ. 07040. pp. 151.

publisher information

Puerto Rican/ Survival Strategies/ Women of Color/ Latina/ Cultural Heritage/ Family/ Acculturation/ Support Systems

PUBLISHED ARTICLE: one or more authors

0345 Baranowski, T.

Bee, D. E., Rassin, D. K., et al. (1983) "Social Support, Social Influence, Ethnicity and the Breast Feeding Decision." Social Science and Medicine 17:21:pp. 1599-1611.

journal title & volume information

Infant Care/ Health Care/ Ethnicity/ Racial Factors/ Women of Color*/ Support Systems/ Cultural Influences/ Breast Feeding

UNPUBLISHED: dissertation

date degree conferred ———

0514 Mansfield, Betty

university conferring degree ———

(1980) "That Fateful Class: Black Teachers of Virginia Freedmen, 1861-1882." Dissertation: Catholic University of America, Washington, D.C. pp. 391. DAI 41(02A)773.

dissertation abstracts international information

African Americans/ People of Color/ Social History/ 19th Century/ Education/ Teachers/ Virginia/ South

vii

UNPUBLISHED: paper presented/working paper

0587 Fong, Pauline L.

date &

conference

(1976) "Economic Status of Asian Women." **Presented: Advisory Council on Women's Educational Programs. San Francisco, Ca.**

Asian American/ Women of Color/ Economic
Status/ Education/ Employment

0421 Brewer, Rose M.

(1987) "Troubled Passage: Labor, Family Formation and the Young Black Working Class." **Author: Department of Sociology, University of Minnesota, Minneapolis, MN. 55455.** Presented: American Sociological Association, Chicago, IL.

author's
current
address

African American/ Women of Color/ Social
Class/ Education/ Family/ Employment/
Higher Education/ Working Class/ Lower Class

CHAPTER IN A BOOK

0447 Eckford, Elizabeth

book
title

(1981) **"The First Day: Little Rock, 1957."** in <u>Growing Up Southern.</u> **Chris Mayfield.** New York: Pantheon. pp.257-261.

chapter
title
book
author

African American/ School Desegregation/
Education/ Civil Rights Movement/ South/
Arkansas/ Race Relations/ People of Color

RACIAL/ETHNIC DESCRIPTOR LIST

African American
African Caribbean
Arab
Asian
   Asian Pacific
   Chinese
   Filipino
   Japanese
   Korean
   Vietnamese
Asian American
   Asian Pacific American
   Chinese American
   Filipino American
   Japanese American
   Korean American
   Vietnamese American
Cajun
Caribbean
Caribbean American
Chicanos
Creole
Hawaiian
Latina
   Chicana

Cuban
Cuban American
Mexican
Puerto Rican
Latinos
Native American
   Apache
   Blackfeet
   Cherokee
   Cheyenne
   Comanche
   Creeks
   Eskimos
   Hopi
   Huron
   Navaho
   Paiute
   Plains
   Seminole
   Sioux
Pacific Islanders
People of Color*
Sikhs
Women of Color*

PARTIAL LIST OF SOURCES REVIEWED

JOURNALS/MAGAZINES:
American Anthropologist
American Journal of Sociology
American Indian Quarterly
American Sociological Review
American Visions
Birth Gazette
Catalyst
Children's Advocate
Contemporary Sociology
El Palacio
Feminist Issues
Feminist Studies
Feminist Teacher
Frontiers
Gender and Society
Hispanic Journal of Behavioral Sciences
Insight
Intercambios Femeniles
Internatl. Migration Review
Journal of American History
Journal of Health and Social Behavior
Journal of Ethnic Studies
Journal of Social & Behavioral Sciences
La Red/The Net
Living Blues
Phylon
Psychology of Women Quarterly
Radical America
Radical Teacher

Sage: A Scholarly Journal of Black Women
Signs: A Journal on Women in Culture and Society
Sociology of Education
Social Forces
Social Problems
Social Science Quarterly
Sociological Spectrum
Sociological Inquiry
Southern Exposure
Southern Sociologist
Teaching Sociology
Western Historical Quarterly
Women's Studies Quarterly

NEWSLETTERS/NEWSPAPERS/ OTHER:
Afro Scholar
Belles Lettres
Bureau of Labor Statistics News
Congressional Caucus for Women's Issues
Feminist Collections (U. of Wisc.)
Footnotes (ASA Newsletter)
Ford Foundation Letter
Interracial Books for Children Bulletin
NWSA-Perspectives
On Campus With Women
National Committee on Pay Equity
Minorities and Women in Business

Psychology of Women Newsletter
Sojourner: The Women's Forum
SE Women's Studies Assn
Newsletter
Southern Feminist
Span Speaking Mental Health
Research
      Ctr. Newsletter
SWS Network
The Unfinished Agenda
Women's Review of Books

Am. Indian Law Review
Bureau of Am. Ethnology Bulletin
California History
Chronicles of Oklahoma
Ethnology
Ethos
Immigration History Newsletter
Integrated Education
Journal for Scientific Study of
Religion
J. of Am. Ethnic History
Journal of Am. Indian Education
J. of Educational Psychology
J. of Educational Research

AUXILIARY SOURCES
AAUW Journal
Akwesasne Notes

The Center for Research on Women is a member of the National Council for Research on Women and regularly receives and reviews newsletters from member centers.

CULTURE

African American

0001   **Albert, Octavia V. Rogers**
(1988) <u>The House of Bondage, or Charlotte Brooks and Other Slaves</u>. New York: Oxford University Press. pp. 224. ISBN 0195052633.

Women of Color/ Writers/ Culture/ African American/ Living Conditions/ Slaves/ Charlotte Brooks/ Civil War/ Slavery/ History/ 19th Century/ Personal Narratives/ Reconstruction/ Literature/ Exploitation

0002   **Allen, Ernest, Jr.**
(1985) "Afro-American Identity: Reflections on the Pre-Civil War Era." <u>Contributions in Black Studies</u> 7:pp. 45-93.

Identity/ Self Concept/ African Americans/ People of Color/ Antebellum/ History/ 19th Century/ Cultural Influences

0003   **Babb, Valerie**
(1986) "The Color Purple: Writing to Undo What Writing Has Done." <u>Phylon</u> 47:2:pp. 107-116.

Women of Color/ Literature/ African American/ Feminist Writing/ Literary Arts/ Women's Culture

0004   **Bailey, Ronald**
(1988) "'Deep South' Revisited: An Assessment of a Classical Text." <u>UCLA Center for Afro-American Studies Newsletter</u> 11:2:pp. 10.

People of Color/ African Americans/ South/ Mississippi/ Reviews/ Race Relations/ Class Differences/ Social Structure/ Living Conditions/ Stratification/ Caste/ Culture

0005   **Bandarage, Asoka**
(1986) "Reflections from Texas." <u>Woman of Power</u> (Fall):4:pp. 36-44.

Women of Color/ African American/ Latina/ Biographies/ Community/ Social Values/ Spirituality/ Racial Discrimination/ Texas/ Sex Discrimination

0006   **Barnes, Annie S.**
(1987) <u>Single Parents in Black America: A Study in Culture and Legitimacy</u>. Bristol, IN: Wyndham Hall. pp. 162. ISBN 1556050240.

African Americans/ People of Color/ Single Parent Families/ Cultural Influences/ Life Styles/ Support Systems/ Family Structure/ Female Headed Households/ Single Mothers/ Single Fathers

0007   **Barnes, Annie S.**
(1975) "The Black Beauty Parlor Complex in a Southern City." <u>Phylon</u> 36(June):2:pp. 149-154.

Women of Color/ African American/ South/ Beauty Parlors/ Social Networks/ Community/ Subculture/ Women's Culture

0008   **Barnett, A. P.**
(1986) "Sociocultural Influences on Adolescent Mothers." in <u>The Black Family: Essays and Studies</u> (3rd Edition). Robert Staples. Belmont, CA: Wadsworth. ISBN

0534072186.

African American/ Social Influences/ Cultural Influences/ Adolescents/ Mothers/ Teenage Mothers/ Women of Color/ Early Childbearing

0009   Bass, M. A.
Owsley, D. W. et al. (1985) "Food Preferences and Food Prestige Ratings by Black Women in East Tennessee." <u>Ecology of Food and Nutrition</u> 16:1:pp. 75-83.

Women of Color/ African American/ Food/ South/ Tennessee/ Nutrition/ Diets/ Cultural Influences

0010   Bell, Roseann P.
Guy-Sheftall, Beverly. (1975) "Images of Black Women, An Introduction to an Unpublished Manuscript." <u>Southern Exposure</u> 3:pp. 62-63.

African American/ Images of Women/ Women of Color/ Stereotypes/ Women's Culture

0011   Bell, Roseann P.
Parker, Bettye J. and Guy-Sheftall, B. (eds.). (1979) <u>Sturdy Black Bridges: Visions of Black Women in Literature</u>. Garden City, NY: Anchor/Doubleday. pp. 422.

African American/ Poetry/ Women's Culture/ Women of Color/ Literary Criticism/ Literature/ Women's History/ Images of Women/ Writers/ Writing/ Race, Class and Gender Studies

0012   Bernstein, Dennis
Blitt, Connie. (1987) "Zora Neale Hurston: Genius of the South." <u>Helicon Nine: Journal of Women's Arts and Letters</u> (Spring):17-18:pp. 48-50.

South/ Zora Neale Hurston/ Cultural Heritage/ Literature/ Writing/ Writers/ Anthropology/ Folk Culture/ African American/ Women of Color

0013   Berry, Jason
Foose, Jonathan and Jones, Tad. (1987) <u>Up from the Cradle of Jazz: New Orleans Music Since World War II</u>. Athens, GA: University of Georgia Press.

People of Color/ Blues/ Music/ African Americans/ Jazz/ Culture/ Louisiana/ Musicians/ Entertainers/ South/ Music History

0014   Bock, Wilbur
(1979) "Farmer's Daughter Effect: The Case of the Negro Female Professionals." <u>Phylon</u> (Spring).

Professional Status/ Social Influences/ African American/ Women of Color/ Cultural Influences

0015   Boles, John B.
(1988) <u>Masters and Slaves in the House of the Lord: Race and Religion in the American South, 1740-1870</u>. Lexington, KY: University of Kentucky Press. pp. 256.

People of Color/ History/ 18th Century/ African Americans/ Essays/ Slavery/ Race/ South/ 19th Century/ European Americans/ Religion/ Churches/ Culture

0016   Braxton, Joanne Margaret
(1984) "Autobiography by Black American Women: A Tradition Within a Tradition." Dissertation: Yale University, New Haven, CT.

African American/ Women of Color/ Autobiographies/ Cultural Heritage/ Traditions/ Writing/ Literature

0017   Brown, Hallie Q.
(1988) <u>Homespun Heroines and Other Women of Distinction</u>. New York: Oxford University Press. pp. 352. ISBN 0195052374.

Women of Color/ Biographies/ African American/ Writers/ Women's History/ 18th Century/ 19th Century/ Women's Culture

0018   Brown-Guillory, Elizabeth
(1986) "Images of Blacks in Plays by Black Women." Phylon   47(September):3:pp.
230-237.
Literature/ Women of Color/ African American/ Drama/ Images of Women/ Theater/ Performing Arts/
Women's Culture

0019   Brown-Guillory, Elizabeth
(1988) Their Place on Stage: Black Women Playwrights in America. Westport, CT:
Greenwood Press. ISBN 0313259852.
Women of Color/ Drama/ Women's Culture/ African American/ Plays/ Writers/ Scripts/ Playwrights/
Entertainment/ Theatre/ Performing Arts

0020   Center for Afroamerican and African Studies
(1985) Black Immigration and Ethnicity in the United States. Ann Arbor:
University of Michigan Press. pp. 170. ISBN 0313243662.
African Americans/ Social History/ Ethnic Studies/ Demography/ Economics/ Immigrants/ People of
Color

0021   Christensen, Harold T.
Johnson, Leonard B. (1978) "Premarital Coitus and the Southern Black: A
Comparative View." Journal of Marriage and the Family 40(Nov):pp. 721-732.
Women of Color/ Coitus/ African American/ Sexuality/ South/ Sexual Permissiveness/ Comparative
Studies/ Sexual Behavior/ Premarital Relationships/ Cultural Influences

0022   Clark, Maxine L.
(1986) "Dating Patterns of Black Students on White Southern Campuses." Journal of
Multicultural Counseling and Development 14(April):2:pp. 85-93.
African American/ Male Female Relationships/ Higher Education/ South/ Dating/ Women of Color/
Dominant Culture

0023   Clarke, Cheryl
(1988) Living as a Lesbian. Ithaca, NY: Firebrand Books. pp. 96. ISBN 0932379125.
Women of Color/ Violence/ African American/ Anger/ Literature/ Life Styles/ Poetry/ Sex/ Lesbianism/
Lesbian Culture

0024   Collins, Patricia Hill
(1988) "Finding a Voice: The Black Women's Blues Tradition." Presented: Society
for the Study of Social Problems Annual Meeting, Atlanta, GA.
African American/ Women of Color/ Traditions/ Entertainment/ Culture/ South/ Social Movements/
Black Studies/ Music/ Blues

0025   Cuffaro, S. T.
(1978) "Discriminant Analysis of Sociocultural Motivation and Personality
Differences among Black, Anglo and Chicana Female Drug Abusers in a Medium
Security Prison." Dissertation: U.S. International University, San Diego, CA.
Women of Color/ Research Methods/ Chicana/ Latina/ Personality/ Treatment/ Drug Abuse/ Prisoners/
Socialization/ Correctional Facilities/ African American/ Motivation/ Behavior/ European American/
Comparative Studies/ Cultural Influences

0026   Darling, Marsha Jean
(1987) "The Disinherited Source: Rural Black Women's Memories." Michigan
Quarterly Review (Spring).
Women of Color/ Women's History/ African American/ Memory/ Testimonial Literature/ Rural Women/
Recall/ Oral Traditions/ Rural Conditions/ Research Methods/ Women's Culture

0027   **Davis, Allison**
Gardner, Burleigh B. et al. (1988) <u>Deep South: A Social Anthropological Study of Caste and Class</u>. Los Angeles: University of California Los Angeles Center for Afro-American Studies. (Originally published 1941)   pp. 567.
People of Color/ Caste/ African Americans/ Socioeconomic Status/ South/ Mississippi/ Social Structure/ Anthropology/ Social Stratification/ Class/ Culture/ Stratification/ Class Differences/ Economic Structure/ Social History/ 1930-1939

0028   **Diedrich, Maria**
(1986) "'My Love is as Black as Yours is Fair': Premarital Love and Sexuality in the Antebellum Slave Narrative." <u>Phylon</u>   47(September):3:pp. 238-247.
Sexual Behavior/ Premarital Relationships/ Antebellum/ History/ Slavery/ Slaves/ Oral Tradition/ Sexuality/ African American/ Social Attitudes/ Women of Color/ Women's Culture

0029   **Dillman, Caroline Matheny**
(ed.). (1988) <u>Southern Women</u>. New York: Hemisphere Publications.   pp. 226. ISBN 0891168389.
African American/ European American/ Cultural Identity/ Women of Color/ Images of Women/ South/ Plantations/ History

0030   **Drake, St. Clair**
(1988) <u>Black Folk Here and There: An Essay in History and Anthropology</u>. Los Angeles: University of California Los Angeles Center for Afro-American Studies. pp. 387.
People of Color/ African Americans/ Anthropology/ History/ Black Studies/ Ethnic Studies

0031   **Dubin, Steven C.**
(1987) "Symbolic Slavery: Black Representations in Popular Culture." <u>Social Problems</u> 34(April):2:pp. 122-140.
Women of Color/ Image/ Stereotypes/ Institutionalized Discrimination/ Bias/ Cultural Heritage/ Racial Discrimination/ Social Relations/ African American/ Popular Culture/ Material Culture

0032   **Ebele, Eko**
(1986) "Beyond the Myth of Confrontation: A Comparative Study of African and African-American Female Protagonists." <u>Phylon</u> 47(September):3:pp. 219-229.
Women of Color/ African American/ Images of Women/ Self Concept/ Identity/ Stereotypes/ Mother Daughter Relationships/ Cultural Influences

0033   **Ellis, W.**
(1980) "Exploratory Investigation of Potential Societal and Intra-familial Factors Contributing to Child Abuse and Neglect." Available: U.S. Department of Health and Human Services, Washington, DC. (Prepared in cooperation with National Committee for Black Child Development). pp. 59.
Women of Color/ African American/ Child Abuse/ Child Neglect/ Culture Conflict/ Economic Factors/ Social Influences/ Racial Discrimination/ Social Services/ Family Influence/ Family Relationships

0034   **Farley, Reynolds**
Allen, Walter R. (1987) <u>Differentiation and Stratification: Age Groups, Class, Gender, Race and Ethnic Groups</u>. New York: Russell Sage Foundation. pp. 493.
African Americans/ Economy/ European Americans/ Occupational Segregation/ Social Change/ Integration/ Social Inequality/ Education/ Segregation/ People of Color/ Diversity/ Racial and Ethnic Differences

0035   Fields, Barbara Jeanne
(1983) "The Nineteenth-Century American South: History and Theory." Plantation Society in the Americas 2(April):pp. 7-27.

South/ Culture/ People of Color/ Slavery/ History/ 19th Century/ African Americans/ Plantations/ European Americans/ Subculture

0036   Franklin, Clyde W. II
(1986) "Black Male-Female Conflict: Individually Caused and Culturally Nurtured." in The Black Family: Essays and Studies (3rd Edition). Robert Staples. Belmont, CA: Wadsworth. ISBN 0534072186.

African American/ Male Female Relationships/ Women of Color/ Cultural Influences/ Couples/ Personal Relationships

0037   Gates, Henry Louis
(ed.). (1988) The Schomburg Library of Nineteenth-Century Black Women Writers. New York: Oxford University Press. (30 Volumes) ISBN 0195052676.

African American/ Writing/ Women of Color/ Literary Tradition/ History/ 19th Century/ Research Resources/ Writers/ Literature/ Literary Arts/ Women's Culture

0038   Gatewood, Willard B., Jr.
(1976) "Kate D. Chapman Reports on the 'Yankton Colored People, 1889'." South Dakota History 7(Winter):1:pp. 28-35.

Women of Color/ African American/ History/ 19th Century/ South Dakota/ North Central/ Culture

0039   Gatewood, Willard B., Jr.
(1988) "Aristocrats of Color: South and North: The Black Elite, 1880-1920." Journal of Southern History 54(February):pp. 3-20.

People of Color/ Elites/ Upper Class/ African Americans/ South/ Social History/ North/ Culture

0040   Georgia Writer's Project
(1987) Drums and Shadows: Survival Studies among the Georgia Coastal Negroes. Athens, GA: University of Georgia Press.

People of Color/ Cultural Identity/ African Americans/ Culture Conflict/ South/ Georgia/ History/ 1930-1939/ Cultural Heritage/ Interviews/ Assimilation Patterns/ Survival Strategies

0041   Gilkes, Cheryl Townsend
Dodson, Jualyne. (1986) "Something Within: Social Change and Collective Endurance in the Sacred World of Black Christian Women." in Women and Religion in America: Volume Three--20th Century. Rosemary Reuther and Rosemary Keller (eds.). New York: Harper and Row. pp. 80-128.

African American/ Women of Color/ Religion/ Religious Practices/ Community/ Social Change/ Support Systems/ Churches/ Cultural Influences

0042   Gillespie, Diane
Spohn, Cassia. (1987) "Adolescents' Attitudes towards Women in Politics: The Effect of Gender and Race." Gender & Society 1(June):2:pp. 208-217.

Women of Color/ African American/ Cultural Influences/ Social Influences/ Images of Women/ Political Participation/ Race, Class and Gender Studies/ Adolescents/ Elected Officials/ Women's Roles

0043   Gilman, Sander L.
(1985) "Black Bodies White Bodies: Toward an Iconography of Female Sexuality in Late Nineteenth-Century Art, Medicine and Literature." Critical Inquiry

12(Autumn):1.

African American/ Women of Color/ Art Symbols/ Images of Women/ Sexuality/ Popular Culture/ Social History/ 19th Century/ Literary Arts/ Medical Sciences/ Iconography

0044   Ginorio, Angela B.
(1979) "A Comparison of Puerto Ricans in New York with Native Puerto Ricans, Caucasians, Black Americans on Two Measures of Acculturation: Gender Role and Racial Identification." Dissertation: Fordham University, New York, NY. DAI Vol. 40(B)983-84.

Latina/ Puerto Rican/ African American/ European American/ Women of Color/ Acculturation/ Gender Roles/ Cultural Identity/ Comparative Studies/ Ethnicity

0045   Gossage, Leslie
(1987) "Black Women Independent Filmmakers: Changing Images of Black Women." IRIS: A Journal about Women 17(Spring/Summer):pp. 4-11.

Women of Color/ African American/ Images of Women/ Film/ Mass Media/ Stereotypes/ Entertainment/ Women's Culture

0046   Hampton, Robert L.
(1986) "Race, Ethnicity, and Child Maltreatment: An Analysis of Cases Recognized and Reported by Hospitals." in The Black Family: Essays and Studies (3rd Edition). Robert Staples. Belmont, CA: Wadsworth. ISBN 0534072186.

People of Color/ Child Abuse/ Comparative Studies/ Family Violence/ Racial and Ethnic Differences/ African Americans

0047   Harrison, Daphne Duval
(1988) Black Pearls: Blues Queens of the 1920's. New Brunswick, NJ: Rutgers University Press. pp. 295.

Music/ Music History/ African American/ Entertainment/ Women of Color/ Performing Arts/ Women's History/ 1920-1929/ Blues/ Entertainers/ Popular Culture

0048   Higginbotham, Elizabeth
Watts, Sarah. (1988) "The New Scholarship on Afro-American Women." Women's Studies Quarterly 16(Spring/Summer):1&2:pp. 6-21.

African American/ Women of Color/ Social History/ Women's History/ Women's Culture/ Race, Class and Gender Studies/ Curriculum Integration/ Feminist Scholarship

0049   Hoffman, Nancy
(1986) "Black Studies, Ethnic Studies, and Women's Studies: Some Reflections on Collaborative Projects." Women's Studies Quarterly 14(Spring/Summer):1-2:pp. 49-53.

Women of Color/ African American/ Black Studies/ Ethnic Studies/ Women's Studies/ Social Science Research/ Research Methods/ Education/ Curriculum Integration

0050   Holloway, Karla F. C.
(1987) The Character of the Word: The Texts of Zora Neale Hurston. Westport, CT: Greenwood Press. pp. 146.

Women of Color/ African American/ Literature/ Authors/ Writers/ Biographies/ History/ Cultural Heritage

0051   Hopkins, Pauline E.
(1988) Contending Forces: A Romance Illustrative of Negro Life North and South. New York: Oxford University Press. pp. 464. ISBN 0195052587.

Women of Color/ Slavery/ African American/ North/ South/ Novels/ Culture/ Fiction/ Living Conditions/ Writers/ Social Change/ Romances

0052   **Hopkins, Pauline E.**
(1988) <u>The Magazine Novels of Pauline Hopkins</u>. New York: Oxford University Press. pp. 672. ISBN 019505248X.

Women of Color/ African American/ Entertainment/ Magazines/ Fiction/ Political Action/ Writers/ Novels/ Social Change/ Popular Culture

0053   **Howell, C. Diane**
(1978) "Black Concepts of the Ideal Black Woman." Dissertation: University of California-Berkeley, Berkeley, CA. DAI Vol. 39(08B)4103.

African American/ Women of Color/ Images of Women/ Social Attitudes/ Personal Values/ Beauty Standards/ Stereotypes/ Women's Culture

0054   **Jewell, Karen Sue**
(1976) "An Analysis of the Visual Development of a Stereotype: The Media's Portrayal of Mammy and Aunt Jemina as Symbols of Black Womanhood." Dissertation: Ohio State University, Columbus, OH.

Women of Color/ Mammies/ Women's Culture/ African American/ Mass Media/ Images of Women/ Stereotypes/ Institutional Racism/ Media Portrayal

0055   **Jewell, Karen Sue**
(1985) "Will the Real, Black, Afro-American, Mixed, Colored, Negro Please Stand Up." <u>Journal of Black Studies</u> 16(September):1:pp. 57-75.

Women of Color/ African American/ Social Movements/ Black Movement/ Institutional Racism/ Affirmative Action/ Cultural Identity/ Social Perception/ Images of Women/ Stereotypes/ Social Change

0056   **Johnson, Audrey Louise**
(1977) "The Perceptions and Social Characteristics Related to Occupational Mobility of Black Women and Interracial Assimilation of Blacks in America." Dissertation: New School for Social Research, New York, NY.

Women of Color/ Interracial Relations/ African American/ Social Characteristics/ Occupational Mobility/ Assimilation Patterns

0057   **Jones, Bessie**
Hawes, Bess Lomax. (1987) <u>Step It Down: Games, Plays, Songs, and Stories from the Afro-American Heritage</u>. Athens, GA: University of Georgia Press.

People of Color/ Stories/ Plays/ African Americans/ Cultural Identity/ Cultural Heritage/ Entertainment/ Folk Culture/ Songs/ Traditions

0058   **Jones, Jacqueline**
(1986) "Class, Gender, and Racial-Cultural Perspectives on the Lives of Black and Poor White Women in the Rural South." Presented: American Farm Women in Historical Perspective, National Conference, Madison, WI.

Women of Color/ Women Living in Poverty/ African American/ European American/ Race, Class and Gender Studies/ Comparative Studies/ Cultural Influences/ Life Styles/ South/ Rural Areas

0059   **Jones, L. V.**
(1984) "White-Black Achievement Differences: The Narrowing Gap." <u>American Psychologist</u> 39:pp. 1207-1213.

Academic Achievement/ Education/ African American/ Comparative Studies/ Women of Color/ European American/ Racial and Ethnic Differences

0060 Larison, Cornelius W.
Lobdell, Jared C. (ed.). (1988) <u>Silvia Dubois, A Biografy of the Slav Who Whipt Her Mistres and Gand Her Fredom</u>. New York: Oxford University Press. (originally published 1969, Negro Universities Press) pp. 124. ISBN 0195052390.

Women of Color/ Oral History/ African American/ History/ 19th Century/ Slaves/ Folk Culture/ Slavery/ Silvia Dubois/ Biographies/ Interviews

0061 Leeper, Fran
(1985) <u>Dignity: Lower Income Women Tell of Their Lives and Struggle</u>. Ann Arbor: University of Michigan. pp. 290.

Women of Color/ African American/ Rural Conditions/ Urban Areas/ Survival Strategies/ Race, Class and Gender Studies/ Women Living in Poverty/ Networks/ South/ Women's Culture

0062 Lesnoff-Cavavaglia, G.
(1982) "The Black Granny and the Soviet Babushka: Commonalities and Contrasts." in <u>Minority Aging: Sociological and Social Psychological Issues</u>. R.C. Manuel (ed.). Westport, CT: Greenwood Press.

Women of Color/ African American/ Healers/ Older Adults/ Senior Citizens/ Cultural Influences/ Comparative Studies

0063 Lorde, Audre
(1979) "Manchild: A Black Lesbian Feminist's Response." <u>Conditions Four</u> 2(Winter):1:pp. 30-36.

Women of Color/ African American/ Feminism/ Feminist Writing / Lesbians/ Lesbian Experience/ Lesbian Culture

0064 Mapp, Edward
(1975) "Black Women in Films: A Mixed Bag of Tricks." in <u>Black Films and Film-Makers: A Comprehensive Anthology from Stereotype to Superhero</u>. Lindsay Patterson (ed.). New York: Dodd, Mead. pp. 196-205.

African American/ Women of Color/ Images of Women/ Film/ Stereotypes/ Media Portrayal/ Entertainment/ Popular Culture

0065 Marks, Carole
(1987) "Demography and Race." <u>American Behavioral Scientist</u> 30(Mar/Apr):4.

Women of Color/ African American/ Demography/ Population Distribution/ Racial Factors/ Race, Class and Gender Studies/ Racial and Ethnic Differences

0066 Massey, Donald S.
Condran, Gretchen A. and Denton, Nancy A. (1987) "The Effect of Residential Segregation on Black Social and Economic Well-Being." <u>Social Forces</u> 66(September):1:pp. 29-56.

African American/ Women of Color/ Declining Neighborhoods/ Racial Discrimination/ Heads of Households/ Poverty/ Lower Class/ Social Status/ Assimilation Patterns/ Housing/ Self Concept/ Segregated Housing

0067 Meleis, Afaf Ibrahim
Sorrell, Leila. (1981) "Arab American Women and their Birth Experiences." <u>The American Journal of Maternal Child Nursing</u> 6(May/June):3:pp. 171.

African American/ Women of Color/ Arab/ Birthing/ Maternal and Infant Welfare/ Cultural Influences/ Health Care Delivery/ Family/ Families

0068 Nitoburg, E. L.
(1986) "The First World War and Black America." <u>Modern and Contemporary</u>

History 6:pp. 50-63.

World War I/ History/ People of Color/ African American/ Social Change/ Assimilation Patterns

0069 Okazawa-Rey, Margo
Robinson, Tracey, and Ward, Janie Victoria. (1986) "Black Women and the Politics of Skin Color and Hair." Women's Studies Quarterly 14(Spring/Summer):1-2:pp. 13-14.

Women of Color/ African American/ Coalition Politics/ Literary Arts/ Literature/ Self Concept/ Race, Class and Gender Studies/ Hair Styles/ Images of Women/ Beauty Standards/ Women's Culture

0070 Roach, Hildred
(1985) Black American Music: Past and Present. Melbourne, FL: Krieger Publishing. pp. 210. ISBN 0898746108.

People of Color/ African Americans/ Music/ Musicians/ Music History/ Composers/ Performing Arts/ Entertainment/ Minority Experience/ Popular Culture

0071 Smith, Eleanor J.
(1981) "African and African American Cultural Connections." Nip Magazine (September):pp. 7.

People of Color/ Africa/ African Americans/ Cultural Heritage/ Culture/ Cultural Identity

0072 Smith, Eleanor J.
(1979) "And Black Women Made Music." Heresies Third World Women: The Politics of Being Other 2:4:pp. 58-64.

Women of Color/ Entertainment/ African American/ Music/ Popular Culture

0073 Smith, Jessie Carney
(1988) Images of Blacks in American Culture: A Reference Guide to Information Sources. Westport, CT: Greenwood Press.

African American/ Research Resources/ Women's Studies/ Culture/ Women of Color/ History/ Stereotypes/ Images of Women

0074 Snow, Loudell
(1977) "Popular Medicine in a Black Neighborhood." in Ethnic Medicine in the Southwest. Edward H. Spicer (ed.). Tucson, AZ: University of Arizona Press.

Women of Color/ South West/ African American/ Help Seeking Behavior/ Health Care/ Medical Sciences/ Cultural Influences/ Neighborhoods/ Life Styles/ Folk Medicine/ Coping Strategies/ Home Remedies

0075 Stanback, Marsha Houston
(1987) "Claiming Our Space, Finding Our Voice: Feminist Theory and Black Women's Talk." Presented: Speech Communication Association, Boston, MA.

Women of Color/ Communication/ African American/ Black Feminism/ Feminist Theory/ Consciousness Raising/ Women's Culture

0076 Susie, Deborah Ann
(1988) In the Ways of Our Grandmothers: A Cultural View of 20th Century Midwifery in Florida. Athens, GA: University of Georgia Press. pp. 272.

Women of Color/ African American/ Midwifery/ Folk Medicine/ Cultural Influences/ Health Care Providers/ Images of Women/ Stereotypes/ Florida/ South/ Maternal and Infant Welfare

0077 Tate, Claudia
(1983) Black Women Writers at Work. New York: Continuum Publishing. ISBN

0826402321.

Women of Color/ African American/ Black Studies/ Authors/ Writing/ Race, Class and Gender Studies/ Literature/ Minority Experience/ Women's History/ Images of Women/ Popular Culture

0078   Tate, Claudia
(1987)   "The Social System Which Labels Some as Writers, Others as Black Writers." <u>Women and Language</u> 10(Spring):2:pp. 21.

African American/ Writing/ Writers/ Social Structure/ Women of Color/ Language/ Images of Women/ Stereotypes/ Labeling/ Literature/ Popular Culture

0079   Taylor, Jerome
Jackson, Beryl. (1988) "Influence of Religious Orientation and Cultural Identity on Alcohol Consumption and Prescription Drug Usage in a Sample of Black Inner City Women." Presented: Nat'l. Council on Family Relations Annual Conference, Philadelphia, PA.

African American/ Women of Color/ Alcohol Use/ Prescription Drugs/ Inner City/ Religious Experience/ Economy/ Cultural Identity/ Urban Areas/ Substance Abuse/ Religious Influences

0080   Terrell, Mary Church
Baxter, Annette K. (ed.). (1980) <u>A Colored Woman in a White World</u>. Washington, D.C.: Ayer Co. ISBN 0405128614.

African American/ Social Movements/ Social Perception/ Women's History/ 20th Century/ Dominant Culture/ Women of Color/ Cultural Heritage

0081   Tracy, Susan Jean
(1983)   "Images of Women, Blacks and Poor Whites in Antebellum Southern Literature." Dissertation: Rutgers University, New Brunswick, NJ. pp. 662.

Images of Women/ South/ Literature/ African American/ Women of Color/ Antebellum/ Culture/ Women's History/ 19th Century/ European American/ Poverty

0082   Udry, J. Richard
Billy, John O. G. (1987) "Initiation of Coitus in Early Adolescence." <u>American Sociological Review</u> 52(Dec):6:pp. 841-855.

Women of Color/ Sex Education/ African American/ Social Behavior/ Comparative Studies/ Adolescents/ Coitus/ Sexual Behavior/ Sexual Permissiveness/ Cultural Influences

0083   Uriarte, Miren
(1986)   "Contribution to a Dialogue."   <u>Women's Studies Quarterly</u> 14(Spring/Summer):1-2:pp. 32-35.

Women of Color/ African American/ Teaching/ Race Relations/ Educational Programs/ Cultural Groups/ Educational Methods

0084   Vass, Winifred K.
(1988) <u>The Bantu-Speaking Heritage of the United States</u>. Los Angeles: University of California Los Angeles Center for Afro-American Studies. pp. 122.

People of Color/ Cultural Heritage/ African Americans/ Language/ African/ Cultural Influences/ Speech/ Communication

0085   Washington, Mary H.
(ed.). (1987) <u>Invented Lives: Narratives of Black Women, 1860-1960</u>. Garden City, NY: Doubleday.

African American/ Women of Color/ Oral Tradition/ Social History/ 19th Century/ 20th Century/ Women's History/ Testimonial Literature/ Women's Culture

0086   Wells, Sharon
(1982) <u>Forgotten Legacy: Blacks in Nineteenth Century Key West</u>. Key West, FL: Historic Key West Preservation Board, 500 Whitehead Street. pp. 60.
African Americans/ People of Color/ South/ Florida/ Social History/ 19th Century/ Legal Status/ Demograpy/ Trends/ Folklore/ Cultural Identity/ Curriculum Integration

0087   Wilkinson, Doris Y.
(1987) "The Doll Exhibit: A Psycho-Cultural Analysis of Black Female Role Stereotypes." <u>Journal of Popular Culture</u> 21:2:pp. 19-29.
Women of Color/ Sex Stereotypes/ African American/ Sex Roles/ Gender Roles/ Popular Culture/ Sex Role Development/ Beauty Standards/ Cultural Influences

0088   Wright, Josephine
(1985) "Philosophy and Definition of Black Women's Research in Afro-American Music." Presented: National Conference on Black Music, University of Michigan. August.
Women of Color/ Entertainment/ African American/ Music/ Cultural Identity/ Cultural Heritage/ Music Industry/ Research

Asian American

0089   Armor, John
Wright, Peter. (1988) <u>Manzanar</u>. New York: Random House. pp. 167. ISBN 0812917276.
Japanese American/ Politics/ Asian American/ World War II/ History/ Inequality/ Internment/ Racial Discrimination/ Photography/ Cultural Heritage

0090   Cabanilla, Gerardo
(1982) "Health and Ethnomedicine: Implications of Alternative Health Care of Philipinos." Asian American Women Research Project, University of California Los Angeles Asian American Studies Center, Los Angeles, CA.
Asian/ Women of Color/ Philipinos/ Health Care Delivery/ Family/ Roles/ Health/ Illness/ Folk Medicine/ Health Seeking Behavior/ Cultural Influences

0091   Calhoun, Mary Atchity
(1986) "The Vietnamese Woman: Health/Illness Attitudes and Behaviors." in <u>Women, Health and Culture</u>. Phyllis Noerager Stern. New York: Hemisphere.
Asian American/ Vietnamese/ Women of Color/ Illness/ Wellness/ Health Seeking Behavior/ Cultural Influences/ Attitudes/ Racial and Ethnic Differences

0092   Chai, Alice Yun
(1978) "Korean Women: An Urban Profile." <u>Impulse: Honolulu West Center</u>. (Winter).
Women of Color/ Immigrants/ Korean/ Asian/ Living Conditions/ Urban Areas/ Acculturation/ Cultural Heritage

0093   Daniels, Roger
(1986) "Chinese and Japanese in North America: The Canadian and American Experiences Compared." <u>Canadian Review of American Studies</u> 17(Summer):pp. 173-187.
Women of Color/ Chinese/ Asian/ Japanese/ Ethnic Studies/ Acculturation/ Assimilation Patterns/ Cultural Identity

0094   **Fournier, Merlinda**
(1987) "Hmong Stories and Story Cloth." <u>The World and I</u> 2(September):9:pp. 615-639.

Asian/ Women of Color/ Oral Tradition/ Acculturation/ Craft Arts/ Textile Making/ Cultural Heritage/ Folk Literature/ Storytelling/ Laotian/ Hmong/ Immigrants/ Refugees

0095   **Gillenkirk, Jeff**
Motlow, James (eds.). (1987) <u>Bitter Melon: Stories from the Last Rural Chinese Town in America</u>. University of Washington, Seattle, WA. pp. 168.

Women of Color/ Chinese American/ Immigrants/ History/ Racial Discrimination/ Rural Areas/ Asian American/ Cultural Heritage

0096   **Kibria, Nazli**
(1987) "New Images of Immigrant Women: A Study of Women's Social Groups among Vietnamese Refugees." Available: Working Paper #173, Wellesley College Center for Research on Women, Wellesley, MA.

Asian/ Vietnamese/ Images of Women/ Low Income Households/ Women of Color/ Social Environment/ Social Clubs/ Urban Areas/ Women's Groups/ Immigrants/ Refugees/ Lower Class/ Assimilation Patterns

0097   **Kim, Elaine H.**
(1986) "A Korean Woman in L.A. 'First Experiences'." <u>Contact</u> 7(Winter/Spring):38-40:pp. 21-23.

Women of Color/ Immigrants/ Asian/ Korean/ Racial and Ethnic Differences/ Cultural Identity/ Culture Conflict/ California/ Pacific/ Acculturation

0098   **Kim, Elaine H.**
(1987) "Defining Asian American Realities Through Literature." <u>Cultural Critique</u> 6(Spring):pp. 87-111.

Women of Color/ Images of Women/ Asian American/ Cultural Identity/ Literature/ Realism/ Writers/ Writing

0099   **Kumagai, Gloria L.**
(1987) "The Asian Woman in America." in <u>Racism and Sexism</u>. Paula S. Rothenberg. New York: St. Martin's Press.

Women of Color/ Race, Class and Gender Studies/ Asian American/ Sex Discrinination/ Racial Discrimination/ Double Bind/ Women's Culture

0100   **Lin, Chien**
(1985) "The Intergenerational Relationships among Chinese Immigrant Families: A Study of Filial Piety." Dissertation: University of Illinois-Chicago, Chicago, IL. pp. 243. DAI Vol. 46(06A)1748.

Immigrants/ Chinese/ Asian/ Women of Color/ Family Relationships/ Parent Child Relationships/ Family Structure/ Cultural Influences

0101   **Rubinowitz, Paula**
(1987) "Eccentric Memories: An Interview with Maxine Hong Kingston." <u>Michigan Quarterly Review</u> (Spring).

Women of Color/ Asian American/ Memory/ Recall/ Interviews/ Writers/ Literature/ Women's Culture/ Biographies

0102   **So, Alvin Y.**
Ito, Karen L. (1982) "The Perception of Gender and Ethnic Group Health Problems by Asian American Doctors." Working Paper #8. Health Care Alternatives of Asian American Women Project, University of California Los Angeles Asian

American Studies Center, Los Angeles, CA.

Physical Health/ Mental Health/ Asian American/ Women of Color/ Physicians/ Ethnic Studies/ Gender/ Cultural Influences/ Health Care Delivery/ Health Care Providers

0103   Sone, Monica
(1979) <u>Nisei Daughter</u>. Seattle: University of Washington Press. pp. 238.

Women of Color/ Japanese American/ Asian American/ Women's History/ World War II/ Education/ Cultural Identity/ Autobiographies/ Assimilation Patterns

0104   Srole, Carole
Yu, Eui-Young and Phillips, E. H. (1987) "Converging Paths: Korean and U.S. Women, 1900-1980." in <u>Korean Women in Transition: At Home and Abroad</u>. Center for Korean-American and Korean Studies, Los Angeles, CA.

Women of Color/ Korean/ Asian/ Asian American/ Culture Conflict/ Korean American/ Cultural Identity/ Assimilation Patterns/ Acculturation/ Cultural Heritage

0105   Yanagida, E.
Marsella, A. J. (1978) "The Relationship between Depression and Self Concept Discrepancy among Different Generations of Japanese-American Women." <u>Journal of Clinical Psychology</u> 34:3:pp. 654-659.

Asian American/ Self Concept/ Women of Color/ Cultural Identity/ Japanese American/ Depression/ Mental Health/ Assimilation Patterns/ Emotional States

Latina

0106   Alcalay, Rina
(1984) "Hispanic Women in the US: Work and Family Relations." <u>Migration Today</u> 12:3:pp. 13-20.

Women of Color/ Balancing Work and Family Life/ Latina/ Immigration/ Women's Culture

0107   Alvarez, M.
(1985) "Health Conditions of Mexican Women Immigrants: A Review of the Literature." <u>Border Health</u> 1:3:pp. 48-52.

Women of Color/ Border Studies/ Latina/ Mexicans/ Immigrants/ Low Income Households/ Health Care Costs/ Health Care Services/ Cultural Influences

0108   Alvarez, Robert R., Jr.
(1987) <u>Familia: Migration and Adaptation in Baja and Alta California, 1880-1975</u>. Berkeley: University of California Press. pp. 228.

Women of Color/ Latina/ Migration Patterns/ Immigrants/ Social Adjustment/ Acculturation/ Assimilation Patterns/ History/ 20th Century/ California/ Pacific/ Family/ Families

0109   Bandarage, Asoka
(1986) "Reflections from Texas." <u>Woman of Power</u> (Fall):4:pp. 36-44.

Women of Color/ African American/ Latina/ Biographies/ Community/ Social Values/ Spirituality/ Racial Discrimination/ Traditions/ Culture/ South West/ Texas/ Sexual Discrimination

0110   Burgess, Norma J.
(1988) "Role Diversity among Mexican-Origin Women in the U.S." Author: Dept. of Sociology and Anthropology, Mississippi State University, P. O. Drawer C, Mississippi State, MS 39762. Presented: Mid-South Sociological Association,

Mobile, AL. October.

Chicana/ Latina/ Images of Women/ Women of Color/ Stereotypes/ Gender Roles/ Family/ Families/ Cultural Identity/ Male Female Relationships/ Wage Earning Wives/ Household Division of Labor/ Employment/ Homemakers

0111   Castillo, Adelaida R. del

Torres, Maria. (1988) "The Interdependency of Educational Institutions and Cultural Norms: The Hispana Experience." in The Broken Web: The Educational Experience of Hispanic American Women. Theresa McKenna and Flora Ida Ortez (eds.). Encino, CA: Floricanto Press, Tomas Rivera Center.

Latina/ Chicana/ Social Attitudes/ Cultural Heritage/ Discrimination/ Academic Achievement/ Women of Color/ Values/ Education

0112   Clark, W. A. V.

Mueller, Milan. (1988) "Hispanic Relocation and Spatial Assimilation: A Case Study." Social Science Quarterly 69 (June):2:pp. 468-475.

Women of Color/ Assimilation Patterns/ Latina/ Acculturation/ Migration/ Social Mobility

0113   Cortes, Carlos E.

(1985) "Chicanas in Film: History of an Image." in Chicano Cinema: Research, Reviews and Resources. Gary D. Keller. Binghamton, NY: Bilingual Review Press. pp. 94-108.

Latina/ Chicana/ Media Portrayal/ Images of Women/ Women of Color/ Film/ Stereotypes/ Folk Culture

0114   Coyle, Laurie

Hershatter, Gail et al. (1980) "Women at Farah: An Unfinished Story." in Mexican Women in the United States: Struggles Past and Present. M. Mora and A. R. del Castillo. Los Angeles: Chicana Studies Research Center, University of California Los Angeles. pp.117-143.

Latina/ Mexican/ Race, Class and Gender Studies/ Women of Color/ Women's History/ Acculturation/ Women's Culture

0115   Cuffaro, S. T.

(1978) "Discriminant Analysis of Sociocultural Motivation and Personality Differences among Black, Anglo and Chicana Female Drug Abusers in a Medium Security Prison." Dissertation: U.S. International University, San Diego, CA.

Women of Color/ Research Methods/ Chicana/ Latina/ Personality/ Treatment/ Drug Abuse/ Prisoners/ Socialization/ Correctional Facilities/ African American/ Motivation/ Behavior/ European American/ Comparative Studies/ Cultural Influences

0116   Deutsch, Sarah

(1987) "Women and Intercultural Relations: The Case of Hispanic New Mexico and Colorado." SIGNS: Journal of Women in Culture and Society 12(Summer):4:pp. 719-739.

Latina/ Women of Color/ West/ New Mexico/ Colorado/ Relationships/ Cultural Groups/ Crosscultural Studies/ Social Relations/ Household Workers/ Discrimination

0117   Deutsch, Sarah

(1987) No Separate Refuge: Culture, Class, and Gender on an Anglo-Hispanic Frontier in the American Southwest, 1880-1940. New York: Oxford University

Press.

Women of Color/ Latina/ Race, Class and Gender Studies/ Comparative Studies/ European American/ Cultural Influences/ Community/ South West/ Assimilation Patterns/ Stereotypes/ Acculturation/ Images of Women/ History/ 20th Century/ Labor Force Participation

0118 Doran, Terry
Satterfield, Janet and Stade, C. (1988) <u>A Road Well Traveled: Three Generations of Cuban American Women</u>. Newton, MA: WEEA Publishing, EDC, 55 Chapel, St. Suite 245, 02160.

Women of Color/ Latina/ Subculture/ Women's History/ Testimonial Literature/ Racial Discrimination/ Bias/ Cuban American/ Language/ Immigrants/ Cultural Heritage/ Assimilation Patterns/ Acculturation/ Socioeconomic Status/ Family/ Families

0119 Flynn, Patricia
Santana, Aracelly. (1980) "Latin American Women--One Myth--Many Realities." <u>NACLA Report on the Americas</u> 14(September):pp. 2-35.

Images of Women/ Latina/ Stereotypes/ Minority Studies/ Women of Color/ Women's Culture

0120 Ginorio, Angela B.
(1979) "A Comparison of Puerto Ricans in New York with Native Puerto Ricans, Caucasians, Black Americans on Two Measures of Acculturation: Gender Role and Racial Identification." Dissertation: Fordham University, New York, NY. DAI Vol. 40(B)983-84.

Latina/ Puerto Rican/ African American/ European American/ Women of Color/ Acculturation/ Gender Roles/ Cultural Identity/ Comparative Studies/ Ethnicity

0121 Gutierrez, Ramon A.
(1986) "Unraveling America's Hispanic Past: Internal Stratification and Class Boundaries." <u>Aztlan</u> 17(Spring):pp. 79-101.

People of Color/ Race, Class and Gender Studies/ Chicanos/ Latinos/ Stratification/ Discrimination/ Folk Culture

0122 Harwood, A.
(1981) "Puerto Rican Americans." in <u>Ethnicity and Medical Care</u>. A. Harwood. Cambridge, MA: Harvard University Press.

Puerto Ricans/ Folk Medicine/ Latinos/ People of Color/ Health Seeking Behavior/ Nervousness/ Mental Health/ Health Care Providers/ Cultural Influences

0123 Horno-Delgado, Asuncion
Ortega, Eliana et al. (1989) <u>Breaking Boundaries: Latina Writing and Critical Readings</u>. Amherst, MA: University of Massachusetts Press. pp. 280.

Latina/ Literature/ Women of Color/ Writing/ Literary Criticism/ Chicana/ Cultural Heritage/ Ethnic Studies

0124 Houston, M.
Kramer, R. and Barret, J. (1984) "Female Predominance in Immigration to U.S. Since 1930: A First Look." <u>International Migration Review</u> 18:4:pp. 908-959.

Women of Color/ Demography/ Latina/ Migration Patterns/ Immigration/ Population Distribution/ History/ 20th Century/ Immigrants/ Assimilation Patterns

0125 Jordan, Rosan A.
(1985) "The Vaginal Serpent and Other Themes from Mexican American Women's Lore." in <u>Women's Folklore, Women's Culture</u>. Rosan A. Jordan and Susan J. Kalcik.

Philadelphia: University of Pennsylvania. pp. 26-44.

Women of Color/ Latina/ Chicana/ Folklore/ Images of Women/ Women's Culture

0126 Jorge, Angela
(1986) "The Black Puerto Rican Woman in Contemporary Society." in The Puerto Rican Woman. Edna Acosta-Belen. New York: Praeger. pp. 134-141. ISBN 0030524660.

Puerto Rican/ Latina/ Racial Discrimination/ Social Status/ Women of Color/ Assimilation Patterns

0127 Juffer, June
(1988) "Valley So Low." Southern Exposure 16(Winter):4:pp. 19-23.

Texas/ South/ Immigration/ Political Refugees/ Economic Refugees/ Central Americans/ Latinos/ Border Studies/ Foreign Policy/ People of Color/ Acculturation/ Cultural Identity

0128 Laosa, Luis M.
(1980) "Maternal Teaching Strategies in Chicano and Anglo-American Families: The Influence of Culture and Education on Maternal Behavior." Child Development 51(September):3:pp. 759-765.

Parent Child Relationships/ Mothers/ Behavior/ Chicana/ Latina/ Women of Color/ European American/ Teaching/ Education/ Cultural Influences/ Child Development/ Family Influence

0129 Low, Setha M.
(1981) "The Meaning of Nervios." Culture, Medicine and Psychiatry 5:pp. 350-357.

Puerto Rican/ Latina/ Women of Color/ Nervousness/ Mental Health/ Physical Health/ Cultural Influences

0130 Low, Setha M.
(1984) "The Biomedical Response to Nervios." Author: Department of Landscape Architecture and Regional Planning, University of Pennsylvania, Philadelphia, PA 19104.

Puerto Rican/ Latina/ Women of Color/ Nervousness/ Mental Health/ Physical Health/ Cultural Influences/ Health Care Providers/ Medical Sciences

0131 Low, Setha M.
(1985) "Culturally Interpreted Symptoms or Culture-Bound Syndromes: A Cross-Cultural Review of Nerves." Social Science and Medicine 21:2:pp. 187-196.

Puerto Ricans/ Kentucky/ South/ Latinos/ People of Color/ Appalachia/ Poverty/ Nervousness/ Folk Medicine/ Lower Class/ Mental Health/ Physical Health/ Home Remedies/ Cultural Influences/ New York/ North East/ Health Seeking Behavior/ Comparative Studies

0132 Melville, Margarita B.
(1978) "Mexican Women Adapt to Migration." International Migration Review 12:2:pp. 225-235.

Women of Color/ Stress/ Latina/ Mexicans/ Coping Strategies/ Migration/ Extended Family/ Acculturation Process/ Assimilation Patterns/ Illegal Immigrants

0133 Morlas, Sylvia
(1985) "Chicano-Produced Celluloid Mujeres." in Chicana Cinema: Research, Reviews, and Resources. Gary D. Keller. Binghamton, NY: Bilingual Reviews and Resources.

Latina/ Chicana/ Media Portrayal/ Images of Women/ Stereotypes/ Women of Color/ Film/ Women's Culture

0134 Pottlitzer, Joanne
(1988) <u>Hispanic Theater in the United States and Puerto Rico</u>. New York: Ford Foundation. pp. 85. ISBN 091658433X.
Latinos/ Puerto Ricans/ Entertainment/ The Arts/ Theater/ Cultural Influences/ Poliltical Activism/ Political Influence/ People of Color

0135 Reissman, Catherine Kohler
(1987) "When Gender is not Enough: Women Interviewing Women." <u>Gender & Society</u> 1(June):2:pp. 172-207.
Women of Color/ Latina/ Interview/ Research Methods/ Cultural Influences/ Marriage/ Norms

0136 Rivera, Eugenio
(1987) "The Puerto Rican Colony of Lorain, Ohio." <u>Centro</u> 2(Spring):1:pp. 11-23.
Women of Color/ Ohio/ North Central/ Latina/ Puerto Rican/ Community/ Subculture/ Assimilation Patterns/ Acculturation Process

0137 Salgado de Snyder, V. Nelly
(1987) "The Role of Ethnic Loyalty among Mexican Immigrant Women." <u>Hispanic Journal of Behavioral Sciences</u> 9(September):3:pp. 287-298.
Women of Color/ Latina/ Mexican/ Women's Roles/ Immigrants/ Cultural Identity/ Cultural Heritage

0138 Trujillo, Roberto G.
Rodriguez, Andres (eds.). (1986) <u>Literatura Chicana: Creative and Critical Writings through 1984</u>. Berkeley: Floricanto Press, pp. 104. ISBN 09157450406.
Chicana/ Latina/ Literature/ Bibliographies/ Research Resources/ Women of Color/ Women's Culture

0139 Valdes, Guadalupe
Cardenas, Manuel. (1981) "Positive Speech Accommodation in the Language of Mexican American Bilinguals: Are Women Really More Sensitive." <u>Hispanic Journal of Behavioral Sciences</u> 3(December):4:pp. 347-359.
Chicana/ Latina/ Women of Color/ Women's Language/ Bilingualism/ Speech/.Women's Culture

0140 Veyna, Angelina F.
(1984) "Women in Early New Mexico: A Preliminary View." Presented: Annual Conference of the National Association for Chicano Studies, Austin, TX. March.
Women of Color/ Women's History/ Latina/ South West/ New Mexico/ Women's Culture

0141 Veyna, Angelina F.
(1986) "Tribute to a Living Art Form and the Future of Chicano Art." Presented: Annual Conference of the National Association for Chicano Studies, El Paso, TX. April.
People of Color/ Chicanos/ Creativity/ Art/ Cultural Influences/ Latinos

0142 Veyna, Angelina F.
(1987) "Our Lives in Eighteenth Century New Mexico." Presented: The Women's West: Race, Class, and Social Change Conference, San Francisco State University. August.
Women of Color/ South West/ New Mexico/ Latina/ Chicana/ 18th Century/ Women's History/ Race, Class and Gender Studies/ Women's Culture

0143 Vigil, James Diego
(1988) "The Nexus of Class Culture and Gender in the Education of Mexican American Females." in <u>The Broken Web: The Education Experience of Hispanic</u>

American Women. Teresa McKenna and Flora Ida Ortiz (eds.). Encino, CA: Floricanto Press and Tomas Rivera Center. pp. 79-107. ISBN 0942177002.

Latina/ Chicana/ Occupational Options/ Education/ Discrimination/ Cultural Heritage/ Acculturation/ Inequality/ Women of Color/ Gender Studies/ Class Differences

0144   **Wagenheim, Olga Jimenez**
(1981) "The Puerto Rican Woman in the 19th Century: An Agenda for Research." Revista/Review Interamericana 11(Summer):2:pp. 196-203.

Women of Color/ Sex Discrimination/ Latina/ Puerto Rican/ Women's History/ 19th Century/ Exploitation/ Colonialism / Women's Culture

0145   **Warren, Nancy Hunt**
(1987) Village of Hispanic New Mexico. Seattle: University of Washington Press. pp. 136.

Latina/ Rural Areas/ History/ Acculturation/ Subculture/ New Mexico/ South West/ Women of Color/ Cultural Heritage

0146   **Wells, Miriam**
(1986) "Power Brokers and Ethnicity: The Rise of a Chicano Movement." Aztlan 17(Spring):pp. 47-77.

People of Color/ Chicanos/ Latinos/ Ethnicity/ Social Movements/ Power/ Consciousness Raising

0147   **Weyr, Thomas**
(1988) Hispanic USA. New York: Harper and Row. pp. 384. ISBN 0060390666.

Latinos/ People of Color/ Acculturation/ Social Change/ Demographic Transition/ Population Characteristics/ Cultural Heritage

0148   **Williams, Mary Willson**
(1984) "Sex Role Orientation: A Cross Cultural Study of Sex Role Strain." Dissertation: University of New Mexico, Albuquerque, NM. DAI Vol. 45(08A)2075.

Latina/ Mental Health/ Sex Roles/ Sex Role Conflict/ Crosscultural Studies/ European American/ Women of Color/ Sex Role Development/ Cultural Influences

0149   **Zentella, Ana C.**
(1987) "Growing Up Female in the Puerto Rican Community: The Role of Language." in Women and Languages in Transition. Joyce Penfield. Albany: State University of New York Press. pp. 224. ISBN 088706485X.

Puerto Rican/ Latina/ Women of Color/ Life Cycles/ Community/ Socialization/ Language/ Speech/ Roles/ Sociolinguistics/ Verbal Communication/ Women's Language/ Women in Transition/ Home Life/ Women's Culture

Native American

0150   **Agnito, Rosemary**
Agnito, Joseph. (1981) "Resurrecting History's Forgotten Women: A Case Study from the Cheyenne Indians." Frontiers: A Journal of Women Studies 6(Fall):3:pp. 9-16.

Women of Color/ Native American/ Cheyenne/ Biographies/ Traditions/ Sex Roles/ Women's Roles/ Women's History/ Women's Culture

0151   **Anderson, Gary Clayton**
(1984) Kinsmen of Another Kind. Lincoln, NE: University of Nebraska Press. ISBN

0803210183.

People of Color/ 1860-1869/ Native American/ Sioux/ Race Relations / History/ 19th Century/ Cultural Influences

0152   Awiakta, Marilou
(1988) "Rebirth of a Nation." Southern Style (Sept/Oct):pp. 12-13. (Whittle Publications, 505 Market St., Knoxville, TN 37902).

Native American/ Cherokee/ Women of Color/ Social Movements/ Oklahoma/ South West/ Leadership/ Cultural Heritage

0153   Begay, Shirley
(1983) Kinnaalda: A Navajo Puberty Ceremony. Rough Rock, AZ: Navajo Curriculum Center.

Women of Color/ Native American/ Navajo/ Anthropology/ Rites/ Ceremonies/ Religious Acts/ Sex Roles/ Religious Practices/ Spiritualism/ Life Cycles/ Physical Development/ Cultural Heritage

0154   Bol, Marsha Clift
(1985) "Dakota Women's Artistic Strategies in Support of the Social System." American Indian Culture and Research Journal 9:1.

Native American/ Acculturation Process/ Cultural Heritage/ Craft Arts/ Kinship/ Women of Color/ North Dakota/ North Central/ Social Structure

0155   Bradley, James W.
(1987) Evolution of the Onondaga Iroquois: Accomodating Change, 1500-1655. Syracuse, NY: Syracuse University Press. pp. 252.

People of Color/ Native Americans/ Iroquois/ Assimilation Patterns/ Acculturation/ Cultural Heritage/ Culture Conflict/ Cultural Identity/ American Indian Studies

0156   Brant, Beth
(1988) A Gathering of Spirit -- A Collection by North American Women. Ithaca, NY: Firebrand Books. pp. 248. ISBN 0932379559.

Women of Color/ Literature/ Native American/ Life Styles/ Women's Culture

0157   Brooks, Maria
(1981) "Remembering the Reindeer Queen." Frontiers: A Journal of Women Studies 6(Fall):3:pp. 59-61.

Native American/ Women of Color/ Acculturation/ Cultural Heritage/ Folk Culture/ Folk Literature

0158   Camavena, Pat
(1986) "Women in Theatre Festival 86." Woman of Power (Fall):4:pp. 73-75.

Women of Color/ Native American/ Performing Arts/ Theater/ Folk Dance/ Visual Arts/ Women's Culture

0159   Devens, Carol A.
(1986) "Separate Confrontations: Indian Women and Christian Missions, 1630-1900." Dissertation: Rutgers University, New Brunswick, NJ.

Native American/ History/ 17th Century/ Missionaries/ Religion/ 18th Century/ Women of Color/ 19th Century/ Cultural Influences

0160   Griffen, Joyce
(1982) "Life is Harder Here: The Case of the Urban Navajo Women." American Indian Quarterly 6(Spring/Summer):1-2:pp. 90-104.

Women of Color/ Kinship/ Native American/ Navajo/ Urban Areas/ Acculturation/ Religion/ Women's Culture

0161   Gump, James
(1988) "The Subjugation of the Zulus and Sioux: A Comparative Study." <u>Western Historical Quarterly</u> 19(Jan):pp. 21-36.
People of Color/ Native Americans/ Sioux/ Comparative Studies/ Crosscultural Studies/ Racial and Ethnic Differences

0162   Herring, Rebecca J.
(1985) "Creation of Indian Farm Women: Field Matrons and Acculturation on the Kiowa-Comanche Reservation." in <u>At Home on the Range: Essays on the History of Western Social and Domestic Life</u>. J. Wonder. Westport, CT: Greenwood Press. pp. 39-56.
Women of Color/ Farming/ Rural Areas/ Native American/ Kiowa Comanche/ Assimilation Patterns/ Acculturation/ West/ Social History/ Domestic Arrangements

0163   Hungry Wolf, Beverly
(1980) <u>The Ways of My Grandmothers</u>. New York: Morrow, Quill. pp. 256.
Women of Color/ Culture/ Native American/ Women's Roles/ Tradition/ Tribal Customs/ Customs/ Cultural Heritage

0164   Jahner, Elaine
(1985) "Woman Remembering: Life History as Exemplary Pattern." in <u>Women's Folklore, Women's Culture</u>. Rosan A. Jordan and Susal J. Kalcik. Philadelphia: University of Pennsylvania Press. pp. 214-233.
Women of Color/ Native American/ Oral History/ Acculturation/ Assimilation Patterns/ Testimonial Literature/ Women's History/ Folklore

0165   Joe, Jennie R.
(1982) "Cultural Influences on Navajo Mothers with Disabled Children." <u>American Indian Quarterly</u> 6(Spring/Summer):1-2:pp. 170-190.
Women of Color/ Cultural Influences/ Native American/ Navajo/ Parent Child Relationships/ Child Rearing Practices/ Motherhood/ Special Education/ Disabilities

0166   Johnson, Broderick H.
(1977) <u>Stories of Traditional Navajo Life and Culture</u>. Tsaile, AZ: Navajo Community College Press.
Women of Color/ Native American/ Navajo/ Traditions/ Culture/ Folk Literature/ Cultural Heritage

0167   Jones, David E.
(1987) <u>Sanapia: Comanche Medicine Women</u>. Prospect Heights, IL: Waveland. pp. 107.
Native American/ Comanche/ Women of Color/ Folk Medicine/ Folk Healer/ Medical Anthropology/ Health Care Providers/ Cultural Heritage/ Biographies/ Traditions/ Rites

0168   Kopp, Judy
(1986) "Crosscultural Contacts: Change in Diet and Nutrition of the Navajo Indians." <u>American Indian Culture and Research Journal</u> 10:4:pp. 1-30.
People of Color/ Acculturation/ Native Americans/ Navajo/ Change/ Cultural Influences/ Crosscultural Studies/ Nutrition/ Diet

0169   La Duke, Winona
(1986) "Interview with Roberta Blackgoat, Dine' Elder." <u>Woman of Power</u> (Fall):4:pp. 29-31.
Women of Color/ Social Change/ Native American/ Dine'/ Cultural Identity/ Leadership/ Cultural Influence/ Social Movements/ Relocation/ Protest Actions/ Roberta Blackgoat/ Social Action

0170   **Leighton, Dorothea**
(1982) "As I Knew Them: Navajo Women in 1940." <u>American Indian Quarterly</u> 6(Spring/Summer):1-2:pp. 34-51.
Women of Color/ Native American/ Navajo/ Sex Roles/ Child Rearing Practices/ Ethnography/ Women's History/ 1940-1949

0171   **Liberty, Margot**
(1982) "Hell Came with Horses: Plains Indian Women in the Equestrian Era." <u>Montana</u> 10(Summer):19.
Women of Color/ Montana/ West/ Native American/ Women's Roles/ History/ Social Change/ Animals/ Women's Culture

0172   **Mathes, Valerie Sherer**
(1980) "American Indian Women and the Catholic Church." <u>North Dakota History</u> 47(Fall):4:pp. 20-25.
Native American/ Religion/ Nuns/ Missionaries/ Women of Color/ North Dakota/ North Central/ Catholicism/ Assimilation Patterns

0173   **Milligan, B. Carol**
(1984) "Nursing Care and Beliefs of Expectant Navajo Women, Parts I and II." <u>American Indian Quarterly</u> 7(Spring/ Summer):3-4:pp. 83.
Women of Color/ Acculturation Process/ Native American/ Navajo/ Assimilation Patterns/ Childbirth/ Maternal and Infant Welfare/ Health Care/ Cultural Influences/ Physical Health/ Pregnancy

0174   **Muga, David A.**
(1987) "Native Americans and the Nationalities Question: Premises for a Marxist Approach to Ethnicity and Self-Determination." <u>Nature, Society, and Thought</u> 1(Fall):pp. 7-26.
People of Color/ Native Americans/ Marxism/ Ethnicity/ Self Determination/ Class/ Nationality/ Social Movements

0175   **Oshana, Maryann**
(1981) "Native American Women in Westerns: Reality and Myth." <u>Frontiers: A Journal of Women Studies</u> 6(Fall):3:pp. 53-57.
Women of Color/ Native American/ Images of Women/ Stereotypes/ Film/ Women's Culture/ Racial Discrimination

0176   **Paper, Jordan**
(1983) "The Post-Contact Origin of an American Indian High God: The Suppression of Feminine Spirituality." <u>American Indian Quarterly</u> 7(Fall):4:pp. 1-24.
Women of Color/ Native American/ Religion/ Spiritualism/ Women's Culture

0177   **Perdue, Thelma**
(1985) "Southern Indians and the Cult of True Womanhood." in <u>The Web of Southern Social Relations: Women, Family and Education</u>. Walter J. Fraser, Jr. et al. (eds.). Athens, GA: University of Georgia Press. pp. 35-51.
Native American/ Women of Color/ Status/ South/ Cult of True Womanhood/ Cultural Heritage/ Matrilineal Kinship/ Patrilineal Kinship/ Power

0178   **Peterson, Susan C.**
(1983) "Holy Women and Housekeepers: Women Teachers on South Dakota Reservations, 1885-1910." <u>South Dakota History</u> 13(Fall):pp. 245-260.
Women of Color/ Native American/ History/ 19th Century/ Education/ Acculturation/ Teaching/ South Dakota/ North Central/ Traditions/ Customs/ Cultural Heritage/ Roles

0179 **Quick-To-See Smith, Jaune**
(1987) "Women of Sweetgrass, Cedar, and Sage." Women's Studies Quarterly 15(Spring/Summer):1-2:pp. 35-41.
Native American/ Women of Color/ Cultural Influences/ Craft Arts/ Artists/ Jewelry Makers/ Photographers/ Basketry/ Beadwork/ Cultural Heritage/ Traditions/ Exhibitions

0180 **Roessel, Ruth**
(1981) Women in Navajo Society. Rough Rock, AZ: Navajo Curriculum Center Press. pp. 184. ISBN 0936008016.
Women of Color/ Cultural Influences/ Native American/ Navajo/ Acculturation/ Biographies/ Folk Healers/ Alternative Lifestyles/ Cultural Heritage

0181 **Schilz, Thomas F.**
Schilz, Joyde Lynn Dickson. (1987) "Amazons, Witches and 'Country Wives': Plains Indian Women in Historical Perspective." Annals of Wyoming 59(Spring):pp. 48-56.
Native American/ Plains/ Images of Women/ Women of Color/ History/ West/ Wyoming/ Witchcraft/ Amazons/ Folk Healers/ Marriage/ Women's Culture

0182 **Sutter, Virginia**
(1981) "Today's Strength from Yesterday's Tradition--The Continuity of American Indian Woman." Frontiers: A Journal of Women Studies 6(Fall):3:pp. 53-57.
Women of Color/ Native American/ Acculturation/ Ceremonies/ Rites/ Cultural Heritage/ Traditions/ Customs

0183 **Tyon, Gracie**
(1981) "The Way of My Grandmother, My Mother, and Me." Frontiers: A Journal of Women Studies 6(Fall):3:pp. 51-52.
Women of Color/ Native American/ Kinship/ Mother Daughter Relationships/ Cultural Heritage/ Customs/ Traditions/ Family/ Families

0184 **Williams, Walter L.**
(1988) The Spirit and the Flesh: Sexual Diversity in American Indian Culture. Boston: Beacon Press. pp. 364. ISBN 0807046116.
Tribal Culture/ Native Americans/ Androgyny/ People of Color/ Sexuality/ Cultural Influences/ History/ Sex Roles/ Gender Roles

0185 **Wright, Anne L.**
(1982) "An Ethnography of the Navajo Reproductive Cycle." American Indian Quarterly 6(Spring/Summer):1-2:pp. 52-70.
Women of Color/ Acculturation/ Menstruation/ Menopause/ Fertility/ Ethnography/ Native American/ Navajo/ Reproductive Cycle/ Reproductive Health

0186 **Wright, J. Leitch**
(1986) Creeks and Seminoles: The Destruction and Regeneration of the Muscogulge People. Lincoln: University of Nebraska Press. pp. 383.
People of Color/ Cultural Identity/ Native Americans/ American History/ American Indian Studies/ Creeks/ Cultural Heritage/ Seminoles/ Culture/ Culture Conflict

Southern

0187 **Bass, M. A.**
Owsley, D.W. et al. (1985) "Food Preferences and Food Prestige Ratings by Black

Women in East Tennessee." <u>Ecology of Food and Nutrition</u> 16:1:pp. 75-83.

Women of Color/ African American/ Food/ South/ Tennessee/ Nutrition/ Diets/ Cultural Influences

0188   Bernstein, Dennis
Blitt, Connie. (1987) "Zora Neale Hurston: Genius of the South." <u>Helicon Nine:</u> <u>Journal of Women's Arts and Letters</u> (Spring):17-18:pp. 48-50.

South/ Zora Neale Hurston/ Cultural Heritage/ Literature/ Writing/ Writers/ Anthropology/ Folk Culture/ African American/ Women of Color

0189   Berry, Jason
Foose, Jonathan and Jones, Tad. (1987) <u>Up from the Cradle of Jazz: New Orleans</u> <u>Music Since World War II</u>. Athens, GA: University of Georgia Press.

People of Color/ Blues/ Music/ African Americans/ Jazz/ Culture/ Louisiana/ Musicians/ Entertainers/ South/ Music History

0190   Boles, John B.
(1988) <u>Masters and Slaves in the House of the Lord: Race and Religion in the</u> <u>American South, 1740-1870</u>. Lexington: University Press of Kentucky. pp. 256.

People of Color/ History/ 18th Century/ African Americans/ Essays/ Slavery/ Race/ South/ 19th Century/ European Americans/ Religion/ Churches/ Culture

0191   Clark, Maxine L.
(1986) "Dating Patterns of Black Students on White Southern Campuses." <u>Journal of</u> <u>Multicultural Counseling and Development</u> 14(April):2:pp. 85-93.

African American/ Male Female Relationships/ Higher Education/ South/ Dating/ Women of Color/ Dominant Culture

0192   Collins, Patricia Hill
(1988) "Finding a Voice: The Black Women's Blues Tradition." Presented: Society for the Study of Social Problems Annual Meeting, Atlanta, GA.

African American/ Women of Color/ Traditions/ Entertainment/ Culture/ South/ Social Movements/ Black Studies/ Music/ Blues

0193   Davis, Allison
Gardner, Burleigh B. et al. (1988) <u>Deep South: A Social Anthropological Study of</u> <u>Caste and Class</u>. Los Angeles: University of California Los Angeles Center for Afro-American Studies. pp. 567.

People of Color/ Caste/ African Americans/ Socioeconomic Status/ South/ Mississippi/ Social Structure/ Anthropology/ Social Stratification/ Class/ Culture/ Stratification/ Class Differences/ Economic Structure

0194   Dillman, Caroline Matheny
(ed.). (1988) <u>Southern Women</u>. New York: Hemisphere Publishing. pp. 226. ISBN 0891168389.

African American/ European American/ Cultural Identity/ Women of Color/ Images of Women/ South/ Plantations/ History

0195   Esman, Marjorie R.
(1985) <u>Henderson, Louisiana: A Culture Adaptation in a Cajun Community</u>. New York: Holt, Rinehart and Winston. ISBN 0030028485.

Cajun/ South/ Louisiana/ Cultural Identity/ Acculturation Process/ Assimilation Patterns/ Subculture

0196   **Exley, Jo Ella Powell**
(1985) <u>Texas Tears and Texas Sunshine: Voices of Frontier Women</u>. College Station, TX: Texas A & M University Press. pp. 264.
Texas/ History/ South West/ Autobiographies/ Rural Living/ Life Styles/ Farming/ Women's Culture

0197   **Fields, Barbara Jeanne**
(1983) "The Nineteenth-Century American South: History and Theory." <u>Plantation Society in the Americas</u> 2(April):pp. 7-27.
South/ Culture/ People of Color/ Slavery/ History/ 19th Century/ African Americans/ Plantations/ European Americans/ Subculture

0198   **Gatewood, Willard B., Jr.**
(1988) "Aristocrats of Color: South and North: The Black Elite, 1880-1920." <u>Journal of Southern History</u> 54(February):pp. 3-20.
People of Color/ Elites/ Upper Class/ African Americans/ South/ Social History/ North/ Culture/ Social Class

0199   **Georgia Writer's Project**
(1987) <u>Drums and Shadows: Survival Studies among the Georgia Coastal Negroes</u>. Athens, GA: University of Georgia Press.
People of Color/ Cultural Identity/ African Americans/ Culture Conflict/ South/ Georgia/ History/ 1930-1939/ Cultural Heritage/ Interviews/ Assimilation Patterns/ Survival Strategies

0200   **Heinmiller, Janet**
(1980) "Women and the Catholic Church in Louisiana: A Study of Religion and the 'Other'." Presented: Southwestern Sociological Association Annual Meeting.
South/ Louisiana/ Catholicism/ Religion/ European American/ Women of Color*/ Churches/ Traditionalism/ Sex Role Stereotyping/ Gender Roles/ Subculture/ Women's Culture

0201   **Hoffert, Sylvia**
(1985) "Yankee Schoolmarms and the Domestication of the South." <u>Southern Studies</u> 24(Summer):pp. 188-201.
Northern/ South/ Social Reform/ Education/ Social Change/ Teaching/ Schools/ History/ 19th Century/ Civility/ Customs/ Cultural Influences

0202   **Hopkins, Pauline E.**
(1988) <u>Contending Forces: A Romance Illustrative of Negro Life North and South</u>. New York: Oxford University Press. pp. 464. ISBN 0195052587.
Women of Color/ Slavery/ African American/ North /South/ Novels/ Culture/ Fiction/ Living Conditions/ Writers/ Social Change/ Romances

0203   **Jones, Jacqueline**
(1986) "Class, Gender, and Racial-Cultural Perspectives on the Lives of Black and Poor White Women in the Rural South." Presented: American Farm Women in Historical Perspective, National Conference, Madison, WI.
Women of Color/ Women Living in Poverty/ African American/ European American/ Race, Class and Gender Studies/ Comparative Studies/ Cultural Influences/ Life Styles/ South/ Rural Areas

0204   **Juffer, June**
(1988) "Valley So Low." <u>Southern Exposure</u> 16(Winter):4:pp. 19-23.
Texas/ South/ Immigration/ Political Refugees/ Economic Refugees/ Central Americans/ Latinos/ Border Studies/ Foreign Policy/ People of Color/ Acculturation/ Cultural Identity

0205   **Low, Setha M.**
(1985) "Culturally Interpreted Symptoms or Culture-Bound Syndromes: A Cross-Cultural Review of Nerves." Social Science and Medicine 21:2:pp. 187-196.
Puerto Ricans/ Kentucky/ South/ Latinos/ People of Color/ Appalachia/ Poverty/ Nervousness/ Folk Medicine/ Lower Class/ Mental Health/ Physical Health/ Home Remedies/ Cultural Influences/ New York/ North East/ Health Seeking Behavior/ Comparative Studies

0206   **McLaurin, Melton A.**
(ed.). (1987) Separate Pasts: Growing Up White in the Segregated South. Athens, GA: University of Georgia. pp. 176.
Social History/ South/ Culture/ Racial Discrimination/ Prejudice/ Segregation/ Subculture

0207   **Moser, Charlotte**
(1988) Clyde Connell: The Art and Life of a Louisiana Woman. Austin, TX: University of Texas Press. pp. 94.
South/ Louisiana/ Women's Culture/ Biographies/ Clyde Connell/ Artists/ Artistic Styles and Genres

0208   **Perdue, Thelma**
(1985) "Southern Indians and the Cult of True Womanhood." in The Web of Southern Social Relations: Women, Family and Education. Walter J. Fraser, Jr. et al. (eds.). Athens, GA: University of Georgia Press. pp. 35-51.
Native American/ Women of Color/ Status/ Southern/ Cult of True Womanhood/ Cultural Heritage/ Matrilineal Kinship/ Patrilineal Kinship/ Power

0209   **Seidel, Kathryn Lee**
(1987) "The Southern Belle in American Literature: The Necessary Fantasy." Helicon Nine: Journal of Women's Art and Letters (Spring):17-18:pp. 40-47.
South/ Stereotypes/ Literature/ Images of Women/ Cult of True Womanhood/ Separate Spheres/ Feminine Mystique/ Women's Culture

0210   **Spitzer, Nick**
(1977) "Cajuns and Creoles: The French Gulf Coast." Southern Exposure 5:2-3:pp. 140-156.
Music/ South/ Louisiana/ Cajuns/ Creoles/ Cultural Influences/ Racial and Ethnic Differences

0211   **Stowe, Steven M.**
(1987) Intimacy and Power in the South: Ritual in the Lives of the Planters. Baltimore: Johns Hopkins University Press. pp. 309.
Plantations/ Elites/ Rites/ Language/ South/ 19th Century/ Courtship Customs/ Race, Class and Gender Studies/ Life Styles/ Family/ History/ 18th Century/ Cultural Heritage

0212   **Struebing-Beazley, Kristen**
Hero, Danella P. (1987) "Salvaged Memories: A Dialogue on Selected New Orleans Artists, Southern Writers and Common Sensibility." Helicon Nine: Journal of Women's Arts and Letters (Spring):17-18:pp. 60-92.
Louisiana/ South/ Southern/ Writers/ Writing/ Artists/ Art/ Popular Culture

0213   **Susie, Deborah Ann**
(1988) In the Ways of Our Grandmothers: A Cultural View of 20th Century Midwifery in Florida. Athens, GA: University of Georgia Press. pp. 272.
Women of Color/ African American/ Images of Women/ Stereotypes/ Midwifery/ Folk Medicine/ Cultural Influences/ Health Care Providers/ Florida/ South/ Maternal and Infant Welfare

0214   **Tracy, Susan Jean**
(1983) "Images of Women, Blacks, and Poor Whites in Antebellum Southern Literature." Dissertation: Rutgers, State University of New Jersey, New Brunswick, NJ. pp. 662.

Images of Women/ South/ Literature/ African American/ Antebellum/ Culture/ Women's History/ 19th Century/ European American/ Poverty

0215   **Wells, Sharon**
(1982) <u>Forgotten Legacy: Blacks in Nineteenth Century Key West</u>. Historic Key West Preservation Board, 500 Whitehead Street, Key West, FL 33040. pp. 60.

African Americans/ People of Color/ South/ Florida/ Social History/ 19th Century/ Legal Status/ Demograhy/ Trends/ Folklore/ Cultural Identity/ Curriculum Integration

0216   **Wilson, Kenneth**
(1987) "Gender Relations in the South: Are Southern Families Unique." Presented: American Sociological Association, Chicago, IL. Author: Sociology/Anthropology Dept., East Carolina University, Greenville, NC 27834.

South/ Families/ Sex-Gender Systems/ Male Female Relationships/ Conflict Resolution/ Gender Roles/ Cultural Influences

0217   **Wolfe, Margaret Ripley**
(1987) "Twentieth-Century Feminism: Southern Styles." <u>Helicon Nine: Journal of Women's Arts and Letters</u> (Spring):17, 18:pp. 148-157.

Southern/ Feminism/ Women's Movement/ Cultural Feminism/ Cultural Influences/ Women's History/ 20th Century

*Women of Color**

0218   **Angel, Ronald J.**
Worobey, Jacqueline Lowe. (1987) "Ethnicity, the Feminization of Poverty, and Children's Health." Presented: American Sociological Association, Chicago, IL. August. Author: Sociology Dept., Rutgers University, New Brunswick, NJ 08903.

Women of Color*/ Children/ Ethnicity/ Single Mothers/ Women Living in Poverty/ Socioeconomic Status/ Disadvantaged/ Racial and Ethnic Differences/ Physical Health/ Living Conditions

0219   **Arnold, Regina A.**
(1980) "Socio-Structural Determinants of Self Esteem and the Relationship Between Self Esteem and Criminal Behavior Patterns of Imprisoned Minority Women." Dissertation: Bryn Mawr College, Bryn Mawr, PA. pp. 161.

Women of Color*/ Prisoners/ Criminals/ Correctional Facilities/ Social Indicators/ Self Esteem/ Personality Traits/ Behavior Modification/ Deviant Behavior/ Culture

0220   **Baskin, David**
Nelson, M. (1980) "Clinical Diagnosis: New Light on Ethnic Differences." Presented: Annual Conference of the American Psychological Association, Montreal, Canada.

Women of Color*/ Mental Health Treatment/ Comparative Studies/ Diagnoses/ Race Bias/ Racial and Ethnic Differences

0221 Brenzel, Barbara
(1983) "History of 19th Century Women's Education: A Plea For Inclusion of Class, Race and Ethnicity." Available: Working Paper #114, Wellesley College Center for Research on Women.

Feminist Scholarship/ Higher Education/ Educational Opportunities/ Social History/ 19th Century/ Women of Color*/ Race, Class and Gender Studies/ Social Class/ Ethnicity

0222 Cafferty, Pastora San Juan
Chestang, Leon (eds.). (1976) The Diverse Society: Implications for Social Policy. Silver Spring, MD: National Association of Social Workers. pp. 176. ISBN 0871010720.

People of Color*/ Cultural Identity/ Ethnicity/ Ethnic Groups/ Social Policy/ Identity/ Cultural Groups

0223 Clark, Ann L.
(1981) Culture and Childbearing. Philadelphia: F. A. Davis Company. pp. 248.

Women of Color*/ Medical Sciences/ Maternal and Infant Welfare/ Cultural Influences/ Childbearing/ Health Care Professionals

0224 Collins, Patricia Hill
(1989) "Toward a New Vision: Race, Class and Gender as Catagories of Analysis and Connection." Curriculum Integration Paper #7, Center for Research on Women, Memphis State University, Memphis, TN 38152. pp. 28.

Race, Class and Gender Studies/ Diversity/ Women of Color*/ Oppression/ Power/ Racial and Ethnic Differences/ Stereotypes/ Cultural Influences/ Social Change/ Education/ Teaching

0225 Davis, C. E.
Rowland, C. K. (1979) "Assessing the Consequences of Ethnic, Sexual, and Economic Representation on State Grand Juries." Justice System Journal 5(Winter):2:pp. 197-203.

Women of Color*/ Race, Class and Gender Studies/ Socioeconomic Status/ Juries/ Criminal Justice/ Criminal Litigation/ Income/ Lower Class/ Disadvantaged Persons/ Racial and Ethnic Differences

0226 Dill, Bonnie Thornton
(1988) "Our Mothers' Grief: Racial Ethnic Women and the Maintenance of Families." Journal of Family History 13:4:pp. 415-431.

Women of Color*/ Survival Strategies/ Resistance/ Families/ Cultural Heritage/ Family Influence/ Support Systems

0227 Epstein, Cynthia Fuchs
(1988) Deceptive Distinctions: Sex, Gender, and the Social Order. New Haven, CT: Yale University Press. pp. 304.

Women of Color*/ Separate Spheres/ Socialization/ Sex Discrimination/ Inequality/ Social Influences/ Gender Roles/ Social Control/ Sex Differences/ Social Status/ Segregation/ Women's Culture

0228 Ferrero, Pat
Hedges, Elaine and Silber, J. (1987) Hearts and Hands: The Influence of Women and Quilts on American Society. San Francisco: Quilt Digest Press. pp. 112.

Women of Color*/ Abolition/ Women's History/ 19th Century/ Women's Roles/ Craft Arts/ Women's Culture/ Social Movements/ Social Influences/ Suffrage Movement/ Civil War

0229 Fulani, Lenora
(1988) The Psychopathology of Everyday Racism and Sexism. New York: Practice

Press.

Women of Color*/ Psychology/ Racial Discrimination/ Sexual Exploitation/ Sex Discrimination/ Poverty/ Social Status/ Assimilation/ Stress/ Cultural Heritage

0230 **Fullilove, Mindy**
Hunt, Phern and Jackson, Sylvia (eds.). (1984) <u>Women in Psychotherapy: Issues of Sex, Class and Race</u>. Tenderloin Mental Health Clinic, Department of Psychiatry, San Francisco General Hospital, University of CA, San Francisco, CA.

Women's Studies/ Women of Color*/ Psychotherapy/ Ethnic Studies/ Race, Class and Gender Studies

0231 **Furstenberg, Frank F.**
Morgan, S. Philip et al. (1987) "Race Differences in the Timing of Adolescent Intercourse." <u>American Sociological Review</u> 52(August):4:pp. 511-518.

Women of Color*/ Racial and Ethnic Differences/ Adolescents/ Comparative Studies/ Race, Class and Gender Studies/ Sexual Behavior/ Premarital Relations/ Socioeconomic Status/ Peer Influence/ Norms

0232 **Ginorio, Angela B.**
Brown, M. and Buren, C. Van. (1984) "Sexual Harassment of Women Students: Functional and Cultural Discrimination." Author: Women's Information Center AJ-50, University of Washington, Seattle, WA 98195.

Women of Color*/ Sexual Harassment/ Students/ Education/ Discrimination/ Power/ Culture

0233 **Gorelick, Sherry**
(1983) "Between Two Sexisms: Ethnic Women's Response." Presented: American Sociological Association Annual Meeting, Detroit, MI. September.

Women of Color*/ Ethnic Studies/ Sex Discrimination/ Acculturation/ Cultural Influences/ Double Bind

0234 **Graham, Hugh Davis**
(1987) "Sex, Race, Ethnicity, and Scholarly Prizes." <u>OAH Newsletter: Organization of American Historians</u> 15(February):1:pp. 2-3.

Women of Color*/ Ethnic Studies/ Racial Discrimination/ Sex Discrimination in Education/ Higher Education/ Academic Awards

0235 **Harris, R.**
(1980) "An Examination of Effects of Ethnicity, Socioeconomic Status and Generation on Familism and Sex Role Orientations." <u>Journal of Comparative Family Studies</u> 2:pp. 173-193.

Socioeconomic Status/ Sex Roles/ Women of Color*/ Cultural Influences/ Family/ Ethnicity

0236 **Heinmiller, Janet**
(1980) "Women and the Catholic Church in Louisiana: A Study of Religion and the 'Other'." Presented: Southwestern Sociological Association Annual Meeting.

South/ Louisiana/ Catholicism/ Religion/ European American/ Women of Color*/ Churches/ Traditionalism/ Sex Role Stereotyping/ Gender Roles/ Subculture/ Women's Culture

0237 **Jacobs, Carolyn**
Bowles, Dorcas D. (eds.). (1988) <u>Ethnicity and Race: Critical Concepts in Social Work</u>. Silver Spring, MD: National Association of Social Workers. pp. 242. ISBN 0871011557.

People of Color*/ Help Seeking Behavior/ Ethnicity/ Family Life/ Race/ Extended Family/ Social Work/ Culture Conflict/ Ethnic Groups/ Adjustment/ Cultural Identity/ Family Roles

0238 **Lipman-Blumen, Jean**
(1984) <u>Gender Roles and Power</u>. Englewood Cliffs, NJ: Prentice Hall.

Women of Color*/ Sex Roles/ Gender Roles/ Power/ Powerlessness/ Cultural Influences

0239   Luchetti, Cathy
Olwell, Carol. (1982) <u>Women of the West</u>. Berkeley, CA: Antelope Island Press. pp. 240.
Women of Color*/ Women's History/ West/ 19th Century/ 20th Century/ Women's Culture

0240   Mann, Coramae R.
(1987) "Women Who Kill Someone They Don't Really Know." Presented: American Sociological Association, Chicago, IL. Author: Florida State University, School of Criminology, Tallahassee, FL 32306. August.
Women of Color*/ Violence/ Murder/ Economic Factors/ Crimes/ Criminals/ Women's Culture

0241   Manuel, R. C.
(1982) <u>Minority Aging: Sociological and Social Psychological Issues</u>. Westport, CT: Greenwood Press.
Health Care/ Women of Color*/ Older Adults/ Aging/ Cultural Influences/ Comparative Studies/ Life Cycles/ Self Concept/ Social Psychology

0242   Marger, Martin N.
(1985) <u>Race and Ethnic Relations: Americans and Global Perspectives</u>. Belmont, CA: Wadsworth. pp. 336. ISBN 0534041493.
Ethnic Studies/ Stratification/ Women of Color*/ Race Relations/ Racial and Ethnic Differences/ Interracial Relations/ Ethnic Relations

0243   Markides, Kyriakos S.
Mindel, Charles H. (1987) <u>Aging and Ethnicity</u>. Beverly Hills, CA: Sage Publications.
People of Color*/ Life Cycles/ Cultural Influences/ Older Adults/ Aging/ Racial and Ethnic Differences/ Ethnicity/ Comparative Studies

0244   McCluskey, Audrey T.
(1985) <u>Women of Color: Perspectives on Feminism and Identity</u>. Bloomington, IN: Indiana University Press. pp. 177.
Women of Color*/ Feminism/ Gender Identity/ Cultural Identity/ Black Feminism/ Social Movements

0245   Myers, Lena Wright
(1988) "Gender Role Socialization of Women: Racial Consequences." Presented: Society for the Study of Social Problems Annual Meeting, Atlanta, GA.
Gender Roles/ Women of Color*/ Women's Studies/ Social Conflict/ Parenthood/ Racial Discrimination/ Socialization/ Women's Culture

0246   Norton, Anne
(1986) <u>Alternative Americas: A Reading of Antebellum Political Culture</u>. Chicago: University of Chicago Press. pp. 364. ISBN 0226595102.
People of Color*/ Politics/ Culture/ Identity/ History/ 19th Century/ Political Influences/ Civil War/ Cultural Influences/ Cultural Identity/ Antebellum

0247   Persons, Stow
(1987) <u>Ethnic Studies at Chicago, 1905-1945</u>. Urbana, IL: University of Illinois Press. pp. 159.
People of Color*/ Sociology/ Ethnic Groups/ Race Relations/ Ethnicity/ Sociologists/ Ethnic Studies/ Theories/ Illinois/ North Central/ 20th Century/ History

0248 Phinney, Jean S.
Rotheram, Mary Jane (eds.). (1987) <u>Children's Ethnic Socialization</u>. Newbury Park, CA: Sage Publications. pp. 328.

Ethnic Studies/ Cultural Influence/ Self Esteem/ Social Behavior/ Attitudes/ Social Status/ Identity/ Socialization/ Women of Color*

0249 Redfern, Bernice I.
(1989) <u>Women of Color in the United States: A Guide to the Literature</u>. New York: Garland Publishing. pp. 176. ISBN 0824058496.

Women of Color*/ Literature/ Ethnic Studies/ Women's Studies/ Bibliographies/ Research Resources

0250 Sanchez, Carol Lee
(1983) "Sex, Class and Race Intersections: Visions of Women of Color." Available: Women's International Resource Exchange, New York, NY.

Women of Color*/ Assimilation Patterns/ Comparative Studies/ Race, Class and Gender Studies/ Cultural Identity/ Stereotypes/ Acculturation Process/ Integration

0251 Sowell, Thomas
(1978) <u>American Ethnic Groups</u>. Lanham, MD: University Press. pp. 254.

Ethnic Groups/ Ethnicity/ People of Color*/ Minority Groups/ Racial and Ethnic Differences

0252 Sowell, Thomas
(1988) <u>Ethnic America</u>. New York: Laissez Faire Books. pp. 353.

Ethnic Groups/ People of Color*/ Immigrants/ Racial and Ethnic Differences/ Ethnicity/ Ethnic Studies

0253 Swerdlow, Amy
Bridenthal, Renate et al. (eds.). (1988) <u>Household and Kin</u>. New York: Feminist Press. ISBN 0912670681.

People of Color*/ Family Roles/ Race, Class and Gender Studies/ Cultural Influences/ Family/ Kinship/ Nontraditional Family/ Family Structure

0254 Takaki, Ronald
(ed.). (1987) <u>From Different Shores: Perspectives on Race and Ethnicity in America</u>. New York: Oxford Press. pp. 272.

Women of Color*/ Race, Class and Gender Studies/ Identity/ Immigrants/ Ethnic Diversity/ Assimilation/ Stratification/ Race Relations

0255 U.S. Department of Health and Human Services
(1976) "Health Characteristics of Minority Groups, U. W. 1976." U.S. Department of Health, Education and Welfare, Washington, D.C.

Health Care/ Comparative Studies/ Ethnicity/ Physical Health/ Mental Health/ Illness/ Wellness/ People of Color*

0256 Walker, Nancy
Dresner, Zita (eds.). (1988) <u>Redressing the Balance: American Women's Literary Humor from Colonial Times to the 1980's</u>. Jackson, MS: University of Mississippi Press. pp. 454. ISBN 0878053646.

Feminist Perspective/ Household Division of Labor/ Women of Color*/ Entertainment/ Literature/ Humor/ Popular Culture/ Literary Criticism/ Images of Women/ Stereotypes/ Male Female Relationships

0257 Weatherford, Doris
(1987) <u>Foreign and Female: Immigrant Women in America, 1840-1930</u>. New York:

Schocken Books. pp. 288.

Women of Color*/ Immigrants/ Women's History/ 19th Century/ European American/ Cultural Influences/ 20th Century

0258 Whelehan, Patricia

et al. (eds.). (1988) <u>Women and Health: Cross Cultural Perspectives</u>. Granby, MA: Bergin and Garvey. pp. 304. ISBN 0897891392.

Women's Studies/ Anthropology/ Health Care Services/ Family Structure/ Politics/ Women of Color*/ Social Movements/ Cross Cultural Studies/ Stress/ Economics/ Comparative Studies

0259 White, Barbara W.

(1984) <u>Color in a White Society</u>. Silver Spring, MD: National Association of Social Workers. pp. 135. ISBN 087101128x.

People of Color*/ Ethnic Groups/ Social Work/ Minority Groups/ Racial Discrimination/ Dominant Culture/ Sex Discrimination/ Race Relations/ Minority Experience

EDUCATION

African American

0260 Abrahamse, Allan F.
Morrison, Peter A. et al. (1988) <u>Beyond Stereotypes: Who Becomes a Single Teenage Mother?</u> Santa Monica, CA: Rand Corporation. pp. 88. ISBN 0833008322.

African American/ Adolescents/ European American/ Economic Factors/ Women of Color/ Academic Achievement/ Teenage Mothers/ Single Parents/ Single Mothers/ Educationally Disadvantaged/ Images of Women/ Sereotypes/ Family/ Families

0261 Allen, Walter R.
Hall, Marcia L. and Mays, Arlene. (1984) "Dreams Deferred: Black Student Career Goals and Fields of Study in Graduate/Professional Schools." <u>Phylon</u> 45:4:pp. 271-283.

Women of Color/ African American/ Higher Education/ Post Secondary Education/ Career Planning/ Academic Achievement/ Graduate Degrees/ Barrier Free Access/ Occupational Status/ Occupational Mobility

0262 Anderson, James D.
(1988) <u>The Education of Blacks in the South, 1860-1935</u>. Chapel Hill, NC: University of North Carolina. pp. 381.

Education/ 20th Century/ 19th Century/ African Americans/ Educational Opportunities/ South/ History/ Educational Experience/ Educational Methods/ People of Color/ Educational Policy

0263 Anderson, Karen T.
(1988) "Brickbats and Roses: The Career of Lucy Diggs Slowe." in <u>Lone Voyagers: Academic Women in Coeducational Institutions, 1869-1937</u>. Gereldine J. Clifford. New York: Feminist Press. pp. 281-307.

African American/ Deans/ Education Occupation/ Women of Color/ Coeducation/ South/ Washington, D.C./ Women's History/ 20th Century/ Universities/ Higher Education/ College Administrators/ Lucy Diggs Slowe/ Biographies

0264 Avery, Byllye
(1989) "Black Women's Health: A Conspiracy of Silence." <u>Sojourner</u> 14(January):5:pp. 15-16.

African American/ Teenage Pregnancy/ Women of Color/ Violence/ Health Care Services/ Prenatal Care/ Health Care Facilities/ Health Care Delivery/ Discrimination/ Disadvantaged/ Health Education

0265 Blackwell, James E.
(1981) <u>Mainstreaming Outsiders: The Production of Black Professionals</u>. Bayside, NY: General Hall, Inc.

African American/ Women of Color/ Higher Education/ Employment/ Professional Status

0266 Brown, Diane Robinson
(1986) "Complaints of Racial Discrimination at Historically Black Colleges."

Journal of Social and Behavioral Sciences 32(Spring):2:pp. 107-116.

People of Color/ African Americans/ Racial Discrimination/ Higher Education/ Colleges/ Black Colleges

0267 **Butler, Anne S.**
(1987) Black Girls and Schooling: Directory of Strategies and Programs for Black Females K-12. Manhattan, KS: College of Education, Kansas State University. pp. 59.

Directories/ Academic Achievement/ African American/ Student Motivation/ Women of Color/ Self Esteem/ Leadership/ Research Resources/ Parent Influence/ Education/ Educational Equity/ Learning Motivation/ Curriculum Integration

0268 **Byrd, Alicia D.**
(1988) "Adult Educational Efforts of the American Black Church, 1600-1900." Journal of Religious Thought 44(Winter/Spring)pp. 83-92.

People of Color/ African Americans/ History/ Education/ Adult Education/ Religion/ Churches/ Educational Programs/ Support Systems

0269 **Christian, Virgil L., Jr.**
Stroup, Robert H. (1981) "The Effect of Education on Relative Earnings of Black and White Women." Economics of Education Review 1(Winter):1:pp. 113-122.

African American/ European American/ Women of Color/ Wage Earning Women/ Education/ Income/ Wages/ Wage Gap

0270 **Collins, Patricia Hill**
(1986) "The Emerging Theory and Pedagogy of Black Women's Studies." Feminist Issues 6(Spring):1:pp. 3-17.

Women of Color/ Racial Discrimination/ African American/ Sex Discrimination/ Feminist Theory/ Patriarchy/ Course Objectives/ Mothers/ Teaching/ Pedagogy/ Images of Women/ Race, Class and Gender Studies/ Black Feminism

0271 **Comer, James**
(1989) Maggie's American Dream: The Life and Times of a Black Family. Bergenfield, NJ: New American Library. ISBN 0453005888.

Women of Color/ Education/ Southern/ Economically Disadvantaged/ Family/ African American/ Black Studies/ Parenting

0272 **Darlington-Hope, Marian**
Grogan, Janet. (1986) "When Poor Women are Forced to Compete: Teaching Negotiations." Women's Studies Quarterly 14(Spring/Summer):1-2:pp. 36-38.

Women of Color/ African American/ Lower Class/ Women Living in Poverty/ Teaching/ Career Education/ Woman Power/ Self Concept/ Competitive Behavior

0273 **Dudovitz, Resa L.**
(1984) Women in Academe. Elmsford, NY: Pergamon Press.

Women of Color/ African American/ Higher Education/ Employment/ Academia/ Schools/ Universities/ Colleges

0274 **Dyer, Thomas G.**
(1985) "Higher Education in the South Since the Civil War: Historical Issues and Trends." in The Web of Southern Social Relations: Women, Family and Education. Walter J. Fraser, Jr. et al. (eds.). Athens, GA: University of Georgia Press. pp. 127-145.

African American/ European American/ Women of Color/ Higher Education/ Black Colleges/ Women's Colleges/ South/ History/ 19th Century/ Radicals

0275   **Eakin, Sue Lyles**
(1980) "The Black Struggle for Education in Louisiana, 1877-1930s." Dissertation: University of Southwestern Louisiana, Lafayette, LA. DAI Vol. 41(09A)4132.

African Americans/ People of Color/ Social History/ Education/ South/ Louisiana/ 19th Century/ 20th Century

0276   **Edwards, Harry T.**
Nordin, Virginia D. (1979) <u>Higher Education and the Law</u>. Cambridge, MA: Institute for Educational Management, Harvard University.

Women of Color/ African American/ Educational Equity/ Laws/ Higher Education/ Civil Rights Movement

0277   **Edwards, Harry T.**
Nordin, Virginia D. (1982) <u>Higher Education and the Law, 1982/83 Cumulative Supplement</u>. Cambridge, MA: Institution for Educational Management, Harvard University.

African American/ Women of Color/ Higher Education/ Laws/ Educational Equity/ Civil Rights

0278   **Farley, Reynolds**
(1985) "Three Steps Forward and Two Back? Recent Changes in the Social and Economic Status of Blacks." <u>Ethnic and Racial Studies</u> 8(January):1:pp. 4-28. (Special Issue: Ethnicity and Race in the U.S.A.: Toward the Twenty-First Century.).

African Americans/ People of Color/ Trends/ Socioeconomic Status/ Educational Attainment/ Occupational Segregation/ Earnings/ Residential Segregation

0279   **Farley, Reynolds**
Allen, Walter R. (1987) <u>Differentiation and Stratification: Age Groups, Class, Gender, Race and Ethnic Groups</u>. New York: Russell Sage Foundation. pp. 493.

African Americans/ Economy/ European Americans/ Occupational Segregation/ Social Change/ Integration/ Social Inequality/ Education/ Segregation/ People of Color/ Diversity/ Racial and Ethnic Differences

0280   **Forten, Charlotte**
Billington, Ray Allen (ed.). (1981) <u>The Journal of Charlotte Forten: A Free Negro in the Slave Era</u>. New York: W. W. Norton.

Women of Color/ African American/ Autobiographies/ Missionaries/ Teachers/ Education/ South Carolina/ Antebellum

0281   **Giddings, Paula**
(1988) <u>In Search of Sisterhood: Delta Sigma Theta and the Challenge of the Black Sorority Movement</u>. New York: William Morrow.

African American/ Students/ Higher Education/ Women of Color/ Social Organizations/ Sisterhood/ Women's Groups/ Colleges/ Sororities/ Networks/ Support Systems

0282   **Giele, Janet Zollinger**
Gilfus, Mary. (1988) "Race and Cohort Differences in Women's Life Patterns, 1934-1982." Presented: American Sociological Association, Annual Meeting, Atlanta, GA. August.

African American/ Family Roles/ European American/ Career Opportunities/ Higher Education/ Education/ Labor Force Participation/ Life Cycles/ Gender Roles/ Women of Color/ Socialization

0283 **Gregory, Clarence Kenneth**
(1976) "The Education of Blacks in Maryland: An Historical Survey." Dissertation: Columbia University Teachers College, New York, NY. pp. 517. DAI Vol. 37(03A)1729.

African Americans/ People of Color/ Social History/ Education/ Maryland/ East

0284 **Hall, Eleanor R.**
(1975) "Motivation and Achievement in Black and White Junior College Students." Journal of Social Psychology 97:pp. 107-113.

People of Color/ Two Year Colleges/ Students/ Junior Colleges/ Higher Education/ Black Colleges/ Motivation/ African Americans/ Academic Achievement/ European Americans/ Comparative Studies

0285 **Hall, Eleanor R.**
Loesting, L. and Woods, M. L. (1977) "Relationships among Measures of Locus of Control for Black and White Students." Psychological Reports 40:pp. 59-62.

People of Color/ African Americans/ Students/ European Americans/ Education/ Comparative Studies/ Locus of Control

0286 **Harris, Leah-Creque**
(1987) "She Danced to Teach--And They Loved It." American Visions (February):pp. 36-41.

Women of Color/ African American/ Biographies/ History/ Ballet/ Performing Arts/ Artistic Styles and Genres/ Education

0287 **Heintze, Michael Robert**
(1981) "A History of the Black Private Colleges in Texas, 1865-1954." Dissertation: Texas Tech University, Lubbock, TX. pp. 344. DAI Vol. 42(08A)3709.

African Americans/ People of Color/ South West/ Texas/ Social History/ Higher Education/ Private Colleges/ Black Colleges/ 19th Century/ 20th Century

0288 **Higginbotham, Elizabeth**
(1987) "The On-Going Struggle: Education and Mobility for Black Women." Research Paper #7, Center for Research on Women, Memphis State University, Memphis, TN 38152.

African American/ Career Aspirations/ Women of Color/ Racial Discrimination/ Oppression/ Sex Discrimination/ Mobility/ Educational Opportunities

0289 **Hine, Darlene Clark**
Bidelman, Patrick Kay and Herd, Shirley. (1986) The Black Women in the Middle West Project: A Comprehensive Resource Guide: Illinois and Indiana. Indianapolis: Indiana Historical Bureau. pp. 238.

Women of Color/ Essays/ Research Resources/ Oral History/ African American/ Documents/ North Central/ Women's History/ Illinois/ Indiana/ Education

0290 **Hoffman, Nancy**
(1986) "Black Studies, Ethnic Studies, and Women's Studies: Some Reflections on Collaborative Projects." Women's Studies Quarterly 14(Spring/Summer):1-2:pp. 49-53.

Women of Color/ African American/ Black Studies/ Ethnic Studies/ Women's Studies/ Social Science Research/ Research Methods/ Education/ Curriculum Integration

0291 **Ihle, Elizabeth L.**
(1986) "History of Black Women's Education in the South, 1865-Present." Instructional Modules for Educators. Module I, II, III, IV. Available: E. Ihle, James

Madison University, Harrisonburg, VA. Sponsored: Women's Educational Equity Act Program, US Department of Education.

African American/ South/ Schools/ 19th Century/ 20th Century/ Higher Education/ Separate Spheres/ Job Training/ Women of Color/ Women's History/ Teaching/ Segregation/ Vocational Education/ Primary Education/ Secondary Education

0292   **Jerrido, Margaret**
(1981) "Early Black Women Physicians." <u>Women and Health</u> 5(Fall):3:pp. 1-3.

African American/ Women of Color/ History/ 19th Century/ Health Care Occupations/ Physicians/ Biographies/ Medical Sciences/ Professional Status/ Race, Class and Gender Studies/ Medical Education

0293   **Jewell, Karen Sue**
(1985) "The Effects of Race, Class and Gender on Research Methodology in African-American Studies." Presented: Parallel Methodological Issues in Women's Studies and Black Studies, North Central Sociological Association, Louisville, KY.

African American/ Women of Color/ Race, Class and Gender Studies/ Research Methods/ Higher Education/ Research Bias

0294   **Jones, Faustine Childress**
(1981) <u>A Traditional Model of Educational Excellence: Dunbar High School of Little Rock, Arkansas</u>. Washington, D.C.: Howard University Press.

Education/ High Schools/ African American/ South/ Arkansas/ Women of Color/ Academic Achievement

0295   **Jones, L. V.**
(1984) "White-Black Achievement Differences: The Narrowing Gap." <u>American Psychologist</u> 39:pp. 1207-1213.

Academic Achievement/ Education/ African American/ Comparative Studies/ Women of Color/ European American/ Racial and Ethnic Differences

0296   **Kahle, Jane B.**
(1986) "From One Minority to Another." in <u>Perspectives on Gender and Science</u>. J. Harding. Philadelphia: Falmer Press. pp. 63-80.

Women of Color/ Scientific and Technical Occupations/ African American/ Science/ Scientists/ Educational Experience/ Educational Programs/ Double Bind

0297   **Kane, Jacqueline**
Bose, Chris. (1987) "Classism, Racism, and Sexism." in <u>An Inclusive Curriculum: Race, Class, and Gender in Sociological Instruction</u>. Patricia Bell Collins and Margaret L. Andersen (eds.). Washington, D.C.: American Sociological Association.

Women of Color/ Class Division/ African American/ Triple Jeopardy/ Race, Class and Gender Studies/ Discrimination/ Institutional Racism/ Higher Education/ Institutional Sexism/ Teaching/ Curriculum Integration

0298   **Kenkel, William F.**
(1981) "Black-White Differences in Age-At-Marriage-Expectations of Low Income High School Girls." <u>Journal of Negro Education</u> 50(Fall):4:pp. 425-438.

Comparative Studies/ European American/ African American/ Marriage/ High Schools/ Low Income Households/ Education/ Women of Color

0299   **King, Deborah Karyn**
Palmieri, Patricia A. (1987) "Women's Colleges." in <u>Women in Higher Education</u>.

Mariam K. Chamberlain. New York: Russell Sage Foundation.

Women of Color/ Women's Colleges/ African American/ Black Colleges/ Higher Education/ Post Secondary Education

0300 Kohl, Jeanne E.
Harman, Marsha S. (1987) "Attitudes of Secondary School Students toward Computers. Do Gender and Socioeconomic Status Make a Difference?" Presented: American Sociological Association, Annual Meeting, Chicago, IL. Author: Sociology Dept., California State University, Long Beach, CA 90840.

Latina/ African American/ Women of Color/ Socioeconomic Status/ Race, Class and Gender Studies/ Computer Literacy/ Computer Equity/ Education/ Income Distribution/ Computer Avoidance/ High Schools/ Gender

0301 Lang, Dwight
(1987) "Stratification and Prestige Hierarchies in Graduate and Professional Education." Sociological Inquiry 57(Winter):1:pp. 12-27.

Women of Color/ Stratification/ African American/ Status/ Prestige/ Race, Class and Gender Studies/ Civil Rights Movement/ Higher Education/ Financial Aid/ Graduate Degrees/ Academic Rank/ Academic Standards

0302 Lindsay, Beverly
(1984) "Pursuing the Baccalaureate Degree in the U.S.: The Case of African American Women." World Yearbook of Education. pp. 139-152.

African American/ Women of Color/ Higher Education/ Undergraduate Degrees/ Colleges/ Universities/ Academic Aspirations

0303 Lukas, J. Anthony
(1986) Common Ground: A Turbulent Decade in the Lives of Three American Families. New York: Random House. pp. 676. ISBN 0394746163.

Women of Color/ African American/ Class Differences/ Class Consciousness/ School Desegregation/ Desegregation Methods/ Busing/ Family/ Social Movements

0304 Mariam, A. G.
(1989) "The Declining Enrollment of Blacks in Higher Education." The Institute for Urban Research, Morgan State University, "Research Notes" 5(Winter):1:pp. 5-6.

African Americans/ Inequality/ Higher Education/ Discrimination/ Colleges/ Universities/ People of Color/ Academic Achievement/ Racial Discrimination/ Civil Rights Movement

0305 Matson, M. R.
(1983) Black Women's Sex Roles: The Social Content for a New Ideology." Journal of Social Issues 39:3:pp. 101-113.

Women of Color/ African American/ Sex Education/ Sex Roles/ Marital Status/ Homosexuality/ Illegitimacy/ Birth Rates/ Race, Class and Gender Studies/ Male Female Relationships

0306 Mays, Vickie M.
(1988) "Teaching the Psychology of Black Women." in Teaching Psychology. P. Bronstein and K. Quina (eds.). Washington, D.C.: American Psychological Association.

Women of Color/ Curriculum Integration/ African American/ Psychology/ Teaching/ Teacher Education

0307 McAdoo, Harriette Pipes
(1988) Black Families. Newbury Park, CA: Sage Publications. pp. 288.

Family/ Families/ Demography/ African Americans/ Mobility/ Teenage Pregnancy/ People of Color/ Educational Opportunities/ Economic Status/ Children/ Socialization

0308 **McCaul, Robert L.**
(1987) The Black Struggle for Public Schooling In Nineteeth Century Illinois. Carbondale, IL: Southern Illinois University. pp. 193.

People of Color/ Public Schools/ African American/ Educational Opportunities/ Education/ Political Influence/ 19th Century/ History/ Illinois/ North Central/ Educational Equity

0309 **McCrate, Elaine**
(1988) "Teenage Mothers: Poverty's Vicious Cycle." UCLA Center for Afro-American Studies Newsletter 11:2:pp. 6-7.

Women of Color/ Single Mothers/ African American/ Single Parents/ Teenagers/ Educationally Disadvantaged/ Teenage Pregnancy/ Educational Attainment/ Poverty/ Women Living in Poverty

0310 **Morris, Robert C.**
(1981) Reading, 'Riting and Reconstruction: The Education of Freemen in the South. Chicago: University of Chicago Press.

African American/ History/ Reconstruction/ Education/ Freemen/ 19th Century/ Women of Color

0311 **Nettles, Michael T.**
Thoeny, A. R. (1988) Toward Black Undergraduate Student Equity in American Higher Education. Westport, CT: Greenwood Press. pp. 234.

African American/ Academic Freedom/ Higher Education/ Women of Color/ Educational Opportunities/ Racial Equality/ Educational Equity/ Career Aspirations/ Students/ Universities

0312 **Neverdon-Morton, Cynthia**
(1982) "Self Help Programs as Educative Activities of Black Women in the South, 1895-1925." Journal of Negro Education 51(Summer):3:pp. 207-221.

Women of Color/ African American/ South/ Women's History/ Self Help Behavior/ Educational Programs/ Social Services/ Model Programs/ Change Agents/ Advocacy Groups

0313 **Newsome, Imani-Sheila**
(1986) "Work My Soul Must Have: Three Generations of Black Women in Ministry." SAGE: A Scholarly Journal on Black Women 3(Spring):1:pp. 50-52.

Women of Color/ African American/ Biographies/ Religion/ Religious Education/ Ministers/ Clergy/ Women Religious

0314 **Perkins, Linda M.**
(1984) "The Education of Black Women: A Historical Perspective." Presented: Annual Meeting of the Organization of American Historians. April.

Women of Color/ African American/ Education/ Women's History

0315 **Perry, Constance M.**
(1987) "Teaching a Controversial Novel to a Conservative Classroom: The Color Purple." Feminist Teacher 2:3:pp. 25-30.

Women of Color/ African American/ Teaching/ Literature/ Stereotypes/ Images of Women/ Course Objectives/ Curriculum Integration

0316 **Shockley, Ann Allen**
(ed.). (1988) Afro-American Women Writers, 1746-1933: An Anthology and Critical Guide. Boston: G. K. Hall. pp. 495.

Women of Color/ African American/ Writers/ Literary Arts/ Women's History/ Anthologies/ Education

0317   Simms, Margaret C.
(1988) "The Choices that Young Black Women Make: Education, Employment and Family Formation." Available: Working Paper #190, Wellesley College Center for Research on Women, Wellesley, MA.

African American/ Career Aspirations/ Educational Opportunities/ Higher Education/ Decision Making/ Women of Color/ Employment/ Young Adults/ Career Planning

0318   Smith, Elaine M.
(1980) "Mary McLeod Bethune and the National Youth Administration." in <u>Clio Was a Woman: Studies in the History of American Women</u>. Mabel E. Deutrich and Virginia C. Puroy. Washington, D.C.: Howard University Press.

African American/ Leadership/ 20th Century/ Women's History/ 1940-1949/ Education/ Civil Rights/ Employment/ Job Training/ Women of Color/ Mary McLeod Bethune

0319   Smith, Eleanor J.
Smith, Paul M. (1978) "General Education: Relevance for African American Studies." <u>College Student Journal</u> 12(Fall):3:pp. 251-255.

Education/ Nationalism/ African Americans/ Curriculum Integration/ People of Color/ Black Studies

0320   Smith, Willy DeMarcell
Chunn, Eva Wells. (1989) <u>Black Education: A Quest for Equity and Excellence</u>. New Brunswick, NJ: Transaction Publishers. pp. 247. ISBN 0887387810.

African American/ Educational Equity/ Women of Color/ Education/ Educational Opportunities/ Academic Aspirations/ Discrimination

0321   Torrecilha, Ramon S.
(1988) "Migration, Education and Income Differentials on Selected Rural Poor Counties in the South, 1975-80." Presented: Rural Sociological Society.

African Americans/ Employment Patterns/ European Americans/ Low Income Households/ People of Color/ Migration/ Wages/ Rural Areas/ Educational Opportunities/ Comparative Studies/ 1970-1979

0322   Udry, J. Richard
Billy, John O. G. (1987) "Initiation of Coitus in Early Adolescence." <u>American Sociological Review</u> 52(Dec):6:pp. 841-855.

Women of Color/ Sex Education/ African American/ Social Behavior/ Comparative Studies/ Adolescents/ Coitus/ Sexual Behavior/ Sexual Permissiveness/ Cultural Influences

0323   Uriarte, Miren
(1986) "Contribution To A Dialogue." <u>Women's Studies Quarterly</u> 14(Spring/Summer):1-2:pp. 32-35.

Women of Color/ African American/ Teaching/ Race Relations/ Cultural Groups/ Educational Methods/ Educational Programs

0324   Walsh, W. Bruce
Horton, J. and Bingham, R. P. (1979) "A Comparison of the Concurrent Validity of Holland's Theory with College-Degreed Black Women." <u>Journal of Vocational Behavior</u> 13:pp. 242-250.

Women of Color/ Bachelors Degrees/ African American/ Academic Awards/ Comparative Studies/ Employment/ Post Secondary Education/ Academic Achievement/ Higher Education

0325   Ward, Connie
(1980) "The Concurrent Validity of Holland's Theory for Non-College Degreed Black Working Women." Dissertation: Ohio State University, Columbus, OH.

Women of Color/ Work Experience/ African American/ Economic Value of Women's Work/ Black Studies/ Employment/ Educationally Disadvantaged

0326   **Weis, Lois**
(1985) "Without Dependence on Welfare for Life: Black Women in the Community College." The Urban Review 17:4:pp. 233-255.

Community Colleges/ Higher Education/ African American/ Women of Color/ Social Welfare/ Educational Objectives/ Stereotyping/ Images of Women

0327   **Williams, Linda F.**
(1984) "On the Ethics of Research on the Triple Oppession of Black American Women." Humanity and Society 8(November):4:pp. 506-513.

Methodologies/ Women of Color/ African American/ Ethics/ Oppression/ Exploitation/ Theories/ Research Bias/ Feminist Writing/ Race, Class and Gender Studies/ Triple Jeopardy/ Education

0328   **Williams-Burns, Winona**
(1982) "Jane Ellen McAllister: Pioneer for Excellence in Teacher Education." Journal of Negro Education 51(Summer):3:pp. 342-257.

African American/ Higher Education/ Teacher Education/ Women of Color/ Teachers/ Teaching/ Women's History/ Jane Ellen McAllister

0329   **Willie, Charles V.**
(1984) "The Role of Mothers in the Lives of Outstanding Scholars." Journal of Family Issues 5(Sept):3:pp. 291-306.

Women of Color/ Support Systems/ African American/ Parent Child Relationships/ Women's Roles/ Social Mobility/ Family Roles/ Parent Influence/ Scholars/ Education/ Academic Achievement

0330   **Withorn, Ann**
(1986) Dual Citizenship: Women of Color in Graduate School." Women's Studies Quarterly 14(Spring/Summer):1-2:pp. 46-48.

Women of Color/ African American/ Latina/ Higher Education/ Graduate Education/ Racial Discrimination/ Sex Discrimination/ Bias/ Graduate Degrees

0331   **Wyatt-Brown, Bertram**
(1985) "Black Schooling During Reconstruction." in The Web of Southern Social Relations: Women, Family and Education. Walter J. Fraser, Jr. et al. (eds.). Athens, GA: University of Georgia Press. pp. 146-165.

African Americans/ People of Color/ Education/ History/ Reconstruction/ South/ Schools/ Racial Discrimination/ Teaching/ Students/ Oral Tradition

0332   **Yates, Sandra Elizabeth Grady**
(1982) The Relationship of Self-Concept and Other Variables to the Work Value Orientation of Black Females Enrolled in Inner City Schools. San Pedro, CA: R and E Publishers. ISBN 0882476513.

African American/ Women of Color/ Work Ethic/ Urban Areas/ Work Incentives/ Schools/ Students/ Psychological Factors/ Psychological Needs/ Self Concept/ Work Attitudes/ Vocational Education

0333   **Young, Joyce L.**
(1984) "Black Women Faculty in Academia: Strategies for Career Leadership Development." Educational and Psychological Research 4:3:pp. 133-145.

Women of Color/ African American/ Faculty/ Higher Education/ Leadership Skills/ Leadership Training/ Career Planning/ Career Opportunities/ Occupational Patterns/ Institutional Racism/ Institutional Sexism

Asian American

0334 Chai, Alice Yun
(1985) "Toward a Holistic Paradigm for Asian American Women's Studies: A Synthesis of Feminist Scholarship and Women of Color's Feminist Politics." Women's Studies International Forum 8(Spring):2.

Asian American/ Politics/ Women of Color/ Feminist Scholarship/ Women's Studies/ Asian Studies/ Education/ Curriculum Integration

0335 Christensen, Lynn
(1987) Shult, Linda and Wagner, Christina. Asian Women in America: A Bibliography. Available: Women's Studies Librarian, 112A Memorial Library, 728 State Street, Madison, WI 53706.

Education/ Bibliographies/ Asian American/ Research Resources/ Women of Color/ Women's Studies/ Curriculum Integration/ Acculturation

0336 Chu, Judy
(1986) "Asian American Women's Studies Courses: A Look Back at Our Beginnings." Frontiers: A Journal of Women Studies 8:3:pp. 96-101.

Women of Color/ Curriculum Integration/ Asian American/ Higher Education/ Women's Studies/ Teaching/ Feminism/ Bibliographies

0337 James, Thomas
(1988) Exile Within: The Schooling of Japanese Americans, 1942-1945. Cambridge, MA: Harvard University Press. ISBN 0674275268.

Women of Color/ Japanese American/ Women's History/ 1940-1949/ Nonformal Education/ Racial Discrimination/ Asian American/ Internment/ Resistance/ World War II/ Educational Policy/ Children

0338 Kim, Elaine H.
(1984) "Asian American Writers: A Bibliographical Review." American Studies International 22(October):2:pp. 41-78.

People of Color/ Research Resources/ Asian Americans/ Bibliographies / Literature/ Writers/ Literary Arts/ Education

0339 Timpane, M.
(1980) Conference on the Educational and Occupational Needs of Asian-Pacific-American Women. Washington, D.C.: U.S. Government Printing Office.

Asian Pacific American/ Women of Color/ Education/ Employment

Latina

0340 Acosta-Belen, Edna
Sjostrom, Barbara R. (1986) "The Educational and Professional Status of Puerto Rican Women." in The Puerto Rican Woman. Edna Acosta-Belen. New York: Praeger. pp. 64-74. ISBN 0030524660.

Puerto Rican/ Latina/ Educational Status/ Professional Status/ Women of Color/ Employment

0341 Castillo, Adelaida R. del
Frederickson, Jeanie et al. (1988) "An Assessment of the Status of the Education of Hispanic American." in The Broken Web: The Educational Experience of Hispanic American Women. Teresa McKenna and Flora Ida Ortez (eds.). Encino, CA:

Floricanto Press and Tomas Rivera Center. pp. 3-25. ISBN 0942177002.

Latina/ Public Education/ Higher Education/ Academic Performance/ Educational Opportunities/ Policy Making/ Inequality/ Discrimination/ Women of Color

0342 Castillo, Adelaida R. del
Torres, Maria. (1988) "The Interdependency of Educational Institutions and Cultural Norms: The Hispana Experience." in The Broken Web: The Educational Experience of Hispanic American Women. Theresa McKenna and Flora Ida Ortez (eds.). Encino, CA: Floricanto Press and Tomas Rivera Center.

Latina/ Chicana/ Social Attitudes/ Cultural Heritage/ Discrimination/ Academic Achievement/ Women of Color/ Values/ Education

0343 Christensen, Edward W.
Acosta-Belen, Edna. (1986) "The Puerto Rican Woman: A Profile." in The Puerto Rican Woman. New York: Praeger. pp. 51-63. ISBN 0030524660.

Puerto Rican/ Latina/ Education/ Child Rearing/ Employment/ Social Values/ Women of Color

0344 Curry Rodriguez, Julia E.
(1988) "Labor Migration and Familial Responsibilities: Experiences of Mexican Women." in Mexicans at Work. Margarita B. Melville. Houston: University of Houston. pp. 47-64.

Women of Color/ Educational Attainment/ Latina/ Mexican/ Community Relations/ Migration/ Kinship/ Networks/ Illegal Immigrants/ Support Systems/ Labor Force Participation/ Heads of Households/ Balancing Work and Family Life/ Employment

0345 Herrera, F. M.
(1981) "Case of Benign Neglect--The Juvenile Justice System and the At-Risk Hispana Adolescent." U. S. Department of Justice Law Enforcement Assistance Administration, Washington, D.C. pp. 27.

Women of Color/ Latina/ Juvenile Justice System/ Delinquent Behavior/ Education/ Employment/ Health/ Sex Roles/ Women's Roles/ Religious Factors/ Crime Prevention

0346 Jaramillo, Mari Luci
(1988) "Institutional Responsibility in the Provision of Educational Experiences to the Hispanic-American Female Student." in The Broken Web: The Educational Experience of Hispanic American Women. Teresa McKenna and Flora Ida Ortiz (eds.). Encino, CA: Floricanto Press and Tomas Rivera Center. pp. 25-39. ISBN 0942177002.

Latina/ Academic Achievement/ Women of Color/ Socialization/ Educational Opportunities/ Students/ Education/ Teachers/ Higher Education/ Discrimination

0347 Kohl, Jeanne E.
Harman, Marsha S. (1987) "Attitudes of Secondary School Students toward Computers: Do Gender and Socioeconomic Status Make a Difference?" Author: Sociology Department, California State University, Long Beach, CA 90840. Presented: American Sociological Association, Annual Meeting. Chicago, IL.

Latina/ African American/ Women of Color/ Socioeconomic Status/ Race, Class and Gender Studies/ Computer Literacy/ Computer Equity/ Education/ Income Distribution/ Computer Avoidance/ High Schools/ Gender

0348 Laosa, Luis M.
(1980) "Maternal Teaching Strategies in Chicano and Anglo-American Families: The Influence of Culture and Education on Maternal Behavior." Child Development

51(September):3:pp. 759-765.

Parent Child Relationships/ Mothers/ Behavior/ Chicana/ Latina/ Women of Color/ European American/ Teaching/ Education/ Cultural Influences/ Child Development/ Family Influence

0349   **Lee, Valerie**
(1988) "Achievement and Educational Aspirations among Hispanic Female High School Students: Comparison between Public and Catholic Schools." in The Broken Web: The Educational Experience of Hispanic American Women. Teresa McKenna and Flora Ida Ortiz (eds.). Encino, CA: Floricanto Press and Tomas Rivera Center. pp. 137-195. ISBN 0942177002.

Latina/ Women of Color/ Education/ High Schools/ Public Education/ Comparative Studies/ Private Education/ Educational Experience

0350   **Marti, Lillian**
(1988) "Teen Pregnancy Propaganda and the Puerto Rican Adolescent." Centro-Bulletin (Fall):pp. 79-82.

Latina/ Puerto Rican/ Economy/ Women of Color/ Prenatal Care/ Adolescents/ Maternal and Infant Welfare/ Teenage Mothers/ Teenage Pregnancy/ Educational Opportunities

0351   **Martinez, Julio**
Burns, Ada. (1984) Mexican-Americans: An Annotated Bibliography of Bibliographies. San Pedro, CA: R and E Publishers. ISBN 0882477366.

Bibliographies/ Research Resources/ Chicana/ Latina / Women of Color/ Education

0352   **McKenna, Theresa**
Ortiz, Flora Ida (eds.). (1988) The Broken Web: The Educational Experience of Hispanic American Women. Encino, CA: Floricanto Press and Tomas Rivera Center. pp. 264.

Education/ Higher Education/ Equal Educational Opportunity/ Latina/ Dropouts/ Women of Color/ Race, Class and Gender Studies/ Private Schools/ Public Schools

0353   **Ortiz, Vilma**
(1986) "Generational Status, Family Background, and Educational Attainment among Hispanic Youth and Non-Hispanic White Youth." in Latino College Students. Michael Olivas (ed.). New York: Teachers' College Press. ISBN 0807727989.

Latinos/ Comparative Studies/ People of Color/ European Americans/ Educational Attainment/ Family Structure/ Educational Opportunities/ Family History

0354   **Salas, Elizabeth**
(1984) "Chicana Graduate Students in History Departments." Presented: Sixth Berkshire Conference on History of Women, Northampton, MA. June.

Chicana/ Latina/ Women of Color/ Women's History/ Higher Education/ Graduate Degrees/ Curriculum Integration/ Graduate Education

0355   **San Miguel, Guadalupe, Jr.**
(1987) Let All of Them Take Heed: Americans and the Campaign for Equality in Texas, 1910-1981. Austin, TX: University of Texas Press. pp. 278.

Women of Color/ Latina/ Chicana/ History/ 20th Century/ Equality/ Academic Freedom/ Social Movements/ Civil Rights/ Educational Equity

0356   **Soto, Lourdes Diaz**
(1988) "The Home Environment of Higher and Lower Achieving Puerto Rican

Children." <u>Hispanic Journal of the Behavioral Sciences</u> 10(June):2:pp. 161-167.
People of Color/ Educational Aspirations/ Latinos/ Puerto Ricans / Parent Child Relationships/ Parenting/ Home Life/ Academic Achievement/ Family Life/ Parental Attitudes

0357 **Sweeny, Judith**
(1982) "Chicana History: A Review of the Literature." in <u>Essays on La Mujer</u>. Rosaura Sanchez and Rosa Martinez Cruz (eds.). Los Angeles: Chicano Studies Center Publications, University of California Los Angeles. pp. 99-123.
Women of Color/ Latina/ Chicana/ Research Resources/ Women's History/ Bibliographies/ Education

0358 **Veyna, Angelina F.**
(1985) "Anthropological and Historical Inquiry Via Correspondence." Presented: Annual Conference of the National Association for Chicano Studies, Sacramento, CA. March.
Women of Color/ Letters/ Research Methods/ Latina/ Testimonial Literature/ Education/ Women's History/ Correspondence/ Anthropology

0359 **Veyna, Angelina F.**
(1986) "Strategies for Effective Participation in Your Children's Education." Presented: The Annual New Mexico Association of Bilingual Education Conference, Albuquerque, NM. April.
People of Color/ Parent Child Relationship/ Latinos/ Bilingualism/ Education/ Parenting

0360 **Veyna, Angelina F.**
(1986) "Como Puedo Ayudar a Mi Hijo en la Escuela? How Can I Help My Child in School." Presented: The Third Annual CABE Multilingual Parent Conference, Whitney High School, Cerritos, CA. May.
People of Color/ Bilingualism/ Latinos/ Parent Influence/ Children/ Education/ Parent Teacher Relationships/ Students/ Schools

0361 **Veyna, Angelina F.**
(1986) "Integrating Chicana/Latina Studies into the Secondary Curriculum." Presented: The Annual Meeting of the Association of Mexican American Educators, Anaheim, CA. November.
Women of Color/ Chicana/ Latina/ Curriculum Integration/ Secondary Education/ Chicana Studies/ Women's Studies

0362 **Veyna, Angelina F.**
(1987) "Classroom Management and Assessment Strategies for Hispanic LEP Students." Presented: The Annual Conference of the California Association for Bilingual Education, Anaheim, CA. January.
Latinos/ Bilingual Education/ People of Color/ Assessment/ Education/ Students/ Classes

0363 **Veyna, Angelina F.**
(1987) "Chicana Studies: A Personal Experience." Presented: The Annual Chicano, Latino Youth Conference, University of California, Irvine, CA. February.
Women of Color/ Chicana/ Education/ Latina/ Experience/ Chicana Studies

0364 **Veyna, Angelina F.**
(1987) "Testaments and Estate Documentation: Their Contributions to Chicana Studies." Presented: The Annual Conference of the National Association for Chicana Studies, Salt Lake City, UT. April.
Women of Color/ Women's History/ Research Methods/ Inheritance Customs/ Legal Documents/ Latina/ Education

0365 **Vigil, James Diego**
(1988) "The Nexus of Class Culture and Gender in the Education of Mexican American Females." in The Broken Web: The Educational Experience of Hispanic American Women. Teresa McKenna and Flora Ida Ortiz (eds.). Encino, CA: Floricanto Press and Tomas Rivera Center. pp. 79-107. ISBN 0942177002.

Latina/ Chicana/ Occupational Options/ Education/ Discrimination/ Cultural Heritage/ Acculturation/ Inequality/ Women of Color/ Gender Studies/ Class Differences

0366 **Withorn, Ann**
(1986) "Dual Citizenship: Women of Color in Graduate School." Women's Studies Quarterly 14(Spring/Summer):1-2:pp. 46-48.

Women of Color/ African American/ Latina/ Higher Education/ Graduate Education/ Racial Discrimination/ Sex Discrimination/ Bias/ Graduate Degrees

Native American

0367 **Bataille, Gretchen M.**
(1981) American Indian Literature: A Selected Bibliography for Schools and Libraries. Pomona, CA: National Association of Interdisciplinary Ethnic Studies.

Native American/ Bibliographies/ Literature/ Women of Color/ Curriculum Integration/ Research Resources/ Education

0368 **Brumble, H. David III**
(1981) An Annotated Bibliography of American Indian and Eskimo Autobiographies. Lincoln, NE: University of Nebraska Press.

Autobiographies/ Native American/ Eskimos/ Women of Color/ Research Resources/ Curriculum Integration/ Education

0369 **Clow, Richmond L.**
(1985) "Mary Clementine Collins: Missionary at Standing Rock." North Dakota History 52(Spring):2:pp. 10-17.

Native American/ Sioux/ Women's History/ Religion/ Missionaries/ Education/ Social Perception/ Racial Stratification/ North Dakota/ North Central/ Women of Color

0370 **Hodge, William**
(1976) "A Bibliography of Contemporary North American Indians: Selected and Partially Annotated with Study Guide." New York: Interland Publishing.

Bibliographies/ Native American/ Women of Color/ Research Resources/ Curriculum Integration/ Education

0371 **Jacobson, Angeline**
(1977) Contemporary Native American Literature: A Selected and Partially Annotated Bibliography. Metuchen, NJ: Scarecrow Press.

Native American/ Literature/ Bibliographies/ Women of Color/ Research Resources/ Entertainment/ Education

0372 **McAnulty, Sarah**
(1976) "Angel Decora: American Artist and Educator." Nebraska History 57(Summer):2:pp. 143-199.

Native American/ Biographies/ Art/ Angel Decora/ Education/ Schools/ Nebraska/ North Central/ Women of Color/ Women's History

0373   Medicine, Beatrice
(1978) "Learning to Be an Anthropologist and Remaining 'Native'." in <u>Applied Anthropology in America</u>. Elizabeth M. Eddy and William L. Partridge. New York: Columbia University Press. pp. 182-196.

Native American/ Sioux/ Anthropology/ Education/ Methods/ Autobiographies/ Women of Color/ Research Bias

0374   Parent, Elizabeth Anne
(1982) "American Indian Women." Presented: Western Regional Social Scientists' Association, Spring Meeting.

Native American/ Women of Color/ Education/ Family

0375   Peterson, Susan C.
(1983) "Holy Women and Housekeepers: Women Teachers on South Dakota Reservations, 1885-1910." <u>South Dakota History</u> 13(Fall):pp. 245-260.

Women of Color/ Native American/ History/ 19th Century/ Education/ Acculturation/ Teaching/ South Dakota/ North Central/ Traditions/ Customs/ Cultural Heritage/ Roles

0376   Peterson, Susan, C.
(1985) "Doing 'Women's Work': The Grey Nuns at Fact Totten Indian Reservation, 1874-1900." <u>North Dakota History</u> 52(Spring):2:pp. 18-25.

Native American/ Sioux/ 19th Century/ History/ Missionaries/ Nuns/ Education/ Religion/ Women of Color

0377   Scheirbeck, Helen M.
(1980) "Current Educational Status of American Indian Girls." in <u>Conference on the Educational and Occupational Needs of American Indian Women</u>. Washington, D.C.: U. S. Government Printing Office. pp. 63-82.

Native American/ Women of Color/ Education/ Status/ Equal Educational Opportunity/ School Age Children/ Educationally Disadvantaged

0378   Sneed, Roseanna
(1981) "Two Cherokee Women." <u>Frontiers: A Journal of Women Studies</u> 6(Fall):3:pp. 35-38.

Women of Color/ Native American/ Cherokee/ History/ Family/ Acculturation/ Education

0379   Street, Douglas
(1981) "LaFleche Sisters Write to St. Nicholas Magazine." <u>Nebraska History</u> 62(Winter):4:pp. 515-523.

Native American/ Women's History/ Education/ Biographies/ Nebraska/ North Central/ Women of Color/ Sisters/ Family Structure/ LaFleche

Southern

0380   Anderson, James D.
(1988) <u>The Education of Blacks in the South, 1860-1935</u>. Chapel Hill, NC: University of North Carolina Press. pp. 381.

Education/ 20th Century/ 19th Century/ African Americans/ Educational Opportunities/ South/ History/ Educational Experience/ Educational Methods/ People of Color

0381   Dyer, Thomas G.
(1985) "Higher Education in the South Since the Civil War: Historical Issues and Trends." in <u>The Web of Southern Social Relations: Women, Family, and Education</u>.

Walter J. Fraser, Jr. et al (eds.). Athens, GA: University of Georgia Press. pp. 127-145.

African American / European American/ Women of Color/ Higher Education/ Black Colleges/ Women's Colleges/ South/ History/ 19th Century/ Radicals

0382   Eakin, Sue Lyles
(1980) "The Black Struggle for Education in Louisiana, 1877-1930." Dissertation: University of Southwestern Louisiana, Lafayette, LA. DAI Vol. 41(09A)4132.

African Americans/ People of Color/ Social History/ Education/ South/ Louisiana/ 19th Century/ 20th Century

0383   Fraser, Walter J., Jr.
Saunders, R. Frank, Jr., and Wakelyn, Jon R. (eds.). (1985) The Web of Southern Social Relations: Women, Family, and Education. Athens, GA: University of Georgia Press. ISBN 0820309427.

Southern/ Women's History/ Education/ Family/ Social Conditions/ Social Relations/ African American/ Women of Color/ European American/ Relationships

0384   Friedman, Belinda Bundy
(1981) "Orie Latham Hatcher and the Southern Woman's Educational Alliance." Dissertation: Duke University, Durham, NC. DAI Vol. 42(11A)4702.

Southern/ Social Movements/ Educational Reform/ Leadership/ Change Agents/ Orie Latham Hatcher

0385   Heintze, Michael Robert
(1981) "A History of the Black Private Colleges in Texas, 1865-1954." Dissertation: Texas Tech University, Lubbock, TX. pp. 344. DAI Vol. 42(08A)3709.

African Americans /People of Color/ South West/ Texas/ Social History/ Higher Education/ Private Colleges/ Black Colleges/ 19th Century/ 20th Century

0386   Hoffert, Sylvia
(1985) "Yankee Schoolmarms and the Domestication of the South." Southern Studies 24(Summer):pp. 188-201.

North/ South/ Social Reform/ Education/ Social Change/ Teaching/ Schools/ History/ 19th Century/ Civility/ Customs/ Cultural Influences

0387   Ihle, Elizabeth L.
(1986) "History of Black Women's Education in the South, 1865-Present: Instructional Modules for Educators." Module I, II, III, IV. Available: E. Ihle, James Madison University, Harrisonburg, VA. Sponsored: Women's Educational Equity Act Program, US Department of Education.

African American/ South/ Schools/ 19th Century/ 20th Century/ Higher Education/ Separate Spheres/ Job Training/ Women of Color/ Women's History/ Teaching/ Segregation/ Primary Education/ Secondary Education/ Vocational Education

0388   Jones, Faustine Childress
(1981) A Traditional Model of Educational Excellence: Dunbar High School of Little Rock, Arkansas. Washington, D.C.: Howard University Press.

Education/ High Schools/ African American/ South/ Arkansas/ Women of Color/ Academic Achievement

0389   Kett, Joseph F.
(1985) "Women and the Progressive Impulse in Southern Education" in The Web of Southern Social Relations: Women, Family and Education. Walter J. Fraser, Jr. et

al. (eds.). Athens, GA: University of Georgia Press. pp. 166-180.

South/ Education/ Reform Movement/ Educational Reform/ Technical Schools/ Social Structure/ Rural Living

0390   Neverdon-Morton, Cynthia
(1982) "Self Help Programs as Educative Activities of Black Women in the South, 1895-1925." Journal of Negro Education 51(Summer):3:pp. 207-221.

Women of Color/ African American/ South/ History/ Self Help/ Educational Programs/ Social Services/ Model Programs/ Change Agents/ Advocacy Groups

0391   Neverdon-Morton, Cynthia
(1989) Afro-American Women of the South and the Advancement of the Race, 1985-1925. Knoxville, TN: University of Tennessee Press.

African American/ Liberation Struggles/ Women of Color/ Civil Rights/ South/ Human Rights/ Race Relations/ Social Movements/ Social History/ Teachers/ Racial Discrimination/ Professional Occupations

0392   Simpson, Ida Harper
(1988) "The South. Sociological Society's Problems of Minorities." in Fifty Years of the Southern Sociological Society. Ida Harper Simpson. Athens, GA: University of Georgia Press.

Women of Color*/ Social Studies/ Sociology/ South/ Associations/ Group Dynamics/ Mixed Sex Groups/ Professional Status/ Higher Education

0393   Spatig, Linda
(1986) "Connections Between Gender Relations and Everyday Life in an Elementary Classroom." Dissertation: University of Houston, Houston, TX.

South/ Primary Education/ Gender Development/ Male Female Relationships

0394   Spatig, Linda
(1987) "Learning to Manage the Heart: Gender Relations in an Elementary Classroom." Presented: Annual Meeting of American Educational Studies Association. November.

South/ Primary Education/ Gender Development/ Male Female Relationships/ Students/ Schools

0395   Stowe, Steven M.
(1985) "The Not-so-Cloistered Academy: Elite Women's Education and Family Feeling in the Old South." in The Web of Southern Social Relations: Women, Family and Education. Walter J. Fraser, Jr. et al. (eds.). Athens, GA: University of Georgia Press. pp. 90-106.

Southern/ Elites/ History/ Higher Education/ Sisterhood/ Family/ Control/ Marriage

0396   Wyatt-Brown, Bertram
(1985) "Black Schooling During Reconstruction." in The Web of Southern Social Relations: Women, Family and Education. Walter J. Fraser, Jr. et al. (eds.). Athens, GA: University of Georgia Press. pp. 146-165.

African Americans/ People of Color/ Education/ History/ Reconstruction/ South/ Schools/ Racial Discrimination/ Teaching/ Students/ Oral Tradition

Women of Color*

0397 **Andersen, Margaret L.**
(1988) <u>Thinking About Women: Sociological Perspectives on Sex and Gender</u> (2nd Edition). New York: Macmillan.
Women of Color*/ Race, Class and Gender Studies/ Sociology/ Curriculum Integration/ Women's Studies/ Gender Roles/ Sex Roles/ Higher Education

0398 **Andersen, Margaret L.**
(1988) "Moving our Minds: Studying Women of Color and Reconstructing Sociology." <u>Teaching Sociology</u> 16(April): pp. 123-132.
Women of Color*/ Women's Studies/ Sociology/ Teaching/ Social Science Research/ Curriculum Integration/ Sociology of Knowledge/ Scholarship/ Higher Education

0399 **Arnold, Regina A.**
(1984) "Women in Prison: Class, Criminality and Imprisonment." Available: Sarah Lawrence College, Bronxville, NY 10708. pp. 33.
Women of Color*/ Coping Strategies/ Emotional Adjustment/ Prisoners/ Discrimination/ Educational Experience/ Class Differences/ Drug Addiction/ Socioeconomic Status/ Oppression/ Self Concept/ Criminal Justice/ Judiciary System

0400 **Arnot, M.**
(1985) <u>Race and Gender: Equal Opportunities Policies in Education</u>. New York: Pergamon Press. pp. 158.
Women of Color*/ Race, Class and Gender Studies/ Equal Educational Opportunity/ Equal Pay for Equal Work/ Double Bind/ Educational Equity/ Educational Policy

0401 **Artis-Goodwin, Sharon E.**
(1986) "Professional Barriers and Facilitators for Minority Women in Educational Research." Dissertation: Harvard University, Cambridge, MA.
Women of Color*/ Discrimination/ Sponsored Research/ Education

0402 **Astin, Alexander W.**
(1982) <u>Minorities in American Higher Education: Recent Trends, Current Prospects, and Recommendations</u>. San Francisco, CA: Jossey-Bass Publishers.
Employment/ Higher Education/ Women of Color*/ Discrimination

0403 **Baer, Judith**
(1983) <u>Equality Under the Constitution: Reclaiming the Fourteenth Amendment</u>. Ithaca, NY: Cornell University Press.
Women of Color*/ Equality/ Education/ Employment/ Sex Discrimination

0404 **Barnett, Margaret Ross**
Harrington, Charles C. (eds.). (1985) <u>Readings on Equal Education, Volume 8: Race, Sex, and National Origin: Public Attitudes of Desegregation</u>. New York: AMS Press. pp. 273.
Women of Color*/ Race, Class, and Gender Studies/ Racial Discrimination/ SexDiscrimination/ Equal Educational Opportunity/ Desegregation/ Attitudes

0405 **Blake, J. Herman**
(1989) "Creating Climates of Excellence with Diverse Students." Presented: American Conference of Academic Deans Annual Meeting, Washington, D.C.

January.

Curriculum Integration/ Higher Education/ Women of Color*/ Students/ Universities/ Academic Achievement/ Dominant Culture/ Minority Experience/ Minority Groups/ Diversity

0406   **Brenzel, Barbara**
(1983) "History of 19th Century Women's Education: A Plea For Inclusion of Class, Race and Ethnicity." Available: Working Paper #114, Wellesley College Center for Research on Women, Wellesley, MA.

Feminist Scholarship/ Higher Education/ Educational Opportunities/ Social History/ 19th Century/ Women of Color*/ Race, Class and Gender Studies/ Social Class/ Ethnicity

0407   **Cababallo, Elba**
(1986) "Teaching About Racism in Community Agencies." Women's Studies Quarterly 14(Spring/Summer):1-2:pp. 39-41.

Women of Color*/ Racial Discrimination/ Teaching/ Teacher Education/ Educational Programs/ Educational Methods/ Social Agencies/ Welfare Agencies/ Consciousness Raising

0408   **Cannon, Lynn Weber**
Higginbotham, Elizabeth, et al. (1988) "Race and Class Bias in Qualitative Research on Women." Gender & Society 2(Dec):4:pp. 449-462.

Women's Studies/ Women of Color*/ Female Intensive Occupations/ Race, Class and Gender Studies/ Research Bias/ Feminist Perspective/ Research Methods/ Race Bias/ Attitudes

0409   **Chow, Esther N.**
(1985) "Teaching Sex and Gender in Sociology: Incorporating the Perspective of Women of Color." Teaching Sociology 12(April):pp. 299-311.

Sociology/ Women of Color*/ Curriculum Integration/ Teaching/ Higher Education/ Race, Class and Gender Studies

0410   **Chunn, Jay**
Dunston, Patricia and Ross-Sheriff, F. (eds.). (1988) Mental Health and People of Color: Curriculum Development and Change. Washington, D.C.: Howard University Press.

Mental Health/ People of Color*/ Curriculum Integration/ Education/ Change/ Teaching

0411   **Collins, Patricia Hill**
Andersen, Margaret L. (eds.). (1987) "An Inclusive Curriculum: Race, Class, and Gender in Sociological Instruction." Washington, DC: Teaching Resources Center, American Sociological Association.

Women of Color*/ Educational Reform/ Curriculum Integration/ Educational Equity/ Sociology/ Teaching/ Race, Class, and Gender Studies/ Higher Education

0412   **Crain, R. L.**
Carsrud, K. B. (1985) "The Role of the Social Sciences in School Desegratation Policy." in Social Science and Social Policy. R. Lance Shotland and Melvin M. Mark. Beverly Hills, CA: Sage Publications. pp. 376.

Education/ Racial Discrimination/ School Desegregation/ Social Policy/ Social Sciences/ People of Color*

0413   **Dometrius, Nelson C.**
Sigelman, Lee. (1988) "The Cost of Quality: Teacher Testing and Racial-Ethnic Representativeness in Public Education." Social Science Quarterly 69(March):1:pp.

70-82.

Women of Color*/ Teacher Education/ Primary Education/ Teaching/ Secondary Education/ Racial Discrimination/ Public Education/ Job Discrimination

0414   Ford Foundation
(1989) "Early Childhood Services: A National Challenge." Presented: Ford Foundation-Program Paper, New York, March.

Women of Color*/ Low Income Families/ Women's Studies/ Family Roles/ Child Care/ Family Support/ Social Policy/ Legislation/ Educational Opportunities/ Public Policy/ Labor Force Participation

0415   Gibbs, Jewelle Taylor
(1984) "Conflicts and Coping Strategies of Minority Female Graduate Students." in Color in a White Society. B. W. White. Silver Spring, MD: National Association of Social Workers.

Women of Color*/ Interracial Relations/ Coping Strategies/ Higher Education/ Graduate Education/ Survival Strategies

0416   Giele, Janet Zollinger
Gilfus, Mary. (1988) "Race and College Differences in Life Patterns of Educated Women." in Women and Educational Choice. Joyce Antler and Sari Biklen. New York: New York University Press.

Education/ Family Background/ Women's Studies/ Education Attainment/ Higher Education/ Academic Aspiration/ Labor Force Participation/ Comparative Studies/ Employment/ Career Opportunities/ Women of Color*

0417   Ginorio, Angela B.
Brown, M. et al. (1984) "Sexual Harassment of Women Students: Functional and Cultural Discrimination." Author: Women's Information Center AJ-50, University of Washington, Seattle, WA 98195.

Women of Color*/ Sexual Harassment/ Students/ Education/ Discrimination/ Power/ Culture

0418   Gornick, Vivian
Moran, Barbra K. (eds.). (1988) Women in a Sexist Society: Studies in Power and Powerlessness. New York: Mentor. pp. 736. ISBN 0451624599.

Women's Studies/ Education/ Feminist Scholarship/ Women's Movement/ Sex Discrimination/ Anthropology/ Discrimination/ Power/ Powerlessness/ Women of Color*

0419   Graham, Hugh Davis
(1987) "Sex, Race, Ethnicity, and Scholarly Prizes." OAH Newsletter: Organization of American Historians 15(February):1:pp. 2-3.

Women of Color*/ Ethnic Studies/ Racial Discrimination/ Sex Discrimination in Education/ Higher Education/ Academic Awards

0420   Grinstein, Louise S.
Campbell, Paul J. (1987) Women of Mathematics: A Biobibliographic Sourcebook. New York: Greenwood Press. pp. 292.

Women of Color*/ Research Resources/ Mathematics/ Professional Occupations/ Mathematicians/ Biographies/ Bibliographies/ Women's History/ Education

0421   Hall, Eleanor R.
Pollard, Diane S. et al. (1986) "Role Demands and College Experiences of Minority and White Men and Women." Presented: Association for Institutional Research, Annual Meeting, Orlando, FL.

Women of Color*/ Urban Areas/ Comparative Studies/ Career Counseling/ Role Expectations/ Roles/ Student Financial Aid/ European American/ Higher Education/ Minority Experience/ Colleges

0422   Higginbotham, Elizabeth
(1988) "Integrating all Women into the Curriculum." Available: Publication #5, Center for Research on Women, Memphis State University, Memphis, TN 38152.

Women of Color*/ Discrimination/ Women's Studies/ Educational Trends/ Women's History/ Higher Education/ Curriculum Integration

0423   Johnson, Elisabeth
(1986) "We are Women of Color First." Women's Studies Quarterly 14(Spring/Summer):1-2:pp. 19-20.

Women of Color*/ Women Living in Poverty/ Feminist Movement/ Feminist Theory/ Socioeconomic Status/ Race, Class and Gender Studies/ Women's Studies/ Curriculum Integration/ Education

0424   Johnson, Nan E.
(1988) "The Pace of Births over the Life Course: Implications for the Minority-Group Status Hypothesis." Social Science Quarterly 69(March):1:pp. 95-107.

Women of Color*/ Birth Rates/ Family Structure/ Childbearing/ Family Planning/ Post Secondary Education/ Fertility/ Demography

0425   Luttrell, Wendy
(1984) "The Getting of Knowledge: A Study of Working Class Women and Education." Dissertation: University of California, Santa Cruz, CA.

Women of Color*/ Cultural Identity/ Working Class/ Employment Opportunities/ European American/ Sex Stereotypes/ Educational Attainment

0426   Rubinstein, Charlotte S.
(1988) American Women Artists from Early Indian Times to the Present. Poughkeepsie, NY: Apollo Books. pp. 561.

Women of Color*/ Women's History/ Artists/ Biographies/ Craft Art/ Research Resources/ Education

0427   Ruzek, Sheryl B.
(1986) "Integrating Minority Women's Health into the Curriculum." in Teaching Materials on Women, Health and Healing. Adele Clarke, et al. San Francisco: Women, Health and Healing Project, University of CA. pp. 35-43.

Women of Color*/ Curriculum Integration/ Health/ Women's Health Movement/ Higher Education/ Teaching

0428   Schmitz, Betty
(1988) Integrating Women's Studies Into the Curriculum: A Guide and Bibliography. New York: Feminist Press. ISBN 0935312366.

Women's Studies/ Women of Color*/ Curriculum Integration/ Research Resources/ Bibliographies/ Education

0429   Schuster, Marilyn R.
Van Dyne, Susan R. (eds.). (1985) Women's Place in the Academy: Transforming the Liberal Arts Curriculum. Totowa, NJ: Rowman and Littlefield. pp. 336. ISBN 0847674088.

Women's Studies/ Higher Education/ Women of Color*/ Curriculum Integration/ Education/ Teaching

0430   Simpson, Ida Harper
(1988) "The South. Sociological Society's Problems of Minorities." in Fifty Years of the Southern Sociological Society. Ida Harper Simpson. Athens, GA: University of Georgia Press.

Women of Color*/ Social Studies/ Sociology/ South/ Associations/ Group Dynamics/ Mixed Sex Groups/ Professional Status/ Higher Education

0431   **Twin, Stephanie L.**
(1986) <u>Out of the Bleachers: Writings on Women and Sport.</u> New York: Feminist Press. pp. 272.

Women of Color*/ Equal Opportunity/ Education/ History/ Athletes/ Physical Health/ Women's Athletics/ Competitive Behavior/ Sports

0432   **Wenk-Dee, Ann L.**
(1988) "An Examination of the Relationship Between Economic Conditions and Teenage Motherhood in Southeastern Labor Market Areas." Presented: Rural Sociological Society Annual Meeting.

Women of Color*/ Sexuality/ Socioeconomic Status/ Secondary Education/ Teenage Pregnancy/ Employment Opportunities/ Parenting/ Mothers/ Economic Patterns/ South

0433   **Women's Education and Equity Act**
(1987) <u>Minority Woman's Survival Kit</u>. Workshop Manual, Newton, MA: W.E.E.A. Publishing. pp. 74.

Women of Color*/ Labor Force/ Job Discrimination/ Human Rights/ Verbal Communication/ Labor Laws/ Interviews/ Job Hunting/ Teacher Education/ Methods

0434   **Zambrana, Ruth E.**
(1986) "Fundamental Issues in Teaching About Minorities." in <u>Women, Health and Healing Program</u>. Adele Clarke et al. San Francisco: University of California Press. pp. 44-49.

Women of Color*/ Education/ Curriculum Integration/ Women's Studies/ Course Objectives/ Teaching

0435   **Zambrana, Ruth E.**
(1986) "Integrating Minority Women's Health into a Professional School Curriculum." in <u>Women, Health and Healing Program</u>. Adele Clark, et al. San Francisco: University of California Press. pp. 55-60.

Women of Color*/ Medical Education/ Curriculum Integration/ Health/ Teaching/ Higher Education/ Teacher Education

EMPLOYMENT

African American

0436   Alexander, Michael
(1986) "Fishy Business." <u>Southern Exposure</u> 14(September/October):5-6:pp. 32-34.
African American/ South/ Mississippi/ Food Industry/ Factory Workers/ Labor
Disputes/ Labor Unions/ Wage Discrimination/ Job Discrimination

0437   Anderson, Kathie Ruckman
(1982) "Era Bell Thompson: A North Dakota Daughter." <u>North Dakota History</u>
49(Fall):4:pp. 11-18.
African American/ Journalism/ Biographies/ History/ North Central/ Era Bell Thompson/ Authors/
North Dakota/ Women of Color/ Writers/ Employment

0438   Benokraitis, Nijole V.
Feagin, Joe R. (1978) <u>Affirmative Action and Equal Opportunity: Action, Inaction
and Reaction</u>. Boulder, CO: Westview Press.
Women of Color/ Education/ Employment/ Affirmative Action/ Inequality/ Sex Discrimination/ African
American

0439   Benokraitis, Nijole V.
Feagin, Joe R. (1986) <u>Modern Sexism: Blatant, Subtle, and Covert Discrimination</u>.
Englewood Cliffs, NJ: Prentice-Hall.
Women of Color/ Education/ Employment/ Sex Discrimination/ African American/ Microinequities/
Institutional Discrimination

0440   Blackwell, James E.
(1981) <u>Mainstreaming Outsiders: The Production of Black Professionals</u>. Bayside,
NY: General Hall.
African American/ Women of Color/ Education/ Employment/ Professional Status

0441   Brown, Diane Robinson
(1988) "Employment and Health among Older Black Women: Implications for
Their Employment Status." Available: Working Paper #177, Wellesley College
Center For Research On Women, Wellesley, MA.
African American/ Health Care/ European American/ Racial Differences/ Women of Color/
Employment/ Status/ Middle Aged Adults/ Health/ Older Adults/ Employment Opportunity

0442   Buford, Carmen
(1986) "The Effect of Women's Studies and Black Studies on the Self Concept and
Careers of Black Women." Dissertation: University of California Los Angeles, Los
Angeles, CA.
African American/ Women of Color/ Women's Studies/ Black Studies/ Self Concept/ Employment/
Career Choice/ Curriculum Integration

0443   Byerly, Victoria M.
(1985) "Hidden From History: The Cotton Mill Girls." <u>Sojourner</u> 10(May):7:pp. 16-

17.

African American/ Poverty/ European American/ Race Relations/ Women of Color/ Health Hazards/ South/ North Carolina/ Women's History/ Employment/ Economic Value of Women's Work/ Textile Industry

0444   **Campbell, John**
(1984) "Work, Pregnancy and Infant Mortality among Southern Slaves." Journal of Interdisciplinary History 14(Spring):4:pp. 793-812.

Women of Color/ African American/ History/ South/ Slavery/ Infant Mortality/ Birth Rates/ Pregnancy/ Pregnant Workers/ Nutrition/ Farm Workers/ Maternal and Infant Welfare

0445   **Campbell, Randolph B.**
(1988) "Slave Hiring in Texas." American Historical Review 93(Feb.):pp. 107-114.

People of Color/ African Americans/ Texas/ South/ Slavery/ Slaves/ Employment/ History/ 19th Century

0446   **Carlson, Shirley J.**
(1987) "Black Migration to Pulaski County, Illinois 1860-1900." Illinois Historical Journal 80(Spring):pp. 37-46.

Migration/ North Central/ Illinois/ Employment/ Family/ History/ 19th Century/ African Americans/ People of Color

0447   **Caver, Carolyn**
(1986) "Dreaming Again." Southern Exposure 14(September/ October):5-6:pp. 62-64.

Women of Color/ African American/ Wage Discrimination/ Socioeconomic Status/ Lower Class/ Minority Owned Business/ Women Owned Business/ South/ Employment

0448   **Cherry, Robert**
(1989) Discrimination: It's Economic Impact on Blacks, Women and Jews. Lexington, MA: Lexington Books. pp. 256. ISBN 0669204196.

African American/ Sex Discrimination/ Jews/ Racial Discrimination/ Women's Studies/ Minority Studies/ Women of Color/ Politics/ Employment Opportunities/ Economic Patterns/ Comparative Studies/ Economy

0449   **Childress, Alice**
(1986) Like one of the Family: Conversations from a Domestic's Life. Boston: Beacon Press. pp. 237.

Women of Color/ African American/ Household Workers/ Domestic Services/ Images of Women/ Employment

0450   **Christensen, Kimberly**
(1986) "Accounting for the Relative Income Gains of Black Females: 1955-1982." Dissertation: University of Massachusetts, Amherst, MA.

African American/ Women of Color/ Employment/ Economic Status/ Wages/ Income

0451   **Clark-Lewis, Elizabeth**
(1987) "This Work Had A' End: African American Domestic Workers in Washington, D.C., 1910-1940." in To Toil the Livelong Day: America's Women at Work, 1780-1980. Carol Groneman and Mary B. Norton (eds.). Ithaca, NY: Cornell University Press. pp. 196-213.

African American/ Employment Patterns/ Women of Color/ Economic Value of Women's Work/ Domestic Services/ 19th Century/ Women's History/ Race, Class and Gender Studies/ Washington, D.C./ South

0452 **Covermann, Shelley**
Kemp, Alice Abel. (1987) "The Labor Supply of Female Heads of Households: Comparisons with Male Heads and Wives." <u>Sociological Inquiry</u> 57(Winter):1:pp. 32-51.

Women of Color/ Race, Class and Gender Studies/ African American/ Women Living in Poverty/ Female Headed Households/ Employment/ Wages/ Labor Supply/ Single Mothers/ Comparative Studies/ Marital Status

0453 **Darden, Joe T.**
(1988) "The Effect of World War I on Black Occupational and Residential Segregation: The Case of Pittsburgh." <u>Journal of Black Studies</u> 18(March):pp. 297-312.

People of Color/ African Americans/ World War I/ Segregated Housing/ Occupational Segregation/ Pennsylvania/ North East/ Racial Discrimination/ Segregation/ Employment

0454 **Datcher, Linda P.**
(1978) "The Effect of Higher Women's Labor Force Participation Rates on the Relative Earnings of Black and White Families." Dissertation: Massachusetts Institute of Technology, Cambridge, MA.

African American/ European American/ Earnings/ Comparative Studies/ Economic Value of Women's Work/ Labor Force/ Employment/ Women of Color/ Women Working Outside the Home

0455 **Dhooper, Sarijit S.**
Dyars, Lauretta F. (1989) "Stress and Life Satisfaction of Black Social Workers." <u>AFFILIA: Journal of Women and Social Work</u> 4(Spring):1:pp. 70-78.

Social Workers/ Balancing Work and Family Life/ Stress/ Mental Health/ Satisfaction/ African American/ Women of Color/ Employment

0456 **DuPont, Patricia**
Feuer, Carl H. and Kost, J. (1988) "Black Migrant Farmworkers in New York State: Exploitable Labor." <u>Afro-Americans in New York Life and History</u> 12(Jan):pp. 7-26.

People of Color/ Migrant Workers/ African Americans/ Employment/ New York/ North East/ Exploitation/ Labor Force/ Farm Workers

0457 **Dudovitz, Resa L.**
(1984) <u>Women in Academe</u>. Elmsford, NY: Pergamon Press.

Women of Color/ African American/ Higher Education/ Employment/ Academia/ Schools/ Universities/ Colleges

0458 **Edmonds, Linda L.**
(1979) "Clothing Buying Practices and Life Style Differentials between Employed Black and White Women." Dissertation: Virginia Polytechnic Institute and State University, Blacksburg, VA. DAI Vol. 40(05A)2777.

African American/ European American/ Consumerism/ Comparative Studies/ Life Styles/ Employment/ Clothing/ Women of Color

0459 **Foner, Philip S.**
Lewis, Ronald L. (1983) <u>The Black Worker: A Documentary History from Colonial Times to Present</u>. Philadelphia, PA: Temple University Press.

African American/ Labor Force/ Employment/ 19th Century/ Workers/ 17th Century/ History/ 18th Century/ Women of Color/ Exploitation

0460   **Gwartney-Gibbs, Patricia**
Taylor, Patricia A. (1986) "Black Women Workers' Earnings Progress in Three Sectors, 1970-1980." <u>SAGE: A Scholarly Journal on Black Women</u> 3(Spring):1:pp. 20-25.

Women of Color/ Wage Discrimination/ African American/ Employment/ Labor History/ 1970-1979/ Equal Opportunity/ Wage Gap/ Affirmative Action/ Economic Value of Women's Work/ Race, Class and Gender Studies/ Equal Pay for Equal Work/ Socioeconomic Conditions

0461   **Hall, Bob**
(1986) "The Black Belt." <u>Southern Exposure</u> 14(September/ October):5-6:pp. 76-78.

People of Color/ African Americans/ Minority Owned Business/ South/ Lower Class/ Blue Collar Workers/ Wage Discrimination/ Labor Disputes/ South

0462   **Harley, Sharon**
(1978) "Northern Black Female Workers: Jacksonian Era." in <u>The Afro-American Woman: Struggles and Images</u>. Sharon Harley and Rosalyn Terborg-Penn. Port Washington, NY: Kennikat Press.

African American/ Workers/ Women's History/ 19th Century/ Employment/ North

0463   **Helmbold, Lois Rita**
(1987) "Beyond the Family Economy: Black and White Working Class Women during the Great Depression." <u>Feminist Studies</u> 13(Fall):3:pp. 629-655.

Women of Color/ Family Economics/ African American/ Economic Depression/ History/ 1930-1939/ Extended Family/ Comparative Studies/ Economic Value of Women's Work/ Working Class/ European American/ Race, Class and Gender Studies

0464   **Hesse-Biber, Sharlene**
(1986) "The Black Woman Worker: A Minority Group Perspective on Women at Work." <u>SAGE: A Scholarly Journal on Black Women</u> 3(Spring):1:pp. 26-34.

Women of Color/ African American/ Work Experience/ Labor Force/ Slavery/ Socioeconomic Status/ Heads of Households/ Unemployment Rates/ Part Time Workers/ Blue Collar Workers/ Race, Class and Gender Studies/ Job Discrimination

0465   **Higginbotham, Elizabeth**
(1987) "Employment for Professional Black Women in the Twentieth Century." in <u>Ingredients for Women's Employment Policy</u>. Christine Bose and Glenna Spitze (eds.). Albany, NY: State University of New York Press. pp. 73-91. ISBN 0887064213.

Women of Color/ African American/ Professional Status/ Employment Opportunities/ 20th Century/ Professional Occupations

0466   **Higginbotham, Elizabeth**
Cannon, Lynn Weber. (1988) "Rethinking Mobility: Towards a Race and Gender Inclusive Theory." Research Paper #8, Center for Research on Women, Memphis State University, Memphis, TN 38152.

Women of Color/ European American/ Race, Class and Gender Studies/ African American/ Career Mobility/ Upward Mobility/ Occupational Opportunities/ Employment

0467   **Hill, Herbert**
(1987) "Race, Ethnicity, and Organized Labor: The Opposition to Affirmative Action." <u>New Politics</u> 1(Winter):2.

Women of Color/ Affirmative Action/ African American/ Labor Unions/ Race, Class and Gender Studies/ Employment

0468 **Hopson, Jannie**
(1985) "Career Patterns and Characteristics of Black Women in the Metropolitan Atlanta Area." Dissertation: Georgia State University, Atlanta, GA.
Women of Color/ Work Experience/ South/ Georgia/ Occupational Patterns/ Career Choice/.Urban Areas/ Leadership/ African American

0469 **Jacobowitz, T.**
(1983) "Relationship of Sex, Achievement and Science Self Concept to Science Career Preferences of Black Students." Journal of Research in Science Teaching 20:7:pp. 621-628.
African American/ Science and Technical Occupations/ Women of Color/ Academic Achievement/ Career Choice/ Self Concept/ Employment

0470 **Janiewski, Dolores**
(1984) "Subversive Sisterhood: Black Women and Unions in the Southern Tobacco Industry." Available: Southern Women Working Paper #1, Center for Research on Women, Memphis State University, Memphis, TN 38152.
African American/ Labor Force Participation/ Women of Color/ South/ Tobacco Industry/ Factories/ Race, Class and Gender Studies/ European American/ Discrimination/ Occupational Segregation/ Labor Unions/ Employment

0471 **Janiewski, Dolores**
(1987) "Seeking a New Day and a New Way: Black Women and Unions in the Southern Tobacco Industry." in To Toil the Livelong Day: America's Women at Work, 1780-1980. Carol Groneman and Mary B Norton (eds.). Ithaca, NY: Cornell University Press. pp. 161-179.
Tobacco Industry/ Race Relations/ African American/ Economic Value of Women's Work/ Women of Color/ Employment/ Industrialization/ South/ Labor History/ Labor Unions

0472 **Jaret, Charles**
Myers, Lyn. (1987) "Black-White Income Inequality and the Urban System of the South." Presented: American Sociological Association, Chicago, IL. Available: Department of Sociology, Georgia State University, Atlanta, GA 30303.
African American/ Women of Color/ Inequality/ Income Distribution/ Statistical Analysis/ Research Methods/ South/ Urban/ Pay Equity/ Employment

0473 **Jerrido, Margaret**
(1979) "Black Women Physicians: A Triple Burden." Alumnae News (The Medical College of Pennsylvania) 30(Summer):1:pp. 4-5.
African American/ Women of Color/ Physicians/ Medical Sciences/ Health Care Occupations/ Male Dominated Employment/ Race, Class and Gender Studies/ Professional Status/ Triple Jeopardy

0474 **Jewell, Karen Sue**
(1988) "Social Gains: Some Empirical Realities for Black American Men and Women." Presented: Society for the Study of Social Problems Annual Meeting, Atlanta, GA.
African Americans/ Labor Force Participation/ Class/ People of Color/ Race/ Social Change/ Minority Experience/ Employment

0475 **Jones, Barbara A. P.**
(1983) "The Contribution of Black Women to the Incomes of Black Families: An Analysis of the Labor Force Participation Rates of Black Wives." Dissertation:

Georgia State University, Atlanta, GA. DAI Vol. 34(06A)2856.

African American/ Women of Color/ Economic Value of Women's Work/ Earnings/ Family Income/ Labor Force Statistics/ Wage Earning Wives/ Employment

0476   **Jones, Jacqueline**
(1986) "Theoretical Perspectives on the Work of Black and Poor White Women in the Rural South, 1865-1940." Presented: American Farm Women in Historical Perspective, Madison, WI. October. Available: Department of History, Wellesley College Center for Research on Women, Wellesley, MA.

History/ 19th Century/ Employment Patterns/ South/ Agriculture/ Farm Workers/ Rural Living/ Interracial Relations/ African American/ European American/ 20th Century/ Comparative Studies/ Women of Color

0477   **Keckley, Elizabeth**
(1988) Behind the Scenes; or, Thirty Years a Slave, and Four Years in the White House. New York: Oxford University Press. pp. 416. ISBN 0195052595.

Women of Color/ Slavery/ African American/ Civil War/ Personal Narratives/ Memoirs/ History/ 19th Century/ Autobiographies/ Employment/ Slaves

0478   **Kessler-Harris, Alice**
(1987) Women Have Always Worked: A Historical Overview. New York: Feminist Press. pp. 208. ISBN 0912670673.

Women of Color/ African American/ Employment/ Images of Women/ Labor Force/ Household Workers/ Immigrants/ Volunteer Work/ Professional Occupations

0479   **Landry, Bart**
(1988) The New Black Middle Class. Berkeley, CA: University of California Press. pp. 250.

African Americans/ People of Color/ Middle Class/ Socialization Social Class/ Leadership/ Class Formation/ Class Identity/ Employment

0480   **Lehman, Paul**
(1986) "The Edwards Family and Black Entrepreneurial Success." Chronicles of Oklahoma 64(Winter):pp. 88-97.

African Americans/ People of Color/ Entrepreneurs/ Success/ Family/ Employment/ Business Ownership

0481   **Malson, Michelene R.**
(1988) "Understanding Black Single Parent Families: Stresses and Strengths." Available: Wellesley College, Stone Center for Developmental Services and Studies, 106 Central Street, Wellesley, MA 02181-8293.

Single Parents/ Employment/ African American/ Child Care/ Parent Child Relationships/ Women of Color/ Stress/ Female Headed Households/ Family Life/ Support Systems/ Education/ Single Parent Families

0482   **Malveaux, Julianne M.**
Englander, Susan. (1986) "Race and Class in Nursing Occupations." SAGE: A Scholarly Journal on Black Women 3(Spring)1:pp. 41-45.

Women of Color/ African American/ Race, Class and Gender Studies/ Health Care Occupations/ Nursing/ Health Care Workers/ Community Health Services

0483   **Marks, Carole**
(1986) "After Migration: The Incorporation of Black Workers in Northern Industries, 1916-1930." in Research in the Sociology of Work. Ida H. Simpson (ed).

Greenwich, CT: J.A.I. Press.

Women of Color/ Industrialization/ African American/ Employment/ North/ Migration/ Factory Workers/ Labor History/ 20th Century/ Blue Collar Workers

0484   **Marshall, Ray**
Knapp, Charles B. et al. (1978) Employment Discrimination: The Impact of Legal and Adminstrative Remedies. New York: Praeger Publisher.

African American/ Laws/ Women of Color/ Employment/ Discrimination/ Public Policy/ Equal Employment Opportunity/ Double Bind

0485   **McAdoo, Harriette Pipes**
(1988) "Changes in the Formation and Structure of Black Families: The Impact on Black Women." Available: Working Paper #182, Wellesley College Center for Research on Women, Wellesley, MA.

African Americans/ Balancing Work and Family Life/ Family/ Families/ Women of Color/ Culture/ Social Change/ Social Influences/ Family Structure

0486   **McGuigan, Dorothy G.**
(1980) Women's Lives: New Theory Research and Policy. Ann Arbor, MI: Center for Continuing Education of Women, University of Michigan. pp. 451.

Women of Color/ African American/ Women's Roles/ Working Class/ Coping Strategies/ Family/ Wage Discrimination/ Widows/ Public Policy

0487   **Miller, Eleanor M.**
(1987) "'Some Peoples Calls It Crime.' Hustling, the Illegal Work of Underclass Women." in The Worth of Women's Work. Anne Statham et al. Albany, NY: State University of New York Press. pp. 109-132.

Women of Color/ Employment/ African American/ Survival Strategies/ Prostitution/ Lower Class/ Crime/ Deviance/ Economic Value of Women's Work/ Women Living in Poverty

0488   **Morrison, Gwendolyn C. C.**
(1981) "Characteristics of Black Females In Administrative Management Level Employment." Dissertation: Texas Women's University, Denton, TX 76204.

Women of Color/ Professional Occupations/ African American/ Personality Traits/ Employment/ Administrators/ Management/ Careers

0489   **Mossell, Mrs. N. F.**
(1988) The Work of the Afro-American Woman. New York: Oxford University Press. pp. 224. ISBN 019505265X.

African American/ Women of Color/ Achievements/ Womanhood/ Essays/ Balancing Work and Family Life

0490   **Painter, Nell Irvin**
(1987) "Woman Suffrage and Women Workers." in Standing at Armageddon: The United States, 1877-1919. Nell Irvin Painter. New York: Norton. pp. 231-282. ISBN 0393024059.

African American/ Women of Color/ Separate Spheres/ Suffrage/ Club Women/ Employment/ Working Class/ Strikes/ Labor Disputes

0491   **Robinson, Sarah B.**
(1978) "The Occupational Aspirations of Young Black and White Females: Levels, Atypicality, and Work Commitment." Dissertation: University of Texas, Austin,

TX.

Women of Color/ Occupational Aspirations/ Work Ethic/ Work Attitudes/ African American/ European American/ Comparative Studies

0492   Rogers, Laura Simons
(1984) "Locus of Control, Vocational Exploratory Behavior, and Career Choices of Black Women." Dissertation: Rutgers University, New Brunswick, NJ.

Women of Color/ Power/ Behavior/ African American/ Black Studies/ Career Choice/ Locus of Control/ Behavioral Research/ Employment

0493   Royster, Jacqueline Jones
(1986) "Black Women Missionaries: A Letter from Flora Zeto Malkebu to Lucy Hale Tapley." SAGE: A Scholarly Journal on Black Women 3(Spring):1:pp. 58-60.

Women of Color/ African American/ Missionary Societies/ History/ Biographies/ Missionaries/ Religious Workers

0494   Scales-Trent, Judy
(1989) "Black Women and the Constitution: Finding our Place, Asserting our Rights." Harvard Civil Rights-Civil Liberties Law Review 24(Winter):1:pp. 9-44.

Women of Color/ Employment/ Racial Discrimination/ African American/ Doubly Disadvantaged/ Legal System/ Laws/ Equal Protection Under the Law/ Civil Rights/ Civil Liberties/ Constitution/ Power/ Powerlessness/ Court Decisions/ Institutional Discrimination/ Women Living in Poverty

0495   Simms, Margaret C.
(1988) "The Choices that Young Black Women Make: Education, Employment and Family Formation." Working Paper #190, Wellesley College Center for Research on Women, Wellesley, MA.

African American/ Career Aspirations/ Educational Opportunities/ Higher Education/ Decision Making/ Women of Color/ Employment/ Young Adults/ Career Planning

0496   Smith, Elaine M.
(1980) "Mary McLeod Bethune and the National Youth Administration." in Clio Was a Woman: Studies in the History of American Women. Mabel E. Deutrich and Virginia C. Puroy (eds.). Washington, D.C.: Howard University Press.

African American/ Leadership/ 20th Century/ Women's History/ 1940-1949/ Education/ Civil Rights/ Employment/ Job Training/ Women of Color/ Mary McLeod Bethune

0497   Sokoloff, Natalie J.
(1987)   "The Increase of Black and White Women in the Professions: A Contradictory Process." in Ingredients for Women's Employment Policy. Christine Bose and Glenna Spitze (eds.). Albany, NY: State University of New York Press. pp. 53-72.

African American/ Employment Patterns/ European American/ Professional Occupations/ Male Dominated Employment/ Women of Color/ Comparative Studies/ Sex Discrimination/ Higher Education

0498   Sokoloff, Natalie J.
(1987) "The Progress of Black Women and Men in the Professions: Myth or Reality-- A Preliminary Analysis." Presented: 4th Annual Women and Work Conference, University of Texas, Austin, TX. May.

Women of Color/ African American/ Professional Status/ Occupational Mobility/ Male Dominated Employment/ Female Intensive Occupations/ Role Conflicts/ Social Change/ Employment

0499   Sokoloff, Natalie J.
(1988) "Evaluating Gains and Losses by Black and White Women and Men in the

Professions, 1960-1986." <u>Social Problems</u> 35(Feb):1:pp. 36-54.

Women of Color/ Labor Force Participation/ African Amercian/ Employment/ Comparative Studies/
Professional Occupations/ Male Dominated Employment/ Race, Class and Gender Studies

0500 Stanley, Amy Dru
(1988) "Conjugal Bonds and Wage Labor: Rights of Contract in the Age of
Emancipation." <u>The Journal of American History</u> 75(Sept):2:pp. 471-500.

Labor Force/ Employment/ African American/ Wage Labor/ Labor History/ Marriage/ Slavery/
Emancipation/ Legal Status/ Wage Earning Wives/ Women of Color/ Women's Rights/ Coverture/
Property Laws/ Labor Legislation

0501 Thomas, Mary Martha
(1987) <u>Riveting and Rationing in Dixie: Alabama Women and the Second World
War</u>. University, AL: University of Alabama Press. pp. 144.

South/ Alabama/ Women's History/ 1940-1949/ Images of Women/ Factory Workers/ Male Dominated
Employment/ Women's Roles/ Women of Color/ African American/ Job Training/ Military Draft/ World
War II/ Industries/ Trades/ Blue Collar Workers

0502 Torrecilha, Ramon S.
(1988) "Migration, Education and Income Differentials on Selected Rural Poor
Counties in the South, 1975-80." Presented: Rural Sociological Society.

African Americans/ Employment Patterns/ European Americans/ Low Income Households/ People of
Color/ Migration/ Wages/ Rural Areas/ Educational Opportunities/ Comparative Studies/ 1970-1979

0503 Tucker, Susan
(1987) "A Complex Bond: Southern Black Domestic Workers and their White
Employers." <u>Frontiers: A Journal of Women Studies</u> 9:3:pp. 6-13.

Women of Color/ Domestic Services/ African American/ Employment/ Bonding/ Household Workers/
Interracial Relations/ European American

0504 Tucker, Susan
(1988) <u>Telling Memories among Southern Women: Domestic Workers and Their
Employers in the Segregated South</u>. Baton Rouge, LA: Louisiana State University
Press.

South/ Women's History/ Domestic Services/ African American/ Division of Labor/ European American/
Women of Color/ Slavery/ Plantations/ Employment/ Household Workers/ Relationships/ Segregation

0505 Walsh, W. Bruce
Horton, J. and Bingham, R. P. (1979) "A Comparison of the Concurrent Validity of
Holland's Theory with College-Degreed Black Women." <u>Journal of Vocational
Behavior</u> 13:pp. 242-250.

Women of Color/ Bachelors Degrees/ African American/ Academic Awards/ Comparative Studies/
Employment/ Post Secondary Education/ Academic Achievement/ Higher Education

0506 Ward, Connie
(1980) "The Concurrent Validity of Holland's Theory for Non-College Degreed
Black Working Women." Dissertation: Ohio State University, Columbus, OH.

Women of Color/ Work Experience/ African American/ Economic Value of Women's Work/ Black
Studies/ Employment/ Educationally Disadvantaged

0507 White, Shane
(1988) "'We Dwell in Safety and Pursue Our Honest Callings': Free Blacks in New

York City, 1783-1810." <u>The Journal of American History</u> 75(Sept):2:pp. 445-470.

People of Color/ New York/ North East/ African Americans/ Emancipation/ History/ 18th Century/ Freemen/ 19th Century/ Black Studies/ Work Ethic

0508   Williams, Rhonda M.
(1988) "Beyond Human Capital: Black Women, Work and Wages." Available: Working Paper #183, Wellesley College Center for Research on Women, Wellesley, MA.

African American/ Earnings/ Employment Opportunities/ Low Income/ Economic Status/ Employment/ Women of Color/ Career Opportunities/ Economic Value of Women's Work/ Wage Gap

0509   Wilson, William Julius
(ed.). (1989) <u>The Ghetto Underclass: Social Science Perspectives</u>. Newbury Park, CA: Sage Publications, Inc. pp. 256.

People of Color/ Role Models/ Employment/ Family/ Poverty/ Socioeconomic Status/ Economically Disadvantaged/ African American/ Lower Class

0510   Wolf, Jacquelyn H.
(1985) "Professionalizing Volunteer Work in a Black Neighborhood." <u>Social Science Review</u> 59(September):3:pp. 423-434.

African Americans/ People of Color/ Neighborhoods/ Physical Health/ Urban Areas/ Older Adults/ Aging/ Volunteers/ Volunteer Work/ Community

0511   Yancy, Dorothy Cowser
(1986) "Dorothy Bolden, Organizer of Domestic Workers." <u>SAGE: A Scholarly Journal on Black Women</u> 3(Spring):1:pp. 53-55.

Women of Color/ African American/ History/ South/ Biographies/ Dorothy Bolden/ Domestic Services/ Household Labor/ Labor Unions/ Organizing/ Labor Movement/ Working Class

0512   Yates, Sandra Elizabeth Grady
(1982) <u>The Relationship of Self-Concept and Other Variables to the Work Value Orientation of Black Females Enrolled in Inner City Schools</u>. San Pedro, CA: R and E Publishers. ISBN 0882476513.

African American/ Women of Color/ Work Ethic/ Urban Areas/ Work Incentives/ Schools/ Students/ Psychological Factors/ Psychological Needs/ Self Concept/ Work Attitudes/ Vocational Education

Asian American

0513   Chai, Alice Yun
(1986) "Freed from the Elders but Locked into Labor: Korean Immigrant Women in Hawaii." <u>Journal of Women's Studies</u> 13:3:pp. 223-234.

Asian/ Traditional Family/ Labor Force/ Social Mobility/ Occupational Mobility/ Immigrants/ Korean/ Hawaii/ Pacific/ Dominance/ Employment/ People of Color

0514   Chan, Connie
(1986) "Teaching about Asian Women's Activism: The Poetry of Mila Aguilar." <u>Women's Studies Quarterly</u> 14(Spring/ Summer):1-2:pp. 23-25.

Women of Color/ Asian American/ Poetry/ Literary Arts/ Political Activism/ Social Change/ Race, Class, and Gender Studies/ Sex Discrimination/ Labor Unions/ Factory Workers

0515   Geschwender, James A.
Carroll-Seguin, Rita. (1987) "Asian-American Success in Hawaii: Myth, Reality, or Artifact of Women's Labor." Author: State University of New York,

Binghamton, NY. Presented: Political Economy of the World System Conference, State University of New York, Binghamton, NY. March.

Asian American/ Women of Color/ Pacific/ Hawaii/ Employment/ Political Economic System/ Economic Value of Women's Work

0516   **Glenn, Evelyn Nakano**
(1987) "Women, Labor Migration, and Household Work: Japanese American Women in the Pre-War Period." in Ingredients for Women's Employment Policy. Christine Bose and Glenna Spitze (eds.). Albany, NY: State University of New York Press. pp. 93-113. ISBN 0887064213.

Women of Color/ Japanese American/ History/ 1940-1949/ Household Workers/ Labor Supply/ Asian American/ Migration/ Employment

0517   **Glenn, Evelyn Nakano**
(1988) "A Belated Industry Revised: Domestic Service among Japanese-American Women." in The Worth of Women's Work. Anne Statham et al. Albany, NY: State University of New York Press. pp. 57-75.

Women of Color/ Asian American/ Japanese American/ Employment/ Domestic Services/ Working Class/ Household Labor/ Female Intensive Occupations/ Economic Value of Women's Work

0518   **Hossfield, Karen J.**
(1988) "Sex, Race and Class in Silicon Valley: Immigrant Women and the High-Tech Division of Labor." Presented: Society for the Study of Social Problems, Atlanta, GA.

Division of Labor/ California/ Pacific/ Sex Discrimination/ Latina/ Mexican/ Immigrants/ Asian American/ Women of Color/ Electronics Industry/ Race, Class and Gender Studies/ Computers/ Employment/ Economic Value of Women's Work

0519   **Loo, Chalsa**
Ong, Paul. (1982) "Slaying Demon with a Sewing Needle: Feminist Issues for Chinatown's Women." Berkeley Journal of Sociology 27:pp. 77-88.

Women of Color/ Chinese American/ Feminism/ Feminist Perspectives/ Racial Discrimination/ Sex Discrimination/ Political Activism/ Asian American/ Textile Workers/ Employment/ Sewing/ Sewers

0520   **Seguin, Rita Carroll**
Geschwender, James A. (1987) "Ethnicity and Women's Labor Force Activities in Hawaii: The Supplemental Earner Thesis and the Asian Success Myth." Presented: American Sociological Association Annual Meeting, Chicago, IL. August.

Women of Color/ Academic Achievement/ Asian American/ Dependent Children/ Labor Force/ Stereotypes/ Income/ Employment/ Pacific/ Hawaii/ Socioeconomic Status/ Two Income Families

0521   **Timpane, M.**
(1980) Conference on the Educational and Occupational Needs of Asian-Pacific-American Women. Washington, D.C.: U.S. Government Printing Office.

Asian Pacific American/ Women of Color/ Education/ Employment

Latina

0522   **Acosta-Belen, Edna**
Sjostrom, Barbara R. (1986) "The Educational and Professional Status of Puerto Rican Women." in The Puerto Rican Woman. Edna Acosta-Belen. New York:

Praeger. pp. 64-74. ISBN 0030524660.

Puerto Rican/ Latina/ Educational Status/ Professional Status/ Women of Color/ Employment

0523 Alers-Montalvo, Manual
(1985) The Puerto Rican Migrants of New York City. New York: AMS Press. ISBN 0404194001.

Puerto Ricans/ Migrants/ New York/ Latinos/ North East/ People of Color/ Employment

0524 Arroyo, Laure E.
Sanchez, Rosaura; Martinez, Rosa (eds.). (1983) "Industrial and Occupational Distribution of Chicana Workers." in Essays on La Mujer. Los Angeles: Chicana Studies Center Publications, University of California Los Angeles. pp. 150-187.

Employment/ Women of Color/ Latina/ Chicana/ Labor Force/ Occupational Segregation

0525 Bonilla-Santiago, Gloria
(1988) "Hispanic Women in New Jersey: A Survey of Women Raising Families Alone." Available: Hispanic Women's Task Force of New Jersey, School of Social Work, Rutgers University, 327 Cooper St., Camden, NJ 08102.

Women of Color/ Employment/ Latina/ Fertility/ New Jersey/ North East/ Female Headed Households/ Single Parent Families/ Heads of Households/ Educational Level

0526 Burgess, Norma J.
(1988) "Role Diversity among Mexican-Origin Women in the U.S." Author: Dept. of Sociology and Anthropology, Mississippi State University, P. O. Drawer C, Mississippi State, MS 39762. Presented: Mid-South Sociological Association, Mobile, AL. October.

Chicana/ Latina/ Images of Women/ Women of Color/ Stereotypes/ Gender Roles/ Family/ Families/ Cultural Identity/ Male Female Relationships/ Wage Earning Wives/ Household Division of Labor/ Employment/ Homemakers

0527 Christensen, Edward W.
Acosta-Belen, Edna. (1986) "The Puerto Rican Woman: A Profile." in The Puerto Rican Woman. New York: Praeger. pp. 51-63. ISBN 0030524660.

Puerto Rican/ Latina/ Education/ Child Rearing/ Employment/ Social Values/ Women of Color

0528 Curry Rodriguez, Julia E.
(1988) "Labor Migration and Familial Responsibilities: Experiences of Mexican Women." in Mexicans at Work. Margarita B. Melville. Houston, TX: University of Houston. pp. 47-64.

Women of Color/ Educational Attainment/ Latina/ Mexican/ Community Relations/ Migration/ Kinship/ Networks/ Illegal Immigrants/ Support Systems/ Labor Force Participation/ Heads of Households/ Balancing Work and Family Life/ Employment

0529 Deutsch, Sarah
(1987) "Women and Intercultural Relations: The Case of Hispanic New Mexico and Colorado." SIGNS: Journal of Women in Culture and Society 12(Summer):4:pp. 719-739.

Latina/ Women of Color/ West/ New Mexico/ Colorado/ Relationships/ Cultural Groups/ Crosscultural Studies/ Social Relations/ Household Workers/ Discrimination

0530 Dubose, Louis
(1988) "Invisible City." Southern Exposure 16(Winter):4:pp. 24-26.

Salvadorans/ Central Americans/ Illegal Immigrants/ Latinos/ People of Color/ Demography/ Texas/ South West/ Networks/ Support Systems/ Refugees/ Immigrants/ Employment/ Activism

0531 Duron, Clementina
(1984) "Mexican Women and Labor Conflict in Los Angeles: The ILGWU Dressmaker's Strike of 1933." Aztlan 15:1:pp. 145-161.

Latina/ Women of Color/ Textile Industry/ Employment/ Labor Force/ California/ Pacific/ Strikes/ Unions/ 20th Century

0532 Fernandez-Kelly, Maria P.
Garcia, Anna M. (1987) "Invisible Amidst the Glitter: Hispanic Women in the Southern California Electronics Industry." in The Worth of Women's Work. Anne Statham et al. Albany: State University of New York Press. pp. 265-290

Women of Color/ California/ Pacific/ Latina/ Employment/ Working Class/ Blue Collar Workers/ Electronics Industry/ Economic Value of Women's Work

0533 Fernandez-Kelly, Maria P.
(1983) "Mexican Border Industrialization, Female Labor Force, Participation and Migration." in Women, Men, and the International Division of Labor. June Nash and Maria Fernandez-Kelly. Albany: State University of New York Press. pp. 205-223.

Latina/ Mexican/ Maquiladora/ Women of Color/ Employment/ Labor Force/ Immigrants/ Border Studies/ South West

0534 Gonzales, Rosalinda M.
(1978) "Mexican Women and Families: Rural-to-Urban and International Migration." Southwest Economy and Society 4:2:pp. 14-27.

Latina/ Mexican/ Urban Migration/ Women of Color/ Family/ Immigrants/ Employment/ Rural Women

0535 Gonzales, Rosalinda M.
(1984) "The Chicana in the Southwest Labor History 1900-1975." Critical Perspectives of the Third World America 2:1:pp. 26-61.

Women of Color/ Labor Force/ Latina/ Unions/ Employment/ Chicana/ South West/ Labor History/ 20th Century

0536 Green, Susan S.
(1983) "Silicon Valley's Women Workers: A Theoretical Analysis of Sex Segregation in the Electronics Industry Labor Market." in Women, Men, and the International Divison of Labor. June Nash and Maria Fernandez-Kelly. Albany: State University of New York Press. pp. 273-331.

Latina/ Sex Segregation/ Women of Color/ Discrimination/ Employment/ Labor Force/ Electronics Industry/ Occupational Segregation

0537 Guendelman, Sylvia
(1987) "The Incorporation of Mexican Women in Seasonal Migration: A Study of Gender Differences." Hispanic Journal of Behavioral Sciences 9(September):3:pp. 245-264.

Women of Color/ Latina/ Mexican/ Immigrants/ Migrant Workers/ Sex Roles/ Farm Workers/ Traditional Family/ Race, Class and Gender Studies

0538 Guendelman, Sylvia
Perez-Itriago, A. (1987) "Double Lives: The Changing Role of Women in Seasonal Migration." International Journal of Women's Studies 13:pp. 249-271.

Women of Color/ Support Systems/ Latina/ Race, Class and Gender Studies/ Immigrants/ Balancing Work and Family Life/ Women's Roles/ Seasonal Migration/ Farm Workers

0539   **Hossfield, Karen J.**
(1988) "Sex, Race and Class in Silicon Valley: Immigrant Women and the High-Tech Division of Labor." Presented: Society for the Study of Social Problems, Atlanta, GA. August.

Division of Labor/ California/ Pacific/ Sex Discrimination/ Latina/ Mexican/ Immigrants/ Asian American/ Women of Color/ Electronics Industry/ Race, Class and Gender Studies/ Computers/ Employment/ Economic Value of Women's Work

0540   **Jaffe, A. J.**
Cullen, Ruth M. et al. (1986) "The Findings: A Summary." in The Changing Demography of Spanish Americans. A. J. Jaffe and Ruth M. Cullen. New York: Academic Press. pp. 426. ISBN 012379580X.

Latinos/ Fertility Rates/ Demography/ Educational Experience/ Single Mothers/ Employment Opportunities/ Family Income/ People of Color

0541   **Jensen, Joan M.**
(1986) "Canning Comes to New Mexico: Women and the Agricultural Extension Service." in New Mexican Women: Intercultural Perspectives. Joan Jensen and Darlis A. Miller. Albuquerque: University of New Mexico Press. pp. 201-226.

Women of Color/ Agricultural Extension/ Latina/ Food Processing/ New Mexico/ South West/ Employment/ Agriculture

0542   **Jensen, Joan M.**
(1986) "I've Worked, I'm Not Afraid of Work: Farm Women in New Mexico." in New Mexican Women: Intercultural Perspectives. Joan M. Jensen and Darlis A. Miller. Albuquerque: University of New Mexico Press.

Women of Color/ Farm Workers/ Latina/ Employment/ New Mexico/ South West/ Rural Areas/ Agriculture

0543   **Jorgensen, Stephen R.**
Adams, Russell P. (1987)   "Family Planning Needs and Behavior of Mexican American Women: A Study of Health Care Professionals and their Clientele." Hispanic Journal of Behavioral Sciences 9(September):3:pp. 265-286.

Women of Color/ Latina/ Health Care Workers/ Health Care Services/ Contraception/ Family Planning/ Comparative Studies/ Stereotypes/ Immigrants

0544   **Korrol, Virginia Sanchez**
(1979) "On the Other Side of the Ocean: The Work Experiences of Early Puerto Rican Migrant Women." Caribbean Review 8(January/March):1.

Puerto Rican/ Latina/ Migration/ Work Experience/ Labor History/ Women of Color/ Employment/ Labor Force

0545   **Lamphere, Louise A.**
(1986) "Working Mothers and Family Strategies: Portuguese and Colombian Immigrant Women in New England." in International Immigration: The Female Experience. Rita Simon and Caroline Brettell (eds.). Totowa, NJ: Rowman and Allenheld.

Women of Color/ Balancing Work and Family Life/ Latina/ Columbian/ New England/ Immigrants/ Employment/ Family Relationships/ Mothers Working Outside the Home/ Family Roles/ Support Systems/ Coping Strategies

0546   **Luhrs, Joyce**
(1987) "Hispanic Women in History: Where Are They?" NWSA Perspectives

5(Winter):2:pp. 20.

Women of Color/ Immigrants/ Latina/ Labor Force/ Domestic Roles/ Women's History/ Household Workers/ Women's Roles/ Acculturation

0547   Marin, Margie
(1975)   "An Historical View of Chicano/Chicana Organizing."   Cadre 2(Spring):pp. 49-56.

Latina/ Chicana/ Labor History/ Women of Color/ Employment/ Labor Organizing/ Unions

0548   Miller, Tom
(1984)   "Class Reunion: Salt of the Earth Revisited." Cineaste 13:3.

Women of Color/ Latina/ Film/ Labor/ Images of Women/ Strikes/ Employment

0549   Mindiola, T.
(1980)   "The Cost of Being a Mexican Female Worker in the 1970 Houston Labor Market." Aztlan 11:2:pp. 231-247.

Women of Color/ Mexican/ Labor Market/ 1970-1979/ Employment/ Latina/ Chicana/ West/ Texas

0550   Mirande, Alfredo
Enriquez, Evangelina. (1982) "Chicana in the Struggle for Unions" in Introduction to Chicano Studies.   Livie Isauro Duran and H. Russell Bernard.   New York: Macmillan Publishing. pp. 325-337.

Latina/ Chicana/ Organizing/ Women of Color/ Union Membership/ Employment/ Labor Force

0551   Monroy, Douglas
(1980)   "La Costura en Los Angeles, 1933-1939: The ILGWU and the Politics of Domination." in Mexican Women in the U.S.: Struggles Past and Present. Magdalena Mora et al. Los Angeles: Chicano Studies Research Center, University of California Los Angeles. pp. 171-178.

Latina/ Mexican/ Union Membership/ Women of Color/ Labor History/ 1930-1939/ Employment/ Garment Industry/ California/ Pacific/ Labor Unions

0552   Mora, Magdalena
(1981)   "The Tolteca Strike: Mexican Women and the Struggle for Union Representation." in Mexican Immigrant Workers in the U.S. Antonio Rios-Bustamente.   Los Angeles: Chicano Studies Research Center, University of California Los Angeles. pp. 111-117.

Latina/ Mexican/ Union Membership/ Immigrants/ Voluntary Organizations/ Employment/ Organizing/ Strikes/ Women of Color/ Labor Force

0553   National Council of La Raza
(1988)   "Hispanics in the Work Force, Part II: Hispanic Women." Available: National Council of La Raza, Policy Analysis Center, 20 F St. NW, 2nd floor, Washington, D.C.

Latina/ Women of Color/ Labor Force/ Employment Patterns

0554   Pena, Devon G.
(1980)   "Las Maquiladoras: Mexican Women's Class Struggle in the Border Industries." Aztlan 11:2:pp. 159-230.

Latina/ Mexican/ Maquiladora/ Women of Color/ Employment/ Labor Force/ Border Studies/ Class Discrimination/ Race, Class and Gender Studies

0555   **Pena, Devon G.**
(1986) "Between the Lines: A New Perspective on the Industrial Sociology of Women Workers in Transnational Labor Process." in <u>Chicana Voices: Intersections of Class, Race, and Gender</u>. Austin, TX: Center for Mexican American Studies. pp. 77-95.

Latina/ Chicana/ Women of Color/ Employment/ Labor Force/ Race, Class and Gender Studies/ Multinational Corporations

0556   **Rodriguez, Carmen F. Quiones**
(1976) "Families of Working Mothers in Puerto Rico." Dissertation: Ohio State University, Columbus, OH. pp. 209.

Family/ Families/ Working Parents/ Puerto Rican/ Latina/ Women of Color/ Wage Earning Mothers/ Employment

0557   **Romero, Mary**
(1986) "Domestics and the Struggle for Harmony: The Case of Chicana Cleaning Ladies." Presented: National Association for Chicano Studies, El Paso, TX.

Women of Color/ Latina/ Chicana/ Domestic Services/ Household Workers/ Employment/ Relationships

0558   **Romero, Mary**
(1987) "Domestic Work in Transition From Rural to Urban Life: A Case of La Chicana." <u>Women Studies</u> 13:3:pp. 199-220.

Women of Color/ Latina/ Chicana/ Urban Areas/ Household Workers/ Domestic Services/ Rural Areas

0559   **Romero, Mary**
(1987) "Using Qualitative Research Methods to Analyze Chicana Work Experience." Presented: National Association for Chicano Studies, Salt Lake City, UT.

Women of Color/ Latina/ Chicana/ Research Methods/ Work Experience/ Employment

0560   **Romero, Mary**
(1987) "Chicana and Mexicana Experience in the Colonial Labor System as Domestic Workers." Presented: Seventh Berkshire Conference on the History of Women, Wellesley, MA.

Women of Color/ Mexican/ Latina/ Chicana/ Employment/ Domestic Services/ History/ 18th Century/ Labor Force/ Human Resources

0561   **Romero, Mary**
(1987) "Chicana Domestics in Denver, Colorado." Presented: National Women's Studies Association, Atlanta, GA. June.

Women of Color/ Latina/ Domestic Services/ West/ Colorado/ Employment/ Household Workers/ Chicana

0562   **Romero, Mary**
(1988) "Renegotiating Race and Gender Hierarchies in the Everyday Interactions of Chicana Household Workers and Employers." Presented: Society for the Study of Social Problems Annual Meeting, Atlanta, GA. August.

Gender Roles/ Employment/ Workers/ Chicana/ Latina/ Race, Class and Gender Studies/ Household Workers/ Relationships/ Household Labor/ Women of Color/ Domestic Services/ Racial Discrimination

0563   **Romero, Mary**
(1988) "Day Work in the Suburbs: The Work Experience of Chicana Private Housekeepers" in <u>The Worth of Women's Work</u>. Anne Statham et al. Albany:

State University of New York Press. pp. 288.

Women of Color/ Employment/ Latina/ Chicana/ Working Class/ Domestic Services/ Household Labor/ Economic Value of Women's Work/ Female Intensive Occupations

0564   Ruiz, Vicki L.
(1986) "A Promise Fulfilled: Mexican Cannery Workers in Southern California." The Pacific Historian 30:2:pp. 51-61.

Latina/ Mexicans/ Women of Color/ Employment/ California/ Pacific/ Food Preparation Occupations/ Food Industry/ Factory Workers

0565   Sanchez, Rosaura
(1982) "The Chicana Labor Force." in Essays on La Mujer. Rosaura Sanchez and Rosa Martinez Cruz. Los Angeles: Chicano Studies Center Publications. pp. 3-15.

Latina/ Labor Force/ Women of Color/ Chicana/ Employment

0566   Segura, Denise A.
(1986) "Chicanas and Triple Oppression in the Labor Force." in Chicana Voices: Intersections in Class, Race, and Gender. Austin, TX: Center for Mexican American Studies, University of Texas. pp. 47-65.

Latina/ Chicana/ Race, Class and Gender Studies/ Women of Color/ Labor Force/ Employment

0567   Sullivan, T. A.
(1984) "The Occupational Prestige of Women Immigrants: A Comparison of Cubans and Mexicans." International Migration Review 18(Winter):pp. 1045-1062.

Latina/ Cubans/ Women of Color / Employment/ Immigrants/ Mexicans/ Prestige/ Comparative Studies

0568   Taylor, Paul S.
(1980) "Mexican Women in Los Angeles Industry in 1928." Aztlan 11:1:pp. 99-130.

Latina/ Mexicans/ Factory Workers/ Women of Color/ Employment/ California/ Pacific/ Labor History/ 1920-1929

0569   Tiano, Susan Beth
(1985) "Maquiladoras, Women's Work and Unemployment in Northern Mexico." Aztlan 15:2:pp. 341-378.

Latina/ Mexicans/ Employment/ Women of Color/ Maquiladoras/ Border Studies/ Economic Value of Women's Work

0570   Warburton, A. A.
Woods, H. H. and Cane, M. (1982) "Four Families of Agricultural Laborers in South Texas, 1941." in Introduction to Chicano Studies. Livie Isauro and H. Russell Bernard (eds.). New York: Macmillan Publishing. pp. 272-278.

Latina/ Migrant Workers/ Women of Color/ Agriculture/ Family/ History/ 1940-1949/ Texas/ South West

0571   Winegarten, Ruthe
Brewer, Rose and Werden, Frieda. (1986) "A Documentary History of Black Texas Women." Author: Texas Women's History, Box 49084, Austin, TX 78765.

African American/ Chicana/ Latina/ South West/ Texas/ Women of Color/ Employment/ Workers/ Women's History/ Documentaries/ Social Movements/ Social Change

0572   Zambrana, Ruth E.
(1987) "Latinas in the United States." in The American Woman 1987-1988: A Report in Depth. Sarah E. Rix. New York: Norton. ISBN 0393303888.

Latina/ Family Roles/ Women of Color/ Employment/ Images of Women/ Education

0573   **Zavella, Patricia**
(1987) <u>Women's Work and Chicano Families: Cannery Workers of the Santa Clara Valley</u>. Ithaca, NY: Cornell University Press. pp. 192. ISBN 0801417309.
Women of Color/ Latina/ Chicana/ Family/ Women's Roles/ Migrant Workers/ Employment/ California/ Pacific/ Factory Workers/ Food Industry

Native American

0574   **Conte, Christine**
(1982) "Ladies, Livestock, Land and Lucre: Women's Networks and Social Status on the Western Navajo Reservation." <u>American Indian Quarterly</u> 6(Spring/Summer):1-2:pp. 105-124.
Women of Color/ Economic Factors/ Native American/ Navajo/ Social Status/ Kinship/ Economic Value of Women's Work/ Sex Roles/ Women's Roles/ Networks/ Property Ownership

0575   **Ferguson, Helena J. Sheehan**
(1985) "A Study of the Characteristics of American Indian Professional Women in Oklahoma." Dissertation: Ohio State University, Columbus, OH. DAI Vol. 46(06A)1518.
Native American/ Oklahoma/ South Central/ Professional Status/ Women of Color/ Employment

0576   **Herring, Rebecca**
(1986) "Their Work Was Never Done: Women Missionaries on the Kiowa-Comanche Reservation." <u>Chronicles of Oklahoma</u> 64(Spring):pp. 69-83.
Native American/ Kiowa Comanche/ Women of Color/ Missionaries/ Social Change/ Women's Work/ Oklahoma/ South West/ History/ Religious Workers

0577   **Nickless, Pamela Jean**
(1976) "Changing Labor Productivity and the Utilization of Native Women in the American Cotton Textile Industry: 1825-1860." Dissertation: Purdue University, West Lafayette, IN. pp. 223. DAI Vol. 37(10A)6654.
Native American/ Women of Color/ Textile Industry/ History/ 19th Century/ Employment/ Productivity

0578   **Russell, Scott C.**
McDonald, Mark B. (1982) "The Economic Contributions of Women in a Rural Western Navajo Community." <u>American Indian Quarterly</u> 6(Fall/Winter):3-4:pp. 262-282.
Women of Color/ Race, Class and Gender Studies/ Native American/ Navajo/ Economic Value of Women's Work/ Economic Factors/ Arts and Crafts Movement/ Sex Roles/ Women's Roles/ Rural Areas/ West

Southern

0579   **Alexander, Michael**
(1986) "Fishy Business." <u>Southern Exposure</u> 14(September/ October)5-6:pp. 32-34.
Women of Color/ African American/ South/ Mississippi/ Food Industry/ Factory Workers/ Labor Disputes/ Labor Unions/ Wage Discrimination/ Job Discrimination

0580   **Anglin, Mary**
(1987) "Women's Experiences of Waged Labor and the Formation of Class

Consciousness in Appalachia." Author: Lenoir Rhyne College, Hickory, NC 28603.

South/ North Carolina/ Appalachia/ History/ 20th Century/ Resistance/ Labor Disputes/ Employment/ Wages/ Class Consciousness

0581   Audirac, Ivonne

(1988) "The Automation of the Farm's Office: the Impacts of High-Tech Farming on Women." Presented: Rural Sociological Society.

South/ Florida/ Employment Opportunities/ Farming/ Occupational Trends/ Computer Operations/ Technology/ Labor Force Participation/ Images of Women

0582   Barlett, Peggy F.

(1983) "South Georgia Farm Women: Patterns and Consequences." Presented: Southern Association of Agricultural Scientists.

South/ Georgia/ Divison of Labor/. Agriculture/ Household Labor/ Income/ Rural Areas/ Employment/ Farming/ Family Roles/ Women's Roles

0583   Byerly, Victoria M.

(1985) "Hidden From History: The Cotton Mill Girls." Sojourner 10(May):7:pp. 16-17.

African American/ Poverty/ European American/ Race Relations/ Women of Color/ Health Hazards/ Southern/ North Carolina/ Women's History/ Employment/ Economic Value of Women's Work/ Textile Industry

0584   Byerly, Victoria M.

(1986) Hard Times Cotton Mill Girls: Personal Histories of Womanhood and Poverty in the South. Ithaca, NY: Cornell University Press.

Textile Industry/ Autobiographies/ South/ History/ Factory Workers/ Poverty/ Employment/ Women's History/ Wage Earning Women/ Testimonial Literature

0585   Cameron, Cindia

(1988) "Issues and Strategies for Organizing in the Service Economy: Women Office Workers and 9 to 5 in the South." Presented: Society for the Study of Social Problems Annual Meeting, Atlanta, GA.

Labor Force Participation/ Organizing/ Unions/ Economy/ Social Movements/ Work Hours/ Employment Schedules/ Service Occupations/ South/ Office Work/ Employment

0586   Campbell, John

(1984) "Work, Pregnancy and Infant Mortality among Southern Slaves." Journal of Interdisciplinary History 14(Spring):4:pp. 793-812.

Women of Color/ African American/ History/ South/ Slavery/ Infant Mortality/ Birth Rates/ Pregnancy/ Pregnant Workers/ Nutrition/ Farm Workers/ Maternal and Infant Welfare

0587   Campbell, Randolph B.

(1988) "Slave Hiring in Texas." American Historical Review 93(Feb.):pp. 107-114.

People of Color/ African Americans/ Texas/ South/ Slavery/ Slaves/ Employment/ History/ 19th Century

0588   Cardenas, Gilbert

(1976) "Women's Work and Economic Crisis: Some Lessons of the Great Depression." Review of Radical Political Economics 8:3:pp. 73-97.

Immigrants/ Southern/ Labor Force/ Economic Value of Women's Work/ Occupational Status/ History/ 1930-1939/ Working Class/ Employment/ Household Workers/ Texas

0589 Carmichael, James V., Jr.
(1986) "Atlanta's Female Librarians, 1883-1915." Journal of Library History 21(Spring):pp. 376-399.

Southern/ Employment/ History/ 19th Century/ Professional Status/ Georgia

0590 Caver, Carolyn
(1986) "Dreaming Again." Southern Exposure 14(September/ October):5-6:pp. 62-64.

Women of Color/ African American/ Wage Discrimination/ Socioeconomic Status/ Lower Class/ Minority Owned Business/ Women Owned Business/ South/ Employment

0591 Clark-Lewis, Elizabeth
(1987) "This Work Had A' End: African American Domestic Workers in Washington, D.C., 1910-1940." in To Toil the Livelong Day: America's Women at Work, 1780-1980. Carol Groneman and Mary B. Norton. Ithaca, NY: Cornell University Press. pp. 196-213.

African American/ Employment Patterns/ Women of Color/ Economic Value of Women's Work/ Domestic Services/ 19th Century/ Women's History/ Race, Class and Gender Studies/ Washington, D.C./ South

0592 Clinton, Catherine
(1987) "'Women's Work' in the Old South - The Sexual Division of Labor on Plantations." Helicon Nine: The Journal of Women's Arts and Letters (Spring):17-18:pp. 187-193.

Southern/ History/ 19th Century/ Economic Value of Women's Work/ Women's Roles/ Plantations/ Sexual Division of Labor/ Gender Roles/ Sex Roles

0593 Cornfield, Daniel B.
(1988) "Household, Work, and Labor Activism: Gender Differences in the Determinants of Union Membership Participation." Presented: American Sociological Association Annual Meeting.

World War II/ Households/ South/ Tennessee/ Gender Differences/ Women's Movement/ Organizing/ Unions/ Labor Force Participation/ Employment/ Labor Unions/ Women's History/ Social Movements

0594 Hall, Bob
(1986) "The Black Belt." Southern Exposure 14(September/ October):5-6:pp. 76-78.

People of Color/ African Americans/ Minority Owned Business/ South/ Lower Class/ Blue Collar Workers/ Wage Discrimination/ Labor Disputes/ South

0595 Hall, Jacquelyn D.
Lelondis, James et al. (1987) Like A Family: The Making of a Southern Cotton Mill. Chapel Hill, NC: University of North Carolina Press.

Southern/ Working Class Women/ History/ Economy/ Employment/ Blue Collar Workers/ Work/ Community/ Networks/ Labor Force Participation/ Family/ Families/ Employment Patterns/ Society

0596 Hall, Jacquelyn D.
(1988) "Partial Truths." Presented: First Southern Conference on Women's History, Converse College, Spartanburg, SC. June.

South/ Women's History/ Employment/ Working Class/ Family

0597 Hardesty, Connie
Harmon, Mary P. (1986) "The Division of Labor on Family Farms: Task Performance of Women, Children and Hired Labor." Presented: Rural Sociological Society, Annual Meeting.

Rural Areas/ Family Roles/ Agriculture/ Farming/ Family Structure/ South/ Kentucky/ Children/ Job Performance/ Traditional Roles/ Division of Labor/ Farm Workers

0598 Hawkins, Mary S.
Hammonds, Maxine M. (1985) "Comparison of Goals and Managerial Behaviors of Urban Single Female Heads of Households." Presented: Southern Association of Agricultural Scientists Annual Meeting .

Female Headed Households/ Employment Practices/ Single Parents/ Singles/ Urban Areas/ Comparative Studies/ Management Styles/ South/ Texas/ Business/ Managers/ Career Aspirations

0599 Hopson, Jannie
(1985) "Career Patterns and Characteristics of Black Women in the Metropolitan Atlanta Area." Dissertation: Georgia State University, Atlanta, GA.

Women of Color/ Work Experience/ South/ Georgia/ Occupational Patterns/ Career Choice/ Urban Areas/ Leadership/ African American

0600 Janiewski, Dolores
(1984) "Subversive Sisterhood: Black Women and Unions in the Southern Tobacco Industry." Southern Women: The Intersection of Race, Class and Gender Series, Working Paper #1, Center for Research on Women, Memphis State University, Memphis, TN 38152.

African American/ Labor Force Participation/ Women of Color/ South/ Tobacco Industry/ Factories/ Race, Class and Gender Studies/ European American/ Discrimination/ Occupational Segregation/ Labor Unions/ Employment

0601 Janiewski, Dolores
(1987) "Seeking a New Day and a New Way: Black Women and Unions in the Southern Tobacco Industry." in To Toil the Livelong Day: America's Women at Work, 1780-1980. Carol Groneman and Mary B. Norton. Ithaca, NY: Cornell University Press. pp. 161-179.

Tobacco Industry/ Race Relations/ African American/ Economic Value of Women's Work/ Women of Color/ Employment/ Industrialization/ South/ Labor History/ Labor Unions

0602 Jaret, Charles
Myers, Lyn. (1987) "Black-White Income Inequality and the Urban System of the South." Presented: American Sociological Association, Chicago, IL. Author: Department of Sociology, Georgia State University, Atlanta, GA 30303.

African American/ Women of Color/ Inequality/ Income Distribution/ Statistical Analysis/ Research Methods/ South/ Urban/ Pay Equity/ Employment

0603 Jones, Jacqueline
(1986) "Theoretical Perspectives on the Work of Black and Poor White Women in the Rural South, 1865-1940." Author: Dept. of History, Wellesley College, Wellesley, MA. Presented: American Farm Women in Historical Perspective, Madison, WI. October.

History/ 19th Century/ Employment Patterns/ South/ Agriculture/ Farm Work/ Rural Living/ Interracial Relations/ African American/ European American/ 20th Century/ Comparative Studies/ Women of Color

0604 Kenig, Sylvia
(1987) "Gaining Turf but Losing Ground: A Critique of Southern Nursing." Frontiers: A Journal of Women Studies 9:3:pp. 64-70.

Women of Color*/ Employment/ South/ Roles/ Female Intensive Occupations/ Nursing/ Health Care Providers/ Health Care Occupations

0605 Losh-Hesselbart, Susan
(1976) "A Comparison of Attitudes toward Women and Attitudes toward Blacks in a Southern City." <u>Sociological Symposium</u> 17(Fall):pp. 45-68.

South/ African Americans/ People of Color/ Racial Stratification/ Sexual Stratification/ Status/ Stereotypes/ Employment/ Discrimination/ Comparative Studies

0606 Lyson, Thomas A.
(1981) "Sex Differences in Recruitment to Agricultural Occupations among Southern College Students." <u>Rural Sociology</u> 46(Spring):1:pp. 85-99.

South/ Agricultural Occupations/ Employment/ Job Recruitment/ Sex Differences/ Career Choice/ College Students/ Rural Development

0607 Maggard, Sally Ward
(1987) "Appalachian Women on Strike: Mobilization of Miners' Wives and Hospital Workers." Presented: National Women's Studies Association, Atlanta, GA. June. Author: Sociology Department, University of Kentucky, Lexington, KY 40506.

South/ Appalachian/ 1970-1979/ Kentucky/ Labor Disputes/ Resistance/ Employment/ Wives/ Strikes/ Mining Industry/ Health Care Workers/ Extractive Industry

0608 Maggard, Sally Ward
(1987) "Gender and Militance among Working Class Appalachian Women." Presented: American Sociological Association, Chicago, IL. Author: Sociology Department, University of Kentucky, Lexington, KY 40506.

Appalachian/ Southern/ Working Class/ Strikes/ Gender Roles/ Household Division of Labor/ Male Female Relationships/ Protest Actions

0609 Maggard, Sally Ward
(1987) "Women's Participation in the Brookside Coal Strike: Militance, Class, and Gender in Appalachia." <u>Frontiers: A Journal of Women Studies</u> 9:3:pp. 16-21.

South/ Strikes/ Blue Collar Workers/ Militance/ Appalachian/ Extractive Industry/ Labor Unions/ Labor Relations/ Mining Industry/ Race, Class and Gender Studies

0610 McHugh, Cathy L.
(1987) <u>Mill Family: The Labor System in the Southern Cotton Textile Industry</u>. New York: Oxford University Press.

South/ North Carolina/ Employment/ Family/ Families/ Community/ Society/ Textile Industry/ Factory Workers

0611 Portier, Carolyn
(1981) "Raising Cane." <u>Southern Exposure</u> 9:4:pp. 77-83.

Louisiana/ South/ Rural Areas/ Farm Workers/ Life Styles/ Rural Women/ Rural Conditions/ Home Life

0612 Reif, Linda Lobao
Shulman, Michael D. and Michael J. Belyea. (1987) "Supporting Unions: The Case of Southern Textile Workers." Author: The Ohio State University, Department of Rural Sociology, Columbus, OH.

South/ Textile Industry/ Employment/ Labor Unions/ Labor Disputes/ Union Membership

0613 Rosell, Ellen
Reese, Cathy. (1988) "Foreign Direct Investment: A Potential Resource for Poor Rural Counties in Tennessee?" Available: PA Program, University of Central Florida, 1519 Clearlake Rd. Cocoa, FL 32922

Employment/ Factories/ Tennessee/ South/ Industries/ Rural Areas/ Foreign Investment Policy/ Economic Opportunities/ Labor Force Participation/ Low Income Households

0614 **Sacks, Karen Brodkin**
(1988) <u>Caring by the Hour: Woman, Work, and Organizing at Duke Medical Center</u>. Urbana, IL: University of Illinois Press. pp. 239. ISBN 0252014499.

Women of Color/ Collective Bargaining/ African American/ Health Care Facilities/ South/ North Carolina/ Income/ Health Care Workers/ Employment/ Labor Unions/ Cultural Identity

0615 **Smith, Suzanne D.**
Price, Sharon J. (1988) "Women and Plant Closings: Unemployment, Re-Employment and Job Training Enrollment Following Dislocation." Presented: Rural Sociological Society.

Images of Women/ Employment Opportunities/ South/ Georgia/ Factories/ Labor Force Participation/ Occupational Hazards/ Rural Areas/ Job Training/ Urban Areas/ Factory Workers/ Unemployment

0616 **Southeast Women's Employment Coalition**
(1988) <u>Women of the Rural South: Economic Status and Prospects</u>. Lexington, KY: Southeast Women's Employment Coalition, Available: Southeast Women's Employment Coalition, 382 Longview Dr., Lexington, KY 40503. (606) 276-1555.

South/ Rural Areas/ North Carolina/ Development/ South Carolina/ Socioeconomic Status/ West Virginia/ Job Market/ Underground Economy/ Employment Opportunities/ Women's History/ Women Living in Poverty/ African American/ Race, Class and Gender/ Vacations

0617 **Thomas, Mary Martha**
(1987) <u>Riveting and Rationing in Dixie: Alabama Women and the Second World War</u>. University, AL: University of Alabama Press. pp. 144.

South/ Alabama/ History/ 1940-1949/ Images of Women/ Factory Workers/ Male Dominated Employment/ Women's Roles/ Women of Color/ African American/ Job Training/ Military Draft/ World War II/ Industries/ Trades/ Blue Collar Workers/ 20th Century

0618 **Tucker, Susan**
(1988) <u>Telling Memories among Southern Women: Domestic Workers and Their Employers in the Segregated South</u>. Baton Rouge, LA: Louisiana State University Press.

South/ Women's History/ Domestic Services/ African American/ Division of Labor/ European American/ Women of Color/ Slavery/ Plantations/ Employment/ Household Workers/ Relationships/ Segregation

0619 **Wenk-Dee, Ann L.**
(1988) "An Examination of the Relationship Between Economic Conditions and Teenage Motherhood in Southeastern Labor Market Areas." Presented: Rural Sociological Society.

Women of Color*/ Sexuality/ Socioeconomic Status/ Secondary Education/ Teenage Pregnancy/ Employment Opportunities/ Parenting/ Mothers/ Economic Patterns/ South

0620 **Yount, Kristen R.**
(1988) "Co-Worker Harassment of Blue-Collar Women: Situational Origins in Underground Coal Mines." Presented: Society for the Study of Social Problems Annual Meeting, Atlanta, GA.

Labor Force Participation/ Sexual Harassment/ Male Dominated Employment/ Women's Studies/ Economy/ South/ Blue Collar Workers/ Coal Miners/ Extractive Industry/ Job Discrimination

Women of Color*

0621 **Almquist, Elizabeth M.**
(1987) "Labor Market Gender Inequality in Minority Groups." <u>Gender & Society</u> 1(December):4:pp. 400-413.
Women of Color*/ Job Discrimination/ Professional Status/ Academic Achievement/ Labor Force/ Inequality/ Socioeconomic Status/ Race, Class and Gender Studies/ Fertility Rates/ Marital Status/ Employment/ Sex Discrimination/ Population Distribution/ Financial Resources

0622 **Anonymous**
(1987) "Minority Women Vets: 'My Country Didn't Love Me.'" <u>Sojourner</u> 12(January):5:pp. 12-14.
Women of Color*/ Employment/ Sex Discrimination/ Military Personnel/ Veterans/ Armed Services

0623 **Baer, Judith**
(1983) <u>Equality Under the Constitution: Reclaiming the Fourteenth Amendment</u>. Ithaca, NY: Cornell University Press.
Women of Color*/ Equality/ Education/ Employment/ Sex Discrimination

0624 **Barnes, Annie S.**
(1987) Introduction: "Women in the Americas: Relationships, Work, and Power." <u>Urban Anthropology Journal</u>, special issue. Annie S. Barnes (ed.).
Women of Color*/ Employment/ Work/ Relationships/ Male Female Relationships/ Work Experience/ Power/ Control/ Status/ Careers/ Occupational Status/ Women Working Outside the Home/ Labor Force Participation/ Occupations

0625 **Bates, Timothy**
(1988) <u>An Analysis of Income Differentials among Self-Employed Minorities</u>. Available: Los Angeles, CA: University of California Los Angeles Center for Afro-American Studies.
Women of Color*/ Pay Equity/ Income/ Economic Status/ Self Employment/ Minority Groups/ Employment/ Comparative Studies

0626 **Baxandall, Rosalyn**
Gordon, Linda et al. (1976) <u>America's Working Women.</u> New York: Vintage Books. pp. 408.
Women of Color*/ Domestic Services/ Anthologies/ Women's History/ Statistics/ Labor History/ Essays/ Diaries/ Working Class/ Slavery/ Women Working Outside the Home/ Work Experience/ Labor Force

0627 **Beckett, Joyce O.**
(1982) "Working Women: A Historical Review of Racial Differences." <u>Black Sociologist</u> 9(Spring/Summer):pp. 5-27.
Women of Color*/ Wage Earning Women/ Comparative Studies/ Racial and Ethnic Differences/ Women's Roles/ Race, Class and Gender Studies/ Employment

0628 **Berheide, Catherine White**
Steinberg, Ronnie et al. (1987) "Decomposition of Wage Differentials: Inequities by Gender and Race in New York State Government." Presented: American Sociological Association, Chicago, IL. August. Author: Sociology Dept., Skidmore College, Saratoga Springs, NY 12866.
Pay Equity/ Women of Color*/ New York/ North East/ Employment/ Wage Gap/ Wages/ Occupational Segregation/ State Government

0629   Boles, Jacqueline
Tatro, Charlotte. (1978) "Legal and Extra-Legal Methods of Controlling Female Prostitution: A Cross-Cultural Comparison." <u>International Journal of Comparative and Applied Criminal Justice</u> 2:1:pp. 71-85.

Prostitutes/ Social Problems/ Women of Color*/ Female Intensive Occupations/ Legal Issues/ Deviant Behavior/ Criminal Justice/ Crime/ Employment/ Crosscultural Studies/ Criminals/ Sexual Behavior/ Sexual Exploitation

0630   Boles, Jacqueline
Davis, Phillip and Tatro, C. (1983) "False Pretense and Deviant Exploitation: Fortunetelling as a Con." <u>Deviant Behavior</u> 4:pp. 375-394.

Women of Color*/ Deviant Behavior/ Female Intensive Occupations/ Exploitation/ Fortune Tellers/ Employment/ Images of Women

0631   Boneparth, Ellen
Stoper, Emily (eds.). (1988) <u>Women, Power, and Policy: Toward the Year 2000</u> (2nd Edition). Elmsford, NY: Pergamon Press. pp. 340.

Women of Color*/ Policy Making/ Power/ Social Policy/ Women's Rights/ Social Issues/ Reagan Administration/ Women's Movement/ Anthologies/ Work Experience/ Feminism/ Child Care/ Reproduction

0632   Bullush, Jewel
(1986) "Room at the Top: The Case of District Council 37 of the American Federation of State, County, and Municipal Employees in New York." <u>SAGE: A Scholarly Journal on Black Women</u> 3(Spring):1:pp. 35-40.

Women of Color*/ New York/ North East/ Social Movements/ Labor Unions/ Government Workers/ Civil Service/ Educational Programs

0633   Burgess, Norma J.
(1986) "Labor Force Participation, Role Adjustment, and Race: An Analysis of Social Change and Subjective Well-Being among Married Women." Presented: National Council of Family Relations. Available: Mississippi State University, P. O. Drawer C, Mississippi State, MS 39762. pp. 44.

Women of Color*/ Social Change/ Labor Force/ Employment/ Income/ Equilibrium/ Leisure/ Comparative Studies/ Marital Roles/ Wives/ Balancing Work and Family Life/ Marital Adjustment

0634   Burgess, Norma J.
(1987) "Role Conflict and Adaptations: An Examination of Employment Patterns of Black, White and Hispanic Married Women in the United States." Available: Mississippi State University (Research Initiation Program), P. O. Drawer C, Mississippi State, MS 39762. pp. 18.

Women of Color*/ Adjustment/ Stress/ African American/ Employment Patterns/ Chicana/ Latina/ Marital Roles/ Comparative Studies/ European American/ Role Conflict/ Time Management/ Coping Strategies/ Balancing Work and Family Life/ Wives Working Outside the Home

0635   Cardenas, Gilbert
Shelton, B. and Pena, D. (1982) "Undocumented Immigrant Women in the Houston Labor Force." <u>California Sociologist</u> 5:2:pp. 98-118.

Women of Color*/ Texas/ South/ Illegal Immigrants/ Immigrants/ Labor Force Participation/ Minority Employment

0636   Chavkin, Wendy
(ed.). (1984) <u>Double Exposure: Women's Health Hazards on the Job and at Home.</u>

New York: Monthly Review Press. pp. 288.

Race, Class and Gender Studies/ Workers/ Health Hazards/ Health/ Factory Conditions/ Electronics Industry/ Reproductive Hazards at Work/ Nursing/ Occupational Health/ Farms/ Employment/ Women of Color*

0637   Chiswick, Barry
(1980) "Immigrant Earnings Patterns by Sex, Race, and Ethnic Groupings." Monthly Labor Review 103(October):pp. 22-25.

Immigrants/ Economic Equity/ Earnings/ Employment/ Racial Factors/ Women of Color*/ Wage Gap

0638   Cummings, Scott
(1987) "Vulnerability to the Effects of Recession: Minority and Female Workers." Social Forces 65(March):3:pp. 834-857.

Labor Market/ Sex Discrimination/ Racial Discrimination/ Workers/ Minority Employment/ Job Layoffs/ Gender/ 1970-1979/ History/ Socioeconomic Indicators/ Recession/ Women of Color*

0639   Davis, Laura F.
(1988) "Rural Attitudes Toward Women, Work and Welfare." AFFILIA: Journal of Women and Social Work 3(Winter):4:pp. 69-79.

Rural Women/ Stereotyping/ Welfare Mothers/ Attitudes/ Employment/ Women of Color*

0640   Deaux, Kay
Ullman, Joseph. (1987) "Blue Collar Workers in the Steel Mills, 1979." Working Paper: Murray Research Center of Radcliffe College, Cambridge, MA.

Women of Color*/ Sexual Harassment/ Blue Collar Workers/ Job Discrimination/ Male Dominated Occupations/ Sex Discrimination in Employment/ Factory Workers/ Hiring Policies/ Trades/ Affirmative Action

0641   Duron, Clementina
(1975) "Racial Dualism in El Paso Labor Market, 1880-1920." Aztlan 6:pp. 197-218.

Employment/ Labor Force/ 19th Century/ Racial Discrimination/ History/ 20th Century/ Women of Color*/ Texas/ South West

0642   Espinosa, Dula J.
(1987) "The Impact of the Affirmative Action Policy on Ethnic and Gender Employment Inequality." Presented: American Sociological Association Annual Meeting, Chicago, Illinois.

Women of Color*/ Inequality/ Affirmative Action/ Racial Discrimination/ Job Discrimination/ Employment/ Public Policy

0643   Farley, Jennie
(1979) "The Minority Woman: Doubly Protected." in Affirmative Action and the Woman Worker: Guidelines for Personnel Management. Jennie Farley. New York: American Management Association. pp. 93-113.

Women of Color*/ Affirmative Action/ Employment/ Personnel Management/ Affirmative Action Officers

0644   Farley, Reynolds
Allen, Walter. (1987) The Color Line and the Quality of Life in America. New York: Russell Sage Foundation. pp. 448.

Women of Color*/ Quality of Life/ Racial Equality/ Comparative Studies/ Socioeconomic Status/ Fertility/ Mortality/ Migration/ Family Structure/ Educational Experience/ Minority Employment/ Income

0645   Ford Foundation
(1989) "Work and Family Responsibilities: Achieving A Balance." Program Paper Ford Foundation, New York, NY 10017. March.

Women of Color*/ Segregation/ Employment Patterns/ Gender/ Stereotypes/ Employment Opportunities/ Occupational Trends/ Family Roles/ Economically Disadvantaged/ Public Policy/ Balancing Work and Family Life/ Labor Force Participation/ Family Responsibility

0646   Giele, Janet Zollinger
Gilfus, Mary. (1988) "Race and College Differences in Life Patterns of Educated Women." in Women and Educational Choice. Joyce Antler and Sari Biklen. New York: New York University Press.

Education/ Family Life/ Women's Studies/ Education Attainment/ Higher Education/ Academic Aspiration/ Labor Force Participation/ Comparative Studies/ Employment/ Career Opportunities/ Women of Color*

0647   Gluck, Sherna Berger
(1987) Rosie the Riveter Revisited: Women, the War and Social Change. Bergenfield, NJ: Meridian. pp. 304.

World War II/ Blue Collar Workers/ Industries/ Employment/ Labor Force Participation/ Women's History/ Women of Color*/ Oral History/ Factory Workers

0648   Groneman, Carol
Norton, Mary Beth (eds.). (1986) To Toil the Livelong Day: America's Women at Work, 1780-1980. Ithaca, NY: Cornell University Press. pp. 320.

Women of Color*/ Labor History/ Women's History/ Employment/ Working Class/ Political Activism/ Sexual Division of Labor/ Domestic Services/ Tobacco Industry/ Farm Workers/ Slavery/ Industrial Revolution/ Race, Class and Gender Studies

0649   Harriford, Diane Sue
(1985) "Race, Class and Organized Feminism: The New York City Chapter of the Coalition of Labor Union Women." Dissertation: State University of New York-Stony Brook, Stony Brook, NY. pp. 130. DAI Vol. 46(04A)1105.

Labor Unions/ Feminism/ Feminist Organizations/ New York/ North East/ Race, Class and Gender Studies/ Employment/ Women of Color*

0650   Karnig, Albert K.
Welch, Susan and Eribes, Richard A. (1984) "Employment by Women in the Southwest." Social Science Journal 21:4:pp. 41-48.

Women of Color*/ Employment/ South West/ Labor Force/ Sex Discrimination in Employment

0651   Kim, Eun Mee
Silver, Hilary. (1984) "Metropolitan Employment Trends and Gender Inequality of Earnings." Presented: American Sociological Association Annual Meetings, San Antonio, TX.

Women of Color*/ Earnings/ Employment Trends/ Wage Gap/ Discrimination/ Inequality/ Labor Force Participation/ Gender Inequality/ Pay Equity/ Urban Areas

0652   King, Deborah Karyn
(1987) "Old Wine in New Bottles: 'Protective Legislation' in Recent Legal Decisions Affecting Women's Employment." Presented: Society for Study of Social Problems, Chicago, IL. August.

Women of Color*/ Race, Class and Gender Studies/ Comparative Studies/ Job Discrimination/ Equal Protection Under the Law/ Employment Opportunities/ Patriarchy/ Power

0653 **Koziara, Karen Shallcross**
Moskow, Michael H. and Tanner, Lucretia Dewey. (1987) <u>Working Women: Past, Present, Future</u>. Washington, D.C.: Bureau of National Affairs Books. pp. 375.
Labor Force/ Women of Color*/ Minority Employment/ Middle Aged/ Status/ Sex Roles

0654 **Kraly, Ellen P.**
Yamanaka, Keiko. (1987) "Labor Force Participation of U.S. Women of Ethnic Origins in 1940 and 1950." Presented: American Sociological Association, Chicago, IL. Author: International Population Program, Cornell University, Ithaca, NY 14853.
Women of Color*/ Employment/ History/ 1940-1949/ 1950-1959/ Labor Force/ Ethnicity/ Comparative Studies/ Life Cycles

0655 **Kupinsky, Stanley**
(1982) <u>Working Women</u>. New York: Praeger. pp. 300.
Workers/ Labor Force/ Women of Color*/ Employment/ Demography

0656 **Levitan, Sar A.**
Shapiro, Isaac. (1988) <u>Working But Poor: America's Contradiction</u>. Baltimore, MD: The Johns Hopkins University Press. pp. 160.
People of Color*/ Low Income Households/ Poverty/ Minimum Income/ Federal Assistance Programs/ Job Training/ Working Class/ Job Segregation/ Women Living in Poverty/ Labor Market/ Public Policy/ Employment

0657 **Luttrell, Wendy**
(1984) "The Getting of Knowledge: A Study of Working Class Women and Education." Dissertation: University of California, Santa Cruz, CA.
Women of Color*/ Cultural Identity/ Working Class/ Employment Opportunities/ European American/ Sex Stereotypes/ Educational Attainment

0658 **Martin, Molly**
(1988) <u>Hard-Hatted Women: Stories of Struggle and Success in the Trades</u>. Seattle: Seal Press. pp. 265.
Women of Color*/ Employment/ Male Dominated Employment/ Work Hazards/ Affirmative Action/ Wages/ Income/ Construction Industry/ Trades/ Blue Collar Workers

0659 **McLaughlin, Steven D.**
Melber, Barbara D. and Billy, John O. G. (1988) <u>The Changing Lives of American Women</u>. Chapel Hill, NC: University of North Carolina Press. pp. 250. ISBN 0807818135.
Women of Color*/ Attitudes/ Demography/ Stereotypes/ Employment Patterns/ Gender Roles/ Educational Attainment/ Family Roles/ Social Change/ Family Structure/ Social Trends

0660 **Meier, E. L.**
(1980) "New ERISA Agency Considered and Pension Issues of Women and Minorities." <u>Aging and Work</u> 3:2:pp. 135-139.
Women of Color*/ Pension Benefits/ Employment/ Retirement/ Aging/ Older Adults

0661 **Michelson, Maureen R.**
(1986) <u>Women and Work: Photographs and Personal Writings</u>. Pasedena, CA: New Sage Press. pp. 179.
Women of Color*/ Occupational Options/ Images of Women/ Occupations/ Photography/ Occupational Counseling/ Work/ Employment/ Work Experience/ Photographs/ Labor Force

0662   **Michelson, William**
(1984) <u>From Sun to Sun: Daily Obligations and Community Structure in the Lives of Employed Women and Their Families.</u> Totowa, NJ: Rowman and Littlefield. pp. 180. ISBN 0865981493.

Family/ Employment/ Balancing Work and Family Life/ Labor Force Participation/ Households/ Stress/ Parenting/ Mothers/ Women Working Outside the Home/ Family Responsibility/ Neighborhoods/ Communities/ Women of Color*

0663   **Miller, Dorothy**
(1987) "Helping the Strong: An Exploration of the Needs of Families Headed by Women." Available: National Association of Social Workers, Silver Spring, MD. pp. 99.

Women of Color*/ Counseling/ Single Parents/ Poverty/ Family/ Female Headed Households/ Single Mothers/ Family Structure/ Social Work/ Home Life

0664   **Miller, Dorothy**
(1989) "Poor Women and Work Programs: Back to the Future." <u>AFFILIA: A Journal of Women and Social Work</u> 4(Spring): 1:pp. 9-22.

Poverty/ Job Training/ Disadvantaged/ Social Work/ Welfare/ Work Incentive Programs/ Employment/ Women of Color*/ European American

0665   **Mullings, Leith**
(1986) "Uneven Development: Class, Race and Gender in the United States Before 1900." in <u>Women's Work: Development and the Division of Labor.</u> Eleanor Leacock and Helen Safa. New York: Bergen Publishers. pp. 41-57.

Race, Class and Gender Studies/ Economic Growth/ Women of Color*/ Women in Development/ History/ 19th Century/ Division of Labor/ Employment

0666   **Mulroy, Elizabeth A.**
(1988) <u>Women as Single Parents: Confronting Institutional Barriers in the Courts, the Workplace, and the Housing Market.</u> Dover, MA: Auburn House. pp. 300. ISBN 0865691762.

Women of Color*/ Family Structure/ Child Care/ Institutional Discrimination/ Single Mothers/ Single Parents/ Housing/ Employment/ Courts/ Court Decisions/ Welfare Reform/ Policymaking/ Nontraditional Family/ Female Headed Households/ Women Living in Poverty/ Single Parent Families/ Marriage and Family Law

0667   **National Association of Social Workers**
(1984) <u>Research on People of Color.</u> Silver Spring, MD: National Association of Social Workers. pp. 45. ISBN 0871011255.

People of Color*/ Child Welfare/ Research Resources/ Research/ Social Issues/ Social Services/ Older Adults/ Social Work/ Juvenile Delinquency/ Teenage Pregnancy

0668   **National Committee on Pay Equity**
(1987) "Pay Equity: An Issue of Race, Ethnicity and Sex." Available: National Committee on Pay Equity, Washington, D.C.

Women of Color*/ Pay Equity/ Wage Discrimination/ Economic Value of Women's Work/ Employment Patterns/ Male Dominated Occupations/ Occupational Segregation/ Race, Class and Gender Studies

0669   **Nussbaum, Karen**
(1984) "The 9 to 5 National Survey on Women and Stress." Available: 9 to 5 National Association of Working Women, 614 Superior Ave., NW, Cleveland, OH

44113. pp. 55.

Women of Color*/ Coping Strategies/ Support Systems/ Occupational Health/ Race, Class and Gender Studies/ Employment/ Comparative Studies/ Clerical Occupations/ Working Class/ Mental Health/ Stress

0670   **O'Sullivan, Judith**
et al. (1988) "Workers and Allies: Female Participation in the American Trade Union Movement, 1824-1976." Washington, D.C.: Smithsonian Institute. pp. 196.

Women of Color*/ Women's History/ 20th Century/ Labor History/ 19th Century/ Labor Movement/ Employment/ Construction Trades/ Unions/ Activism/ Organizing

0671   **Ogilvie, Marilyn Bailey**
(1986) <u>Women in Science, Antiquity through the Nineteenth Century: A Biographical Dictionary</u>. Cambridge, MA: MIT Press. pp. 254.

Women of Color*/ Women's History/ Biographies/ Scientists/ Women in Science/ Bibliographies/ Research Resources/ Professional Occupations/ Employment

0672   **Price, Dorothy Z.**
Wilhelm, Mari. (1988) <u>Socioeconomic Stress in Rural Families</u>. New York: Human Sciences Press. pp. 81. ISBN 0898854342.

People of Color*/ Rural Areas/ Poverty/ Family/ Rural Women/ Socioeconomic Conditions/ Unemployment/ Employment/ Stress/ Rural Living

0673   **Reskin, Barbara F.**
Hartmann, Heidi I. (eds.). (1986) <u>Women's Work, Men's Work: Sex Segregation on the Job</u>. Washington, DC: National Academy.   pp. 173.

Job Segregation/ Sexual Stratification/ Occupational Status/ Socioeconomic Status/ Occupational Segregation/ Employment Opportunities/ Women of Color*

0674   **Rodgers, Harrell R., Jr.**
(1986) <u>Poor Women, Poor Families: The Economic Plight of America's Female Headed Households</u>. Armonk, NY: M. E. Sharpe. pp. 167.

Women of Color*/ Disadvantaged/ Wage Gap/ Public Policy/ Economic Value of Women's Work/ Women Living in Poverty/ Economic Status/ Female Headed Households/ Family/ Families

0675   **Rosen, Ellen Israel**
(1987) <u>Bitter Choices: Blue-Collar Women in and out of Work</u>. Chicago, IL: University of Chicago Press. pp. 208.

Women's Studies/ Economics/ Working Class/ Blue Collar Workers/ Images of Women/ Factory Workers/ Women of Color*/ Employment/ Unemployment/ Underemployment

0676   **Schrodel, Jean Reith**
(1987) "Women in Trades, 1985." Working Paper: Murray Research Center of Radcliffe College, Cambridge, MA.

Women of Color*/ Blue Collar Workers/ Role Conflict/ Male Dominated Occupations/ Career Choice/ Job Discrimination/ Sex Discrimination in Employment/ Occupational Health/ Occupational Safety/ Labor Unions/ Labor Movement/ Trades

0677   **Smith, Barbara Ellen**
(1987) "Job Inequities Persist for Women." <u>State Government News</u> 30:1:pp. 12-13.

Women of Color*/ Inequality/ Job Discrimination/ Occupational Patterns/ Pay Equity/ Occupational Trends/ Employment/ Discrimination/ Women and Work/ Employment Patterns/ Equal Employment Opportunity/ Occupational Segregation/ Labor Force

0678   **Squires, Gregory D.**
(1987) "Employee Ownership and Equal Opportunity: Ameliorating Race and Gender Wage Inequalities through Democratic Work Organizations." Presented: American Sociological Association Annual Meeting, Chicago, IL. Author: University of Wisconsin, Department of Sociology, Milwaukee, WI 53201.

Women of Color*/ Wage Gap/ Wages/ Pay Equity/ Employment/ Employee Benefits/ Equal Opportunity/ Employee Ownership/ Economic Development

0679   **Stiehm, Judith Hicks**
(1989) Arms and the Enlisted Woman. Philadelphia: Temple. pp. 331.

Women of Color*/ Enlisted Personnel/ European American/ Employment/ Women's History/ 1970-1979/ Military Personnel/ Women in the Military/ Armed Forces

0680   **U.S. Department of Commerce**
(1987) "Who's Minding the Kids?: Child Care Arrangement, Winter 1984-85." Current Population Report. Household and Economic Studies Series P-70, #9. Available: U.S. Government Printing Office, Washington, D.C.

Women of Color*/ Child Care/ Balancing Work and Family Life/ Employment/ Mothers Working Outside the Home/ Women Working Outside the Home/ 1980-1989

0681   **U.S. Department of Health and Human Services**
(1984) Minorities and Women in the Health Fields. Washington, D.C.: Health Resources and Services Administration. pp. 191.

Women of Color*/ Health Care Professionals/ Employment/ Health Care Occupations/ 1980-1989/ Professional Status/ Health Care Workers/ Female Intensive Occupations

0682   **Weeks, Elaine**
Boles, Jacqueline et al. (1986) "The Transformation of Sexual Harassment from a Private Trouble into a Public Issue." Sociological Inquiry 56:4:pp. 432-455.

Women of Color*/ Occupational Stress/ Sexual Attitudes/ Job Discrimination/ Sexual Exploitation/ Employment/ Sexual Harassment/ Social Problems/ Sex Discrimination

0683   **Weick, Ann**
Vandiver, Susan T. (eds.). (1982) Women, Power, and Change. Silver Spring, MD: National Association of Social Workers. pp. 214. ISBN 0871010925.

Women of Color*/ Change/ Living Conditions/ Counseling/ Social Services/ Mental Health/ Social Work/ Crisis Intervention/ Power

0684   **Weiner, Lynn Y.**
(1985) From Working Girl to Working Mother: The Female Labor Force in the United States, 1820-1980. Chapel Hill: University of North Carolina Press. pp. 187.

Women of Color*/ Images of Women/ Labor Force Participation/ Women Working Outside the Home/ Employment/ Work Experience/ Labor History/ Women's History/ Wage Earning Mothers/ 19th Century/ 20th Century/ Wage Earning Wives

0685   **Wenk-Dee, Ann L.**
(1988) "An Examination of the Relationship Between Economic Conditions and Teenage Motherhood in Southeastern Labor Market Areas." Presented: Rural Sociological Society Annual Meeting.

Women of Color*/ Sexuality/ Socioeconomic Status/ Secondary Education/ Teenage Pregnancy/ Employment Opportunities/ Parenting/ Mothers/ Economic Patterns/ South

0686   **White, Barbara W.**
(1984) <u>Color in a White Society</u>. Silver Spring, MD: National Association of Social Workers. pp. 135. ISBN 087101128x.

People of Color*/ Ethnic Groups/ Social Work/ Minority Groups/ Racial Discrimination/ Dominant Culture/ Sex Discrimination/ Race Relations/ Minority Experience

0687   **Willenz, June A.**
(1984) <u>Women Veterans: America's Forgotten Heroines</u>. New York: Continuum. pp. 252.

Women of Color*/ Military/ Military Occupations/ Narratives/ Veterans/ Heroines/ Employment

0688   **Women's Education and Equity Act**
(1987) <u>Management Basics for Minority Women</u>. Newton, MA: W.E.E.A. Publishing. pp. 98.

Women of Color*/ Management/ Management Techniques/ Aspirations/ Teacher Education/ Methods/ Verbal Communication/ Employment

0689   **Women's Education and Equity Act**
(1987) <u>Career Planning for Minority Women</u> Newton, MA: W.E.E.A. Publishing. pp. 76.

Women of Color*/ Career Planning/ Career Strategies/ Career Counseling/ Career Awareness/ Teacher Education/ Methods/ Employment

FAMILY

African American

0690   Abrahamse, Allan F.
Morrison, Peter A. et al. (1988) <u>Beyond Stereotypes: Who Becomes a Single Teenage Mother?</u> Santa Monica, CA: Rand Corporation. pp. 88. ISBN 0833008322.

African American/ Adolescents/ European American/ Economic Factors/ Women of Color/ Academic Achievement/ Teenage Mothers/ Single Parents/ Single Mothers/ Educationally Disadvantaged/ Images of Women/ Stereotypes/ Family/ Families

0691   Allen, Walter R.
(1986) <u>Black American Families, 1965-1984: A Classified, Selectively Annotated Bibliography.</u> Westport, CT: Greenwood Press. pp. 480.

People of Color/ African Americans/ Family/ Families/ Bibliographies/ Research Resources/ History/ 1970-1979

0692   Alliance Against Women's Oppression
(1987) "Teenage Mothers: Setting the Record Straight." Discussion Paper #8, Alliance Against Women's Oppression, San Francisco, CA.

Women of Color/ African American/ Teenage Pregnancy/ Family Influence/ Low Income/ Comparative Studies/ Latina/ Early Childbearing/ Mothers

0693   Ball, Richard E.
(1986) "Marriage: Conducive to Greater Life Satisfaction for American Black Women?" in <u>The Black Family: Essays and Studies</u> (3rd Edition). Robert Staples. Belmont, CA: Wadsworth. ISBN 0534072186.

African American/ Marriage/ Life Styles/ Satisfaction/ Happiness/ Women of Color/ Marital Status/ Single Women/ Singles/ Home Life

0694   Barnes, Annie S.
(1987) <u>Single Parents in Black America: A Study in Culture and Legitimacy.</u> Bristol, IN: Wyndham Hall. pp. 162. ISBN 1556050240.

African Americans/ People of Color/ Single Parent Families/ Cultural Influences/ Life Styles/ Support Systems/ Family Structure/ Female Headed Households/ Single Mothers/ Single Fathers

0695   Barnett, A. P.
(1986) "Sociocultural Influences on Adolescent Mothers." in <u>The Black Family: Essays and Studies</u> (3rd Edition). Robert Staples. Belmont, CA: Wadsworth. ISBN 0534072186.

African American/ Social Influences/ Cultural Influences/ Adolescents/ Mothers/ Teenage Mothers/ Women of Color/ Early Childbearing

0696   Berry, Mary Frances
Blassingame, John W. (1982) "Family and Church: Enduring Institutions." in <u>Long Memory: The Black Experience in America</u>. Mary Frances Berry and John W. Blassingame. New York: Oxford University Press.

Women of Color/ African American/ Family/ Religion/ Religious Factors/ Family Influence/ Institutions/ Support Systems/ Churches

0697   **Braxton, Joanne Margaret**
(1987) "Black Grandmothers: Sources of Artistic Consciousness and Personal Strength." Available: Working Paper #172, Wellesley College Center for Research on Women, Wellesley, MA.

African American/ Family Relationships/ Grandmothers/ Extended Family/ Personal Development/ Cultural Influences/ Women of Color/ Gender Roles/ Support Systems/ Family Roles/ Consciousness Raising/ Artistic Styles and Genres/ Art/ Arts

0698   **Brewer, Rose M.**
(1988) "Black Women in Poverty: Some Comments on Female-Headed Families." SIGNS: Journal of Women in Culture and Society 13:2:pp. 331-339.

African American/ Unemployment/ Female Headed Households/ Welfare/ Poverty/ Women of Color/ Economically Disadvantaged/ Economic Value of Women's Work/ Family Structure

0699   **Brinkley-Carter, Christina**
(1980) "Black Fertility: Recent Demographic and Sociological Influences." in The Black Woman. La Frances Rogers-Rose (ed.). Beverly Hills, CA: Sage Publications. pp. 43-66.

Women of Color/ African American/ Fertility Rates/ Population Characteristics/ Demography/ Marital Status/ Childbearing/ Social Influences

0700   **Brown, Diane Robinson**
Momeni, J. A. (1986) "Housing Characteristics of Black Female Households: An Analysis of Data from the 1970 and 1980 Census." Institute for Urban Affairs and Research, Washington D.C.

Women of Color/ African American/ Housing/ Female Headed Households/ Family Structure/ Single Mothers/ Single Parents/ Family

0701   **Brown, Prudence**
(1977) "Sex Role Attitudes and Psychological Outcomes for Black and White Women Experiencing Marital Dissolution." Journal of Marriage and the Family 39(August):pp. 549-562.

Women of Color/ African American/ Sex Role Behavior/ Mental Health/ Emotional Adjustment/ Separation/ Divorce/ Family Conflict/ European American/ Marriage

0702   **Cantor, Milton**
Rosenthal, K. and Walker, L. (1979) "Social and Family Relationships of Black Aged Women in New York City." Journal of Minority Aging 4:pp. 50-61.

Women of Color/ Older Adults/ African American/ Senior Citizens/ New York/ East/ Networks/ Family Relationships/ Age/ Aging/ Social Relationships/ Support Systems

0703   **Carlson, Shirley J.**
(1987) "Black Migration to Pulaski County, Illinois 1860-1900." Illinois Historical Journal 80(Spring):pp. 37-46.

Migration/ North Central/ Illinois/ Employment/ Family/ History/ 19th Century/ African Americans/ People of Color

0704   **Cason, Candice S.**
(1984) "Telling My Mother's Story - Notes from a Daughter." SAGE: A Scholarly Journal on Black Women 1(Fall):2:pp. 31.

Women of Color/ African American/ Biographies/ Mother Daughter Relationships/ Parent Child Relationships/ Family/ Families

0705 Church, Annette E.
Church, Roberta (eds.). (1974) <u>The Robert R. Churches of Memphis</u>. Ann Arbor, MI: Annette E. Church and Roberta Church.

African Americans/ Tennessee/ South/ Urban Areas/ Leadership/ Elites/ Upper Class/ Family/ Social History/ People of Color/ Political Influence/ Mary C. Terrell

0706 Collier-Watson, B.
Williams, L. N. and Smith, W. (1986) "An Alternative Analysis of Sexism: Implications for the Black Family." in <u>The Black Family: Essays and Studies</u> (3rd Edition). Robert Staples. Belmont, CA: Wadsworth. ISBN 0534072186.

African American/ Families/ Sex Roles/ People of Color/ Sex Discrimination

0707 Comer, James
(1989) <u>Maggie's American Dream: The Life and Times of a Black Family</u>. Bergenfield, NJ: New American Library. ISBN 0453005888.

Women of Color/ Education/ Southern/ Economically Disadvantaged/ Family/ African American/ Black Studies/ Parenting

0708 Creighton-Zollar, Ann
(1982) "Variations in Interdependence between and among Members of Lower Class Urban Black Extended Families." <u>Western Journal of Black Studies</u> 6(Fall):pp. 131-137.

People of Color/ Family Structure/ African Americans/ Family Responsibility/ Lower Class/ Family Roles/ Family/ Kinship/ Extended Family/ Urban Areas

0709 Creighton-Zollar, Ann
(1985) <u>A Member of the Family: Strategies for Black Family Continuity</u>. Chicago: Nelson Hall. (Book appears under author name Zollar).

Family/ Families/ African Americans/ People of Color/ Family Structure/ Family Relations

0710 Creighton-Zollar, Ann
(1986) "Ideological Perspectives on the Black Family: Related Typologies." <u>Free Inquiry Creative Sociology</u> 17(November): pp. 169-172.

People of Color/ African Americans/ Family/ Ideology/ Family Structure/ Family Roles

0711 Creighton-Zollar, Ann
(1987) "Socialization for the Collectivity: The Transmission of Kinship Practices in Black Extended Families." <u>The Griot: Southern Conference on Afro-American Studies</u> (October):pp. 19-27.

People of Color/ African Americans/ Socialization/ Kinship/ Extended Family/ Family

0712 Creighton-Zollar, Ann
Honnold, Julie. (1988) "Socioeconomic Characteristics and Kin Interaction in Black Middletown." <u>Western Journal of Black Studies</u> 12(Spring):pp. 9-18.

People of Color/ Social Status/ African Americans/ Social Class/ Socioeconomic Status/ Economic Conditions/ Kinship/ Extended Family

0713 Davis, Angela Y.
(1985) <u>Violence Against Women and the Ongoing Challenge to Racism</u>. Latham, NY: Kitchen Table Press. (Freedom Organizing Pamphlet #5). pp. 20.

Women of Color/ Violence Against Women/ African American/ Abuse/ Racial Discrimination/ Sex Discrimination/ Crimes Against People/ Home Life

0714 Day-Nawabi, Lumumba
(1986) "Dua Afe: Whole Women, Inc." <u>Woman of Power</u> (Fall):4:pp. 70-71.
Women of Color/ African American/ Midwifery/ Childbirth Training/ Natural Childbirth/ Folk Medicine/ South

0715 Ellis, W.
(1980) "Exploratory Investigation of Potential Societal and Intra-familial Factors Contributing to Child Abuse and Neglect." Available: U.S. Department of Health and Human Services, Washington, DC. (Prepared in cooperation with National Committee for Black Child Development). pp. 59.
Women of Color/ African American/ Child Abuse/ Child Neglect/ Culture Conflict/ Economic Factors/ Social Influences/ Racial Discrimination/ Social Services/ Family Influence/ Family Relationships

0716 Farnham, Christopher
(1987) "Sapphire? The Issue of Dominance in the Slave Family, 1830-1865." in <u>To Toil the Live Long Day: America's Women at Work, 1780-1980</u>. Carol Groneman and Mary Beth Norton. Ithaca, NY: Cornell University Press. pp. 68-87. ISBN 0801494524.
African American/ Family Roles/ Domestic Roles/ History/ 19th Century/ Dominance/ Matriarchy/ Women of Color/ Slavery/ Images of Women/ Female Headed Households/ Family Structure

0717 Fox, Greef
Inazu, Judith. (1982) "The Influence of Mother's Marital History on the Mother-Daughter Relationship in Black-White Households." <u>Journal of Marriage and the Family</u> 44(February):pp. 143-154.
Women of Color/ African American/ Comparative Studies/ Mother Daughter Relationships/ Households/ Marital Stability/ Marital Conflict/ European American/ Family

0718 Fox-Genovese, Elizabeth
(1988) <u>Within the Plantation Household: Black and White Women of the Old South</u>. Chapel Hill, NC: University of North Carolina Press. pp. 563.
Women of Color/ Household Labor/ European American/ African American/ Relationships/ Slavery/ Comparative Studies/ Family/ South/ Women's History/ Plantations

0719 Gibson, R. C.
(1986) "Blacks in An Aging Society." <u>Daedalus</u> 115:1:pp. 349-371.
Women of Color/ African American/ Family/ Support Systems/ Aging/ Older Adults/ Family Structure

0720 Giele, Janet Zollinger
Gilfus, Mary. (1988) "Race and Cohort Differences in Women's Life Patterns, 1934-1982." Presented: American Sociological Association, Atlanta, GA. August.
African American/ Family Roles/ European American/ Career Opportunities/ Higher Education/ Education/ Labor Force Participation/ Life Cycles/ Gender Roles/ Women of Color/ Socialization

0721 Gorum, Jacquelyne Wallace
(1983) "Stress Coping Patterns and Functioning of Black Single Parent Families." Dissertation: Howard University School of Social Work, Washington, D.C. DAI Vol. 45(07A)2255.
African American/ Single Parent Families/ Coping Strategies/ Stress/ Single Mothers/ Female Headed Households/ Women of Color/ Family/ Parenting

0722 Greenstone, Joan
(1984) "Kinship Support for Black and White Unmarried Adolescent Mothers."

Dissertation: University of Chicago, Chicago, IL.

African American/ European American/ Teenage Mothers/ Single Mothers/ Support Systems/ Kinship/ Family/ Adolescents/ Women of Color

0723   Hampton, Robert L.
(1986) "Race, Ethnicity, and Child Maltreatment: An Analysis of Cases Recognized and Reported by Hospitals." in The Black Family: Essays and Studies (3rd Edition). Robert Staples. Belmont, CA: Wadsworth. ISBN 0534072186.

People of Color/ Child Abuse/ Comparative Studies/ Family Violence/ Racial and Ethnic Differences/ African Americans

0724   Hauser, Stuart T.
Kasendorf, E. (1983) Black and White Identity Formation. Melbourne, FL: Krieger Publisher. pp. 252. ISBN 089874055x.

People of Color/ African Americans/ Identity/ Adolescents/ Comparative Studies/ European Americans/ Child Development/ Socialization

0725   Heckel, R. V.
Mandell, E. (1981) "Factor Analytic Study of the Demographic Characteristics of Incarcerated Male and Female Juvenile Offenders." Journal of Clinical Psychology 37(April):2:pp. 426-429.

Women of Color/ African American/ Delinquent Behavior/ Juvenile Justice System/ Demographic Measurements/ Criminals/ Correctional Facilities/ Lower Class/ Adolescents/ Family Influence

0726   Helmbold, Lois Rita
(1987) "Beyond the Family Economy: Black and White Working Class Women during the Great Depression." Feminist Studies 13(Fall):3:pp. 629-655.

Women of Color/ Family Economics/ African American/ Economic Depression/ History/ 1930-1939/ Extended Family/ Comparative Studies/ Economic Value of Women's Work/ Working Class/ European American/ Race, Class and Gender Studies

0727   Hill, Robert B.
Shackleford, L. (1986) "The Black Extended Family Revisited." in The Black Family: Essays and Studies (3rd Edition). Robert Staples. Belmont, CA: Wadsworth. ISBN 0534072186.

African Americans/ Family Structure/ Extended Family/ People of Color

0728   Hooks, Bell
(1984) "Reflections of a 'Good' Daughter: From Black Is a Woman's Color." SAGE: A Scholarly Journal on Black Women 1(Fall):2:pp. 28-29.

Women of Color/ African American/ Daughters/ Parent Child Relationships

0729   Jackson, Beryl Bernice H.
(1982) "Life Satisfaction of Black Climacteric Women in Relation to Specific Life Events." Dissertation: University of Pittsburgh, Pittsburgh, PA. DAI Vol. 43(10A)3440.

African American/ Middle Aged Adults/ Life Cycles/ Menopause/ Satisfaction/ Women of Color/ Home Life

0730   Jackson, Jacquelyne J.
(1986) "Black Grandparents: Who Needs Them?" in The Black Family: Essays and Studies (3rd Edition). Robert Staples. Belmont, CA: Wadsworth. ISBN 0534072186.

African Americans/ Families/ Extended Family/ Grandparents/ People of Color/ Support Systems

0731   **Jewell, Karen Sue**
(1983) "Black Male/Female Conflict: Internalization of Negative Definitions Transmitted through Imagery." <u>Western Journal of Black Studies</u> 7:1:pp. 43-48.
Women of Color/ African American/ Interpersonal Relationships/ Images of Women/ Sex Roles/ Self Concept/ Racial Discrimination/ Stereotypes/ Male Female Relationships/ Home Life

0732   **Jewell, Karen Sue**
(1983) "The Utilization of Formal Social Service Programs and Divorce among Black Men and Women." Presented: Association for Study of African American Life and History, Annual Convention, Detroit, MI. October.
Women of Color/ Counseling/ Conflict Resolution/ African American/ Divorce/ Family Conflict/ Social Services/ Marital Adjustment

0733   **Jewell, Karen Sue**
(1985) "A Look at Sex Equality in the Black Family." Presented: North Central Sociological Association, Louisville, KY. April.
African American/ Women of Color/ Family Roles/ Sexual Equality

0734   **Johnson, Mrs. A. E.**
(1988) <u>Clarence and Corinne; or God's Way</u>. New York: Oxford University Press. pp. 240. ISBN 0195052641.
19th Century/ Novels/ Writers/ Social Problems/ Women of Color/ Alcoholism/ African American/ Family/ Women's Movement/ Social Reform

0735   **Jones, Barbara A. P.**
(1982) "The Economic Status of Black Women." Working Paper: Southern Center for Studies in Public Policy, Atlanta, GA. pp. 18.
Women of Color/ Labor Market/ African American/ Academic Achievement/ Socioeconomic Status/ Women's Roles/ Heads of Households/ Disadvantaged/ Family Structure/ Race, Class and Gender Studies/ Income

0736   **Jones, Barbara A. P.**
(1983) "The Contribution of Black Women to the Incomes of Black Families: An Analysis of the Labor Force Participation Rates of Black Wives." Dissertation: Georgia State University, Atlanta, GA. DAI Vol. 34(06A)2856.
African American/ Women of Color/ Economic Value of Women's Work/ Earnings/ Family Income/ Labor Force Statistics/ Wage Earning Wives/ Employment

0737   **Joseph, Gloria I.**
(1984) "Mothers and Daughters: Traditional and New Populations." <u>SAGE: A Scholarly Journal on Black Women</u> 1(Fall):2:pp. 17-21.
Women of Color/ African American/ Mother Daughter Relationships/ Traditional Roles/ Population Characteristics/ Family/ Parent Child Relationships

0738   **Kaplan, Elaine Bell**
(1988) "Black Teenage Mothers and Their Mothers: The Impact of Teen Pregnancy on the Daughter-Mother Relationship." Presented: Society for the Study of Social Problems Annual Meeting, Atlanta, GA.
African American/ Parenting/ Mothers/ Teenage Pregnancy/ Women of Color/ Parent Child Relationships/ Single Parents/ Early Childbearing/ Mother Daughter Relationships/ Grandparents/ Grandmothers

0739 La Greca, Anthony J.
(1988) "Black Female Headed Households: Central City and Suburban Differences." Presented: Society for the Study of Social Problems Annual Meeting, Atlanta, GA.

Female Headed Households/ Economy/ Single Parents/ Racial Discrimination/ African American/ Women of Color/ Suburbs/ Inner City/ Urban Areas/ Family/ Comparative Studies

0740 Laska, Shirley Bradway
Wright, Beverly Hendrix. (1982) "Composition of Lower-Income Urban Black Families in a Tight Housing Market." Presented: Society for the Study of Social Problems Annual Meeting.

South/ Louisiana/ Female Headed Households/ Urban Areas/ Family Structure/ African American/ Public Housing/ Women of Color/ Economy/ Equal Access/ Housing Costs/ Low Income Families

0741 Leashore, Bogart R.
(1986) "Social Policies, Black Males and Black Families." in The Black Family: Essays and Studies (3rd Edition). Robert Staples. Belmont, CA: Wadsworth. ISBN 0534072186.

African Americans/ Family/ Families/ Social Policy/ People of Color/ Male Female Relationships

0742 Lehman, Paul
(1986) "The Edwards Family and Black Entrepreneurial Success." Chronicles of Oklahoma 64(Winter):pp. 88-97.

African Americans/ People of Color/ Entrepreneurs/ Success/ Family/ Employment/ Business Ownership

0743 Lewis, Earl
(1987) "Afro-American Adaptive Strategies: The Visiting Habits of Kith and Kin among Black Norfolkians during the First Great Migration." Journal of Family History 12(Oct):pp. 407-420.

People of Color/ Virginia/ South/ African Americans/ Kinship/ Support Systems/ Coping Strategies/ Extended Family/ Migration

0744 Lightfoot, Sara Lawrence
(1988) Balm in Gilead: Journey of a Healer. Reading, MA: Addison-Wesley.

African American/ Sex Discrimination/ Women of Color/ Career Aspirations/ Health Care/ Psychiatry/ Child Development/ Biographies

0745 Lindsay, I. Beverly
(1975) "Coping Characteristics of the Black Aged." in No Longer Young: The Older Women in America - Occasional Papers in Gerontology, Series Statement #11. Ann Arbor, MI: Institute of Gerontology, University of Michigan-Wayne State University.

Gerontology/ Coping Strategies/ Women of Color/ African American/ Aged/ Senior Citizen/ Older Adults/ Home Life

0746 Lorde, Audre
(1979) "My Mother's Mortar." Sinister Wisdom 8(Winter):pp. 54-61.

Women of Color/ African American/ Mothers/ Support Systems/ Parent Child Relationships

0747 Malson, Michelene R.
(1988) "Understanding Black Single Parent Families: Stresses and Strengths." Available: Wellesley College, Stone Center for Developmental Services and

Studies, 106 Central Street, Wellesley, MA 02181-8293.

Single Parents/ Employment/ African American/ Child Care/ Parent Child Relationships/ Women of Color/ Stress/ Female Headed Households/ Family Life/ Support Systems/ Education/ Single Parent Families

0748   Matsueda, Ross L.
Heimer, Karen. (1987) "Race, Family Structure and Delinquency: A Test of Differential Association and Social Control Theories." Presented: American Sociological Association Annual Meeting, Chicago, IL. Author: University of Wisconsin, Dept. of Sociology, Madison, WI 53706.

African American/ Women of Color/ Family Structure/ Single Parent Families/ Family Influence/ Juvenile Delinquency/ Social Control/ Learned Behavior

0749   McAdoo, Harriette Pipes
(1988) "Changes in the Formation and Structure of Black Families: The Impact on Black Women." Working Paper #182, Wellesley College Center for Research on Women, Wellesley, MA.

African Americans/ Balancing Work and Family Life/ Family/ Families/ Women of Color/ Culture/ Social Change/ Social Influences/ Family Structure

0750   McAdoo, Harriette Pipes
(ed.). (1988) Black Families. Newbury Park, CA: Sage Publications. pp. 288.

Family/ Families/ Demography/ African Americans/ Mobility/ Teenage Pregnancy/ People of Color/ Educational Opportunities/ Economic Status/ Child Socialization

0751   McGuigan, Dorothy G.
(1980) Women's Lives: New Theory Research and Policy. Ann Arbor, MI: Center for Continuing Education of Women, University of Michigan. pp. 451.

Women of Color/ African American/ Women's Roles/ Working Class/ Coping Strategies/ Family/ Wage Discrimination/ Widows/ Public Policy

0752   McKay, R.
(1986) "One-Child Families and Atypical Sex Ratios in an Elite Black Community." in The Black Family: Essays and Studies (3rd Edition). Robert Staples. Belmont, CA: Wadsworth. ISBN 0534072186.

African American/ Family/ Families/ Children/ Elites/ Upper Class/ Women of Color/ Family Size/ Sex Ratio

0753   Merritt, Carol Elaine
(1986) "Slave Family and Household Arrangement in Piedmont Georgia." Dissertation: Emory University, Atlanta, GA.

African American/ Women of Color/ South/ Georgia/ Slavery/ Family/ Households/ History/ Roles

0754   Mossell, Mrs. N. F.
(1988) The Work of the Afro-American Woman. New York: Oxford University Press. pp. 224. ISBN 019505265X.

African American/ Women of Color/ Achievements/ Womanhood/ Essays/ Balancing Work and Family Life

0755   Mullings, Leith
(1986) "Anthropological Perspectives on the Afro-American Family." American Journal of Social Psychiatry 6:1:pp. 11-16.

African Americans/ People of Color/ Family/ Families/ Anthropology/ Social Environment/ Family Structure

0756   **Omolade, Barbara**
(1987) <u>It's A Family Affair: The Real Lives of Black Single Mothers</u>. Latham, NY: Kitchen Table Press (Freedom Organizing Pamphlet #4.).
Women of Color/ Health Care/ African American/ Female Headed Households/ Single Parent Families/ Single Mothers/ Networks/ Kinship

0757   **Peters, M.**
De Ford, C. (1986) "The Solo Mother." in <u>The Black Family: Essays and Studies</u> (3rd Edition). Robert Staples. Belmont, CA: Wadsworth. ISBN 0534072186.
African American/ Single Mothers/ Single Parent Family/ Family Structure/ Childrearing Practices/ Women of Color/ Female Headed Households

0758   **Philliber, Susan**
(1981) "The Impact of Age of Mother on Mother-Child Interaction Patterns." <u>Journal of Marriage and the Family</u> 43(February):pp. 109-116.
Women of Color/ Coping Strategies/ African American/ Family/ Families/ Maternal Age/ Parent Child Relationships/ Early Childbearing/ Late Childbearing

0759   **Pincus, Samuel Norman**
(1978)   "The Virginia Supreme Court, Blacks, and the Law, 1870-1902." Dissertation: University of Virginia, Charlottesville, VA. pp. 476. DAI Vol. 39(08A)5087.
African American/ People of Color/ Social History/ 19th Century/ Legal Status/ Courts/ Virginia/ South/ Judicial Attitudes/ Marriage and Family Law

0760   **Reid, Pamela T.**
(1982) "Socialization of Black Female Children." in <u>Women: A Developmental Perspective</u>. Phyllis Berman (ed.). Bethesda, MD: National Institute of Health.
Women of Color/ African American/ Socialization/ Child Development/ Individual Development/ Sex Roles

0761   **Rushing, Lawrence Henry**
(1982) "Independence-Conformity: A Comparative Study of White and Black Women." Dissertation: New School for Social Research, New York, NY. pp. 145. DAI Vol. 43(09A)3126.
African American/ European American/ Comparative Studies/ Conforming Behavior/ Independence/ Women of Color/ Peer Influence/ Home Life

0762   **Schoen, Robert**
Kluegel, James. (1988) "The Widening Gap in Black and White Marriage Rates: The Impact of Population Composition and Differential Marriage Propensities." <u>American Sociological Review</u> 53(Dec):pp. 895-907.
African Americans/ Comparative Studies/ European Americans/ People of Color/ Social Differences/ Demography/ Family Structure/ Life Styles/ South/ Marriage Forms

0763   **Schulz, Donald A.**
(1986) "The Role of the Boyfriend in Lower-Class Negro Life." in <u>The Black Family: Essays and Studies</u> (3rd Edition). Robert Staples. Belmont, CA: Wadsworth Publishing. ISBN 0534072186.
African American/ Male Female Relationships/ Roles/ Social Class/ Lower Class/ Women of Color/ Boys/ Men/ Family/ Home Life

0764   **Scott, J.**
Kivett, V. (1980)   "The Widowed, Black, Older Adult in the Rural South:

Implications for Policy." <u>Family Relations</u> 29:pp. 83-90.

Women of Color/ African American/ Older Adults/ Senior Citizens/ Aging/ Rural Areas/ South/ Widows/ Rural Women/ Home Life

0765   Smith, Eleanor J.
Smith, Paul M. (1986) "The Black Female Single-Parent Family Conditions." <u>The Journal of Black Studies</u> 17(Spring):1:pp. 125-134.

Women of Color/ Single Parent Families/ African American/ Single Parents/ Family/ Women Living in Poverty/ Nontraditional Family/ Single Mothers/ Female Headed Households

0766   Staples, Robert
(1986) "Changes in Black Family Structure: The Conflict between Family Ideology and Structural Conditions." in <u>The Black Family: Essays and Studies</u> (3rd Edition). Robert Staples. Belmont, CA: Wadsworth Publishing. ISBN 0534072186.

African Americans/ Family Structure/ People of Color/ Home Life

0767   Staples, Robert
(1986) "Beyond the Black Family: The Trend Toward Singlehood." in <u>The Black Family: Essays and Studies</u> (3rd Edition). Robert Staples. Belmont, CA: Wadsworth Publishing. ISBN 0534072186.

African Americans/ Families/ Social Trends/ Singles/ Life Styles/ People of Color/ Single Parent Families

0768   Staples, Robert
(1986) "Change and Adaptation in the Black Family." in <u>The Black Family: Essays and Studies</u> (3rd Edition). Robert Staples. Belmont, CA: Wadsworth Publishing. ISBN 0534072186.

African Americans/ Families/ Social Trends/ People of Color/ Family Life

0769   Swerdlow, Amy
Bridenthal, Renate et al. (1988) <u>Families in Flux</u>. New York: Feminist Press. pp. 208.

Single Parent Families/ Blended Families/ Social Class/ African American/ People of Color/ Family Structure

0770   Taylor, Robert J.
Chatters, Linda M. and Mays, Vickie M. (1988) "Parents, Children, Siblings, In-Laws, and Non-Kin as Sources of Emergency Assistance to Black Americans." <u>Family Relations: Journal of Applied Family and Child Studies</u> 37:3:pp. 298-304

People of Color/ Parents/ Children/ African Americans/ Help Seeking Behavior/ Extended Family/ Family Problems/ Relationships/ Networks/ Support Systems

0771   Walsh, Lorena S.
(1985) "The Experiences and Status of Women in the Chesapeake, 1750-1775." in <u>The Web of Southern Social Relations: Women, Family and Education</u>. Walter J. Fraser, Jr. et al. (eds.). Athens, GA: University of Georgia Press. pp. 257.

18th Century/ South/ Sex Roles/ Status/ Family/ History/ Early Childbearing/ Slavery/ African American/ European American/ Women of Color/ Property Laws/ Marital Status/ Marriage

0772   Willie, Charles V.
(1984) "The Role of Mothers in the Lives of Outstanding Scholars." <u>Journal of Family Issues</u> 5(Sept):3:pp. 291-306.

Women of Color/ Support Systems/ African American/ Parent Child Relationships/ Women's Roles/ Social Mobility/ Family Roles/ Parent Influence/ Scholars/ Education/ Academic Achievement

0773 Willie, Charles V.
(1986) "The Black Family and Social Class." in The Black Family: Essays and Studies (3rd Edition). Robert Staples. Belmont, CA: Wadsworth Publishing. ISBN 0534072186.

African Americans/ Family/ Social Class/ People of Color

0774 Wilson, William Julius
(ed.). (1989) The Ghetto Underclass: Social Science Perspectives. Newbury Park, CA: Sage Publications. pp. 256.

People of Color/ Role Models/ Employment/ Family/ Poverty/ Socioeconomic Status/ Economically Disadvantaged/ African American/ Lower Class

0775 Wyrick, Eleanor S.
Owens, Otis H. (1977) "Black Women: Income and Incarceration." in Blacks and Criminal Justice. Owens and Bell (eds.). Lexington, MA: Lexington Books. pp. 85-92.

African American/ Women of Color/ Poverty/ Socioeconomic Status/ Prisoners/ Correctional Rehabilitation/ Incarceration/ Low Income Households/ Criminal Justice/ Prisons/ Family Finances

Asian American

0776 Cerroni-Long, E. L.
(1982) "The Curative Use of Japanese 'New Religions' by Los Angeles Japanese Americans." Working Paper #7, University of California Los Angeles Asian American Studies Center, Los Angeles, CA.

Japanese American/ Family/ Asian American/ Roles/ Women of Color/ Religions/ Health Care Delivery/ Health/ Illness

0777 Chai, Alice Yun
(1988) "Women's History in Public: 'Picture Brides' of Hawaii." Women's Studies Quarterly 1-2(Spring/Summer):pp. 51-62.

Women of Color/ Stereotypes/ Asian American/ Family/ Hawaii/ Pacific/ 20th Century/ Marriage/ Immigrants/ Women's History/ Family History/ Oppression/ Wives

0778 Cho, Pill Jay
(1987) "Family Care of the Asian American Elderly." Author: School of Social Work, Grambling State University, Grambling, LA. Presented: American Sociological Association, Chicago, IL. August.

Asian American/ Women of Color/ Older Adults/ Traditions/ Poverty/ Extended Families/ Dependent Care/ Family Finances

0779 Lin, Chien
(1985) "The Intergenerational Relationships among Chinese Immigrant Families: A Study of Filial Piety." Dissertation: University of Illinois-Chicago, Chicago, IL. pp. 243. DAI Vol. 46(06A)1748.

Immigrants/ Chinese/ Asian/ Women of Color/ Family Relationships/ Parent Child Relationships/ Family Structure/ Cultural Influences

0780 Min, Pyong Gap
(1987) "Korean Immigrants' Marital Patterns and Marital Adjustment." Author: Department of Sociology, Georgia State University, Atlanta, GA 30303. Presented:

American Sociological Association, Chicago, IL.

Korean/ Asian/ Immigrants/ Women of Color/ California/ Pacific/ Male Female Relationships/ Marital Adjustment/ Korean American/ Asian American/ Acculturation/ Family

0781 Organization of Pan Asian American Women
(1980) Regional Conference on "Just Us--Young Pan Asian Females and the Juvenile Justice System." U.S. Department of Justice Office of Juvenile Justice and Delinquency Prevention, Washington, D.C. Available: National Institute of Justice/ National Criminal Justice Reference Service, Microfiche Program, Box 6000, Rockville, MD 20850. pp. 37.

Women of Color/ Asian American/ Delinquent Behavior/ Family Conflict/ Traditional Family/ Social Influences/ Juvenile Justice System/ Community Problems

0782 Seguin, Rita Carroll
Geschwender, James A. (1987) "Ethnicity and Women's Labor Force Activities in Hawaii: The Supplemental Earner Thesis and the Asian Success Myth." Presented: American Sociological Association Annual Meeting, Chicago, IL. August.

Women of Color/ Academic Achievement/ Asian American/ Dependent Children/ Labor Force/ Stereotypes/ Income/ Employment/ Pacific/ Hawaii/ Socioeconomic Status/ Two Income Families

Latina

0783 Alliance Against Women's Oppression
(1987) "Teenage Mothers: Setting the Record Straight." Discussion Paper #8, Alliance Against Women's Oppression, San Francisco, CA.

Women of Color/ African American/ Teenage Pregnancy/ Family Influence/ Low Income/ Comparative Studies/ Latina/ Early Childbearing/ Mothers

0784 Alvarez, Robert R., Jr.
(1987) Familia: Migration and Adaptation in Baja and Alta California, 1880-1975. Berkeley: University of California. pp. 228.

Women of Color/ Latina/ Migration Patterns/ Immigrants/ Social Adjustment/ Acculturation/ Assimilation Patterns/ History/ 20th Century/ California/ Pacific/ Family/ Families

0785 Angel, Ronald J.
Worobey, Jacqueline Lowe. (1988) "Single Motherhood and Children's Health." Journal of Health and Social Behavior 29(March):1:pp. 38-52.

Women of Color/ Latina/ Marital Status/ Single Mothers/ Children/ Physical Health/ Health Seeking Behavior/ Maternal and Infant Welfare/ Female Headed Households

0786 Bonilla-Santiago, Gloria
(1988) "Hispanic Women in New Jersey: A Survey of Women Raising Families Alone." Available: Hispanic Women's Task Force of New Jersey, School of Social Work, Rutgers University, 327 Cooper St., Camden, NJ 08102.

Women of Color/ Employment/ Latina/ Fertility/ New Jersey/ North East/ Female Headed Households/ Single Parent Families/ Heads of Households/ Educational Level

0787 Christensen, Edward W.
Acosta-Belen, Edna. (1986) "The Puerto Rican Woman: A Profile." in The Puerto Rican Woman. New York: Praeger. pp. 51-63. ISBN 0030524660.

Puerto Rican/ Latina/ Education/ Child Rearing/ Employment/ Social Values/ Women of Color

0788 Cordasco, Francesco
(1982) <u>The Puerto Rican Community and It's Children on the Mainland: A Source Book for Teachers, Social Workers, and Other Professionals</u> (3rd Edition). Metuchen, NJ: Scarecrow. pp. 469. ISBN 0810815060.
Puerto Ricans/ Latinos/ Children/ People of Color/ Family/ Families

0789 Curry, Rodriguez, Julia E.
(1988) "Labor Migration and Familial Responsibilities: Experiences of Mexican Women." in <u>Mexicans at Work</u>. Margarita B. Melville. Houston: University of Houston Press. pp. 47-64.
Women of Color/ Educational Attainment/ Latina/ Mexican/ Community Relations/ Migration/ Kinship/ Networks/ Illegal Immigrants/ Support Systems/ Labor Force Participation/ Heads of Households/ Balancing Work and Family Life/ Employment

0790 Darabi, Katherine F.
(1987) <u>Childbearing among Hispanics in the United States</u>. Westport, CT: Greenwood Press. pp. 179.
Women of Color/ Latina/ Population Characteristics/ Fertility Rates/ Bibliographies/ Marital Status/ Sexual Behavior/ Abortion/ Contraception/ Childbearing

0791 Darabi, Katherine F.
(1988) <u>El Embarazo Precoz: Childbearing among Hispanic Teenagers in the United States</u>. New York: Columbia University Press.
Women of Color/ Latina/ Childbearing/ Childbirth/ Teenage Pregnancy/ Abortion/ Birth Control/ Early Childbearing/ Fertility

0792 Doran, Terry
Satterfield, Janet and Stade, C. (1988) <u>A Road Well Traveled: Three Generations of Cuban American Women</u>. Newton, MA: WEEA Publishing, EDC, 55 Chapel St., suite 245.
Women of Color/ Latina/ Subculture/ Women's History/ Testimonial Literature/ Racial Discrimination/ Bias/ Cuban American/ Language/ Immigrants/ Cultural Heritage/ Assimilation Patterns/ Acculturation/ Socioeconomic Status/ Family/ Families

0793 Ginorio, Angela B.
(1985) "Violence in the Lives of Latina Women." <u>Working Together--To Prevent Sexual and Domestic Violence</u> 5(3):2-4. Available: Center for the Prevention of Sexual and Domestic Violence, 1914 N. 34th, Suite 205, Seattle, WA 98103.
Women of Color/ Latina/ Domestic Violence/ Spouse Abuse/ Violence Against Women/ Male Female Relationships

0794 Gonzales, Rosalinda M.
(1978) "Mexican Women and Families: Rural-to-Urban and International Migration." <u>Southwest Economy and Society</u> 4:2:pp. 14-27.
Latina/ Mexican/ Urban Migration/ Women of Color/ Family/ Immigrants/ Employment/ Rural Women

0795 Gratton, Brian
Rosales, F. Arturo and DeBano, H. (1988) "A Sample of the Mexican-American Population in 1940." <u>Historical Methods</u> 21(Spring):pp. 80-87.
People of Color/ Chicanos/ Latinos/ History/ 1940-1949/ Demography/ Family

0796 **Guendelman, Sylvia**
(1987) "The Incorporation of Mexican Women in Seasonal Migration: A Study of Gender Differences." Hispanic Journal of Behavioral Sciences 9(September):3:pp. 245-264.

Women of Color/ Latina/ Mexican/ Immigrants/ Migrant Workers/ Sex Roles/ Farm Workers/ Traditional Family/ Race, Class and Gender Studies

0797 **Guendelman, Sylvia**
Perez-Itriago, A. (1987) "Double Lives: The Changing Role of Women in Seasonal Migration." International Journal of Women's Studies 13:pp. 249-271.

Women of Color/ Support Systems/ Latina/ Race, Class and Gender Studies/ Immigrants/ Balancing Work and Family Life/ Women's Roles/ Seasonal Migration/ Farm Workers

0798 **Ito, Karen L.**
(1986) "Pregnancy among Hispanic and Anglo Women: Post Partum Interviews in a San Diego Hospital." Final Report, Health Officers Association of California, Inc., Sacramento, CA.

Latina/ California/ European American/ Women of Color/ Pregnancy/ Childbirth/ Maternal and Infant Welfare/ Comparative Studies

0799 **Jaffe, A. J.**
Cullen, Ruth M. et al. (1986) "The Findings: A Summary." in The Changing Demography of Spanish Americans. A. J. Jaffe and Ruth M. Cullen. New York: Academic Press. pp. 426. ISBN 012379580X.

Latinos/ Fertility Rates/ Demography/ Educational Experience/ Single Mothers/ Employment Opportunities/ Family Income/ People of Color

0800 **Jorgensen, Stephen R.**
Adams, Russell P. (1987) "Family Planning Needs and Behavior of Mexican American Women: A Study of Health Care Professionals and Their Clientele." Hispanic Journal of Behavioral Sciences 9(September):3:pp. 265-286.

Women of Color/ Latina/ Health Care Workers/ Health Care Services/ Contraception/ Family Planning/ Comparative Studies/ Stereotypes/ Immigrants

0801 **Kay, Margarita**
(1980) "Mexican, Mexican American, and Chicana Childbirth." in Twice a Minority: Mexican American Women. Margarita B. Melville. St. Louis, MO: C.V. Mosby. pp. 52-65. ISBN 0801633869.

Double Bind/ Parent Child Relationships/ Childbirth/ Chicana/ Women of Color/ Crosscultural Studies/ Birthing/ Mexican/ Latina

0802 **Lamphere, Louise A.**
(1986) "Working Mothers and Family Strategies: Portuguese and Colombian Immigrant Women in New England." in International Immigration: The Female Experience. Rita Simon and Caroline Brettell (eds.). Totowa, NJ: Rowman and Allenheld.

Women of Color/ Balancing Work and Family Life/ Latina/ Colombian/ New England/ Immigrants/ Employment/ Family Relationships/ Mothers Working Outside the Home/ Family Roles/ Support Systems/ Coping Strategies

0803 **Laosa, Luis M.**
(1980) "Maternal Teaching Strategies in Chicano and Anglo-American Families: The Influence of Culture and Education on Maternal Behavior." Child Development

51(September):3:pp. 759-765.

Parent Child Relationships/ Mothers/ Behavior/ Chicana/ Latina/ Women of Color/ European American/ Teaching/ Education/ Cultural Influences/ Child Development/ Family Influence

0804   Melville, Margarita B.
(1978) "Mexican Women Adapt to Migration." <u>International Migration Review</u> 12:2:pp. 225-235.

Women of Color/ Stress/ Latina/ Mexicans/ Coping Strategies/ Migration/ Extended Family/ Acculturation Process/ Assimilation Patterns/ Illegal Immigrants

0805   Ortiz, Vilma
(1986) "Generational Status, Family Background, and Educational Attainment among Hispanic Youth and Non-Hispanic White Youth." in <u>Latino College Students</u>. Michael Olivas (ed.). New York: Teachers' College Press. ISBN 0807727989.

Latinos/ Comparative Studies/ People of Color/ European Americans/ Educational Attainment/ Family Structure/ Educational Opportunities/ Family History

0806   Perez, Lisandro
(1986) "Immigrant Economic Adjustment and Family Organization: The Cuban Success Story Re-Examined." <u>International Migration Review</u> 20(Spring):1:pp. 4-10.

Cuban/ Latina/ Women of Color/ Immigrants/ Socioeconomic Status/ Acculturation Process/ Family Structure

0807   Perez, Robert G.
(1983) "Effects of Stress, Social Support and Coping Style on Adjustment to Pregnancy among Hispanic Women." <u>Hispanic Journal of Behavioral Sciences</u> 5:2:pp. 141-161.

Women of Color/ Health Care Services/ Latina/ Childbirth/ Childbearing/ Stress/ Support Systems/ Coping Strategies/ Pregnancy

0808   Rodriguez, Carmen F. Quiones
(1976) "Families of Working Mothers in Puerto Rico." Dissertation: The Ohio State University, Columbus, OH. pp. 209.

Family/ Families/ Working Parents/ Puerto Rican/ Latina/ Women of Color/ Wage Earning Mothers/ Employment

0809   Rogler, Lloyd H.
Canino, Ian and Earley, Brian F. (1980) "The Puerto Rican Child in New York City: Stress and Mental Health." Monograph #4, Hispanic Research Center, Fordham University, Bronx, NY.

People of Color/ New York/ North East/ Latinos/ Puerto Ricans/ Coping Strategies/ Adolescents/ Mental Health/ Psychological Stress/ Children

0810   Ruiz, Vicki L.
(1985) "Obreras y Madres: Labor Activism among Mexican Women and Its Impact on the Family." in <u>La Mexicana/Chicana</u>, Renato Rosaldo Lecture Series Monograph, Vol. I. Tucson: University of AZ, Mexican American Studies and Research Center pp. 19-38.

Latina/ Mexican/ Women of Color/ Family/ Employment/ Labor Movement/ Unions/ Activism/ Balancing Work and Family Life/ Chicana

0811 Shapiro, J.
Tittle, K. (1986) "Psychosocial Adjustment of Poor Mexican Mothers of Disabled and Nondisabled Children." American Journal of Orthopsychiatry 56:2:pp. 289-302.

Women of Color/ Psychological Adjustment/ Latina/ Mexican/ Social Adjustment/ Support Systems/ Disabilities/ Children/ Coping Strategies/ Poverty/ Stress/ Mental Health

0812 Soto, Lourdes Diaz
(1988) "The Home Environment of Higher and Lower Achieving Puerto Rican Children." Hispanic Journal of the Behavioral Sciences 10(June):2:pp. 161-167.

People of Color/ Educational Aspirations/ Latinos/ Puerto Ricans/ Parent Child Relationships/ Parenting/ Home Life/ Academic Achievement/ Family Life/ Parental Attitudes

0813 U.S. Dept. of Justice Law Enforcement Assistance Administration
(1981) "Report From the National Hispanic Conference on Law Enforcement and Criminal Justice." U.S. Department of Justice Law Enforcement Assistance Administration, Washington, D.C. pp. 564.

Women of Color/ Latina/ Law Enforcement/ Criminal Justice/ Juvenile Courts/ Correctional Facilities/ Marriage and Family Law

0814 Warburton, A. A.
Woods, H. H. and Cane, M. (1982) "Four Families of Agricultural Laborers in South Texas, 1941." in Introduction to Chicano Studies. Livie Isauro and H. Russell Bernard (eds.). New York: Macmillan Publishing. pp. 272-278.

Latina/ Migrant Workers/ Women of Color/ Agriculture/ Family/ History/ 1940-1949/ Texas/ South West

0815 Westfried, Alex H.
(1980) Ethnic Leadership in a New England Community: Three Puerto Rican Families. Cambridge, MA: Schenkman Books, 190 Concord Avenue. pp. 196.

Puerto Ricans/ Latinos/ Family/ People of Color/ Leadership/ North East/ New England/ Community

0816 Westfried, Alex H.
(1985) Three Puerto Rican Families. Prospect Heights, IL: Waveland Press. pp. 176. ISBN 0881331848.

Puerto Ricans/ Family/ Families/ Latinos/ People of Color/ Community/ Leadership

0817 Zambrana, Ruth E.
(1987) "Latinas in the United States." in The American Woman 1987-1988: A Report in Depth. Sarah E. Rix. New York: Norton. ISBN 0393303888.

Latina/ Family Roles/ Women of Color/ Employment/ Images of Women/ Education

0818 Zavella, Patricia
(1987) Women's Work and Chicano Families: Cannery Workers of the Santa Clara Valley. Ithaca, NY: Cornell University Press. pp. 192. ISBN 0801417309.

Women of Color/ Latina/ Chicana/ Family/ Women's Roles/ Migrant Workers/ Employment/ California/ Pacific/ Factory Workers/ Food Industry

0819 Zentella, Ana C.
(1987) "Growing Up Female in the Puerto Rican Community: The Role of Language." in Women and Languages in Transition. Joyce Penfield. Albany: State University of New York Press. pp. 224. ISBN 088706485X.

Puerto Rican/ Latina/ Women of Color/ Life Cycles/ Community/ Socialization/ Language/ Speech/ Roles/ Sociolinguistics/ Verbal Communication/ Women's Language/ Women in Transition/ Home Life

Native American

0820 Ackerman, Lillian A.
(1987) "The Effect of Missionary Ideals on Family Structure and Women's Roles in Plateau Indian Culture." <u>Idaho Yesterdays</u> 31(Spring/Summer):pp. 64-73.

Women of Color/ Native American/ Family Structure/ Women's Roles/ Missionaries/ Family Responsibility/ Social Bias/ Race Bias

0821 Anderson, Karen Lee
(1982) "Huron Women and Huron Men: The Effects of Demography, Kinship and the Social Division of Labour on Male/Female Relations among the 17th Century Huron." Dissertation: University of Toronto, Toronto, Ontario, Canada. DAI Vol. 44(03A)873.

Native American/ Huron/ 17th Century/ History/ Male Female Relationships/ Domestic Arrangements/ Social Influences/ Family Influence/ Division of Labor/ Kinship/ Women of Color

0822 Hanson, W.
(1980) "The Urban Indian Women and Her Family." <u>Social Casework</u> 51:8:pp. 476-483.

Native American/ Women of Color/ Family Structure/ Urban Areas/ Family/ Families

0823 Joe, Jennie R.
(1982) "Cultural Influences on Navajo Mothers with Disabled Children." <u>American Indian Quarterly</u> 6(Spring/Summer):1-2: pp. 170-190.

Women of Color/ Cultural Influences/ Native American/ Navajo/ Parent Child Relationships/ Child Rearing Practices/ Motherhood/ Special Education/ Disabilities

0824 Knack, Martha C.
(1980) <u>Life is With People: Household Organization of the Contemporary Southern Paiute Indians</u>. Socorro, NM: Ballena Press.

Women of Color/ Native American/ Paiute/ Households/ Family Structure

0825 Kunitz, Stephen J.
Slocumb, John C. (1976) "The Use of Surgery to Avoid Childbearing among Navajo and Hopi Indians." <u>Human Biology</u> 48:pp. 9-21.

Fertility/ Sterilization/ Health/ Childbearing/ Surgery/ Contraception/ Medical Sciences/ Native American/ Hopi/ Navajo/ Women of Color

0826 Leighton, Dorothea
(1982) "As I Knew Them: Navajo Women in 1940." <u>American Indian Quarterly</u> 6(Spring/Summer):1-2:pp. 34-51.

Women of Color/ Native American/ Navajo/ Sex Roles/ Child Rearing Practices/ Ethnography/ Women's History/ 1940-1949

0827 May, Philip
(1983) "Epidemiology of Fetal Alcohol Syndrome among American Indians of the Southwest." <u>Social Biology</u> 30(Winter):pp. 374-387.

Native American/ Alcohol Abuse/ Fetal Alcohol Syndrome/ Childbirth/ Mothers/ South West/ Women of Color/ Maternal and Infant Welfare/ Epidemiology/ Health Care

0828   **Scheirbeck, Helen M.**
(1980) "Current Educational Status of American Indian Girls." in <u>Conference on the Educational and Occupational Needs of American Indian Women</u>. Washington, D.C.: U.S. Government Printing Office. pp. 63-82.
Native American/ Women of Color/ Education/ Status/ Equal Educational Opportunity/ School Age Children/ Educationally Disadvantaged

0829   **Sneed, Roseanna**
(1981)   "Two Cherokee Women." <u>Frontiers: A Journal of Women Studies</u> 6(Fall):3:pp. 35-38.
Women of Color/ Native American/ Cherokee/ History/ Family/ Acculturation/ Education

0830   **Street, Douglas**
(1981)   "LaFleche Sisters Write to St. Nicholas Magazine." <u>Nebraska History</u> 62(Winter):4:pp. 515-523.
Native American/ Women's History/ Education/ Biographies/ Nebraska/ North Central/ Women of Color/ Sisters/ Family Structure/ LaFleche

0831   **Tyon, Gracie**
(1981) "The Way of My Grandmother, My Mother, and Me." <u>Frontiers: A Journal of Women Studies</u> 6(Fall):3:pp. 51-52.
Women of Color/ Native American/ Kinship/ Mother Daughter Relationships/ Cultural Heritage/ Customs/ Traditions/ Family/ Families

Southern

0832   **Babb, Ellen**
St. Julian, Milly. (1986) "Public and Private Lives: Women of St. Petersburg at the Turn of the Century." <u>Tampa Bay History</u> 8(Spring-Summer):pp. 4-27.
South Atlantic/ Florida/ 20th Century/ Women's History/ Women of Color*/ Home Life

0833   **Barlett, Peggy F.**
(1983) "South Georgia Farm Women: Patterns and Consequences." Presented: Southern Association of Agricultural Scientists, Rural Sociology Section.
South/ Georgia/ Gender Divison/ Agriculture/ Household Labor/ Income/ Rural Areas/ Employment/ Farming/ Family Roles/ Women's Roles

0834   **Bellows, Barbara L.**
(1985) "My Children, Gentlemen, Are My Own: Poor Women, the Urban Elite, and the Bonds of Obligation in Antebellum Charleston." in <u>The Web of Southern Social Relations: Women, Family and Education</u>. Walter J. Fraser, Jr., et al, (eds.). Athens, GA: University of Georgia Press.
History/ 19th Century/ Southern/ South Carolina/ Family/ Dominance/ Paternalism/ Single Mothers/ Singles/ Working Class/ Poverty/ Immigrants/ Elite/ Antebellum

0835   **Bleser, Carol K.**
(1985) "The Perrys of Greenville: A Nineteenth Century Marriage." in <u>The Web of Southern Social Relations: Women, Family and Education</u>. Walter J. Fraser, Jr. et al. (eds.). Athens, GA: University of Georgia Press. pp. 72-90.
South Carolina/ History/ Separate Spheres/ Family/ Elite/ Male Female Relationships/ Marriage/ Marital Roles/ Traditional Family/ Control/ Dominance/ Sex Roles

0836   Bynum, Victoria
(1987) "'War Within a War': Women's Participation in the Revolt of the North Carolina Piedmont, 1863-1865." <u>Frontiers: A Journal of Women Studies</u> 9:3:pp. 43-49.

South/ North Carolina/ 19th Century/ 1860-1869/ Women's History/ Slavery/ Female Headed Households/ Resistance/ Civil War/ Social Structure/ Plantations/ Farmers/ Aggressive Behavior/ European American/ Deviant Behavior/ Family/ Separate Spheres

0837   Fiene, Judy
(1988) "The Social Reality of a Group of Rural, Low-Status, Appalachian Women: A Grounded Theory Study." Dissertation: University of Tennessee College of Social Work, Knoxville, TN.

South/ Home Life/ Social Realism/ Rural Women/ Socioeconomic Status/ Appalachia/ Self Concept

0838   Fiene, Judy
(1988) "Perceptions of Family Roles of a Group of Rural, Low-Status, Appalachian Women." Presented: Annual National Institute on Social Work and Human Services in Rural Areas, Ft. Collins, CO. July.

South/ Family Roles/ Rural Women/ Self Concept/ Appalachia/ Socioeconomic Status

0839   Fox-Genovese, Elizabeth
(1988) <u>Within the Plantation Household: Black and White Women of the Old South</u>. Chapel Hill, NC: The University of North Carolina Press. pp. 563.

Women of Color/ Household Labor/ South/ European American/ African American/ Relationships/ Plantations/ History/ Slavery/ Comparative Studies/ Family

0840   Fraser, Walter J., Jr.
Saunders, R. Frank, Jr. and Wakelyn, Jon R. (eds.). (1985) <u>The Web of Southern Social Relations: Women, Family and Education</u>. Athens, GA: University of Georgia Press. ISBN 0820309427.

South/ Women's History/ Education/ Family/ Social Conditions/ Social Relations/ African American/ Women of Color/ European American/ Relationships

0841   Geary, Patrick J.
(1987) <u>Ce'line: Remembering Louisiana, 1850-1871</u>. Ce'line Fre'maux Garcia.(ed.). Athens, GA: University of Georgia Press. pp. 288. ISBN 0820309648.

Southern/ Louisiana/ Middle Class/ Immigrants/ History/ 1850-1859/ Civil War/ 1860-1869/ Family Influence/ Biographies/ European American/ Ce'line Fre'maus Garcia

0842   Hall, Jacquelyn D.
(1988) "Partial Truths." Presented: First Southern Conference on Women's History, Converse College, Spartanburg, SC. June.

South/ Women's History/ Employment/ Working Class/ Family

0843   Hammonds, Maxine, M.
Hawkins, Mary S. (1985) "Increase in the Cost of Living: A Concern of Rural Female Headed Families." Presented: Southern Association of Agricultural Scientists, Rural Sociology Section.

Rural Areas/ Women of Color*/ South/ Texas/ Cost of Living/ Low Income Households/ Female Headed Households/ Women Living in Poverty/ Economic Status/ Families

0844 Hardesty, Connie
Harmon, Mary P. (1986) "The Division of Labor on Family Farms: Task Performance of Women, Children and Hired Labor." Presented: Rural Sociological Society Annual Meeting.

Rural Areas/ Family Roles/ Agriculture/ Farming/ Family Structure/ South/ Kentucky/ Children/ Job Performance/ Traditional Roles/ Division of Labor/ Farm Workers

0845 Lewis, Earl
(1987) "Afro-American Adaptive Strategies: The Visiting Habits of Kith and Kin among Black Norfolkians during the First Great Migration." Journal of Family History 12(Oct):pp. 407-420.

People of Color/ Virginia/ South/ African Americans/ Kinship/ Support Systems/ Coping Strategies/ Extended Family/ Migration

0846 Merritt, Carol Elaine
(1986) "Slave Family and Household Arrangement in Piedmont Georgia." Dissertation: Emory University, Atlanta, GA.

African American/ Women of Color/ South/ Georgia/ Slavery/ Family/ Households/ History/ Roles

0847 Salant, Pricilla
(1983) "Farm Women: Contribution to Farm and Family." Presented: Southern Association of Agricultural Scientists, Rural Sociology Section.

South/ Income/ Agriculture/ Rural Areas/ Family Roles/ Economic Value of Women's Work/ Cultural Identity/ Farming/ Earnings/ Employment Patterns

0848 Schoen, Robert
Kluegel, James. (1988) "The Widening Gap in Black and White Marriage Rates: The Impact of Population Composition and Differential Marriage Propensities." American Sociological Review 53 (Dec):pp. 895-907.

African Americans/ Comparative Studies/ European Americans/ People of Color/ Social Inequalities/ Demography/ Family Structure/ Life Styles/ South/ Marriage Forms

0849 Scott, J.
Kivett, V. (1980) "The Widowed, Black, Older Adult in the Rural South: Implications for Policy." Family Relations 29:pp. 83-90.

Women of Color/ African Americans/ Older Adults/ Senior Citizens/ Aging/ Rural Areas/ South/ Widows/ Rural Women/ Home Life

0850 Stowe, Steven M.
(1987) "Growing up Female in the Planter Class." Helicon Nine: Journal of Women's Arts and Letters (Spring):17-18:pp. 194-205.

Southern/ Plantations/ Separate Spheres/ Elites/ Images of Women/ Women's History/ Gender Roles/ Family

0851 Walsh, Lorena S.
(1985) "The Experiences and Status of Women in the Chesapeake, 1750-1775." in The Web of Southern Social Relations: Women, Family and Education. Walter J. Fraser, Jr. et al. (eds.). Athens, GA: University of Georgia Press. pp. 257.

18th Century/ South/ Sex Roles/ Status/ Family/ History/ Early Childbearing/ Slavery/ African American/ European American/ Women of Color/ Property Laws/ Marital Status/ Marriage

0852 Wilson, Kenneth
(1987) "Gender Relations in the South: Are Southern Families Unique." Presented: American Sociological Association, Chicago, IL. Author: Sociology/Anthropology

Department, East Carolina University, Greenville, NC 27834.

South/ Families/ Sex-Gender Systems/ Male Female Relationships/ Conflict Resolution/ Gender Roles/ Cultural Influences

*Women of Color**

0853 Abramovitz, Mimi
(1988) Regulating the Lives of Women: Social Welfare Policy From Colonial Times to the Present. Boston, MA: South End Press.

Women's History/ 18th Century/ Discrimination/ Marriage and Family Law/ Women of Color*/ 20th Century/ 19th Century/ Economic Value of Women's Work/ Social Policy/ Social Welfare/ Economic Trends

0854 Babb, Ellen
St. Julian, Milly. (1986) "Public and Private Lives: Women of St. Petersburg at the Turn of the Century." Tampa Bay History 8:(Spring/Summer):pp. 4-27.

South Atlantic/ Florida/ 20th Century/ Women's History/ Women of Color*/ Home Life

0855 Danziger, Sandra K.
Nagatoshi, Charles. (1987) "Adolescent Welfare Mothers and the Fathers of their Children: Legal Ties, Family Relationships and Economic Prospects." Author: Institute Research Poverty, 1180 Observatory Drive, Madison, WI 53706.

Women of Color*/ Parent Child Relationships/ Paternity/ Child Support/ Teenage Fathers/ Teenage Mothers/ Legal Responsibility/ AFDC/ Wisconsin/ North Central/ Family/ Families/ Socioeconomic Status

0856 Dill, Bonnie Thornton
(1988) "Our Mothers' Grief: Racial Ethnic Women and the Maintenance of Families." Journal of Family History 13:4:pp. 415-431.

Women of Color*/ Survival Strategies/ Resistance/ Families/ Cultural Heritage/ Family Influence/ Support Systems

0857 Farley, Reynolds
Allen, Walter (eds.). (1987) The Color Line and the Quality of Life in America. New York: Russell Sage Foundation. pp. 448.

Women of Color*/ Quality of Life/ Racial Equality/ Comparative Studies/ Socioeconomic Status/ Fertility/ Mortality/ Migration/ Family Structure/ Educational Experience/ Minority Employment/ Income

0858 Ford Foundation
(1989) "Early Childhood Services: A National Challenge." Presented: Ford Foundation-Program Paper, New York, NY 10017. March.

Women of Color*/ Low Income Families/ Women's Studies/ Family Roles/ Child Care/ Family Support/ Social Policy/ Legislation/ Educational Opportunities/ Public Policy/ Labor Force Participation

0859 Ford Foundation
(1989) "Work and Family Responsibilities: Achieving a Balance." Ford Foundation Program Paper, New York, NY 10017. March.

Women of Color*/ Segregation/ Employment Patterns/ Gender Stereotypes/ Employment Opportunities/ Occupational Trends/ Family Roles/ Economically Disadvantages/ Public Policy/ Balancing Work and Family Life/ Labor Force Participation/ Family Responsibility

0860   **Furstenberg, Frank F.**
Brooks-Gunn, J. et al. (1987) <u>Adolescent Mothers in Later Life</u>. New York:
Cambridge University Press. pp. 204.
Parenting/ Mothers/ Marital Stability/ Teenage Pregnancy/ Stereotypes/ Social Welfare/ Women of
Color*/ Single Parents/ Economic Mobility/ Early Childbearing/ Family

0861   **Hammonds, Maxine M.**
Hawkins, Mary S. (1985) "Increase in the Cost of Living: A Concern of Rural Female
Headed Families." Presented: Southern Association of Agricultural Scientists,
Rural Sociology Section Annual Meetings.
Rural Areas/ Women of Color*/ South/ Texas/ Cost of Living/ Low Income Households/ Female Headed
Households/ Women Living in Poverty/ Economic Status/ Families

0862   **Hardaway, Roger D.**
(1986) "Unlawful Love: A History of Arizona's Miscegenation Laws." <u>Journal of
Arizona History</u> 27(Winter).
Women of Color*/ Marriage and Family Law/ Arizona/ Mountain/ Racial Discrimination/ History/
Laws/ Miscegenation

0863   **Harris, R.**
(1980) "An Examination of Effects of Ethnicity, Socioeconomic Status and Generation
on Familism and Sex Role Orientations." <u>Journal of Comparative Family Studies</u>
2:pp. 173-193.
Socioeconomic Status/ Sex Roles/ Women of Color*/ Cultural Influences/ Family/ Ethnicity

0864   **Hutchings, Nancy**
(1988) <u>The Violent Family: Victimization of Women, Children, and Elders</u>. New
York: Human Sciences Press, pp. 201. ISBN 0898853834.
Family/ Family Conflict/ Abuse/ Pornography/ Child Abuse/ Family History/ Rape/ Social Problems/
Battered Women/ Elder Abuse/ Family Violence/ Women of Color*

0865   **Johnson, Nan E.**
(1988) "The Pace of Births over the Life Course: Implications for the Minority-
Group Status Hypothesis." <u>Social Science Quarterly</u> 69(March):1:pp. 95-107.
Women of Color*/ Birth Rates/ Family Structure/ Childbearing/ Family Planning/ Post Secondary
Education/ Fertility/ Demography

0866   **Levitan, Sar A.**
Belous, Richard and Gallo, Frank. (1988) <u>What's Happening to the American
Family? Tensions, Hopes, Realities</u>. Baltimore: Johns Hopkins University Press.
pp. 224.
People of Color*/ Women Living in Poverty/ Family Structure/ Single Mothers/ Extended Families/
Divorce/ Social Trends/ Single Parents/ Single Parent Families/ Female Headed Households/ Family
Problems/ Family History/ Nuclear Families

0867   **Levitan, Sar A.**
(1988) <u>Programs in Aid of the Poor</u>. Baltimore: Johns Hopkins University Press. pp.
168.
People of Color*/ Federal Assistance Programs/ Poverty/ Public Policy/ Welfare/ Public Assistance/
Social Policy/ Reagan Administration/ Women Living in Poverty/ Family

0868   **Mander, Anica Vesel**
Hofbauer, Sarika Finci. (1976) <u>Blood Ties</u>. Hopkinton, NH: Women's Words

Books.

Women of Color*/ Comparative Studies/ European American/ Matrilineal Kinship/ Women's History/ Autobiographies/ Family/ Networks/ Support Systems

0869 McLanahan, Sara

Garfinkel, Irwin. (1989) "Single Mothers, the Underclass, and Social Policy." The Annuals 501(Jan):pp. 92-104.

Female Headed Households/ Socioeconomic Status/ Single Mothers/ Race, Class and Gender Studies/ Women Living in Poverty/ Child Care/ Health/ Women of Color*/ Income Distribution/ Poverty/ Unemployment/ Social Policy/ Family/ Families/ Welfare Programs

0870 McLaughlin, Steven D

Melber, Barbara D. and Billy, John O. G. (1988) The Changing Lives of American Women. Chapel Hill, NC: University of North Carolina Press. pp. 250. ISBN 0807818135.

Women of Color*/ Attitudes/ Demography/ Stereotypes/ Employment Patterns/ Gender Roles/ Educational Attainment/ Family Roles/ Social Change/ Family Structure/ Social Trends

0871 Michelson, William

(1984) From Sun to Sun: Daily Obligations and Community Structure in the Lives of Employed Women and Their Families. Totowa, NJ: Rowman and Littlefield. pp. 180. ISBN 0865981493.

Family/ Employment/ Balancing Work and Family Life/ Labor Force Participation/ Households/ Stress/ Parenting/ Mothers/ Women Working Outside the Home/ Family Responsibility/ Neighborhoods/ Communities/ Women of Color*

0872 Miller, Dorothy

(1987) "Helping the Strong: An Exploration of the Needs of Families Headed by Women." National Association of Social Workers, Silver Spring, MD. pp. 99.

Women of Color*/ Counseling/ Single Parents/ Poverty/ Family/ Female Headed Households/ Single Mothers/ Family Structure/ Social Work/ Home Life

0873 Mintz, Steven

Kellogg, Susan. (1988) Domestic Revolutions: A Social History of American Family Life. New York: Free Press. pp. 316.

People of Color*/ Family Problems/ Family/ Family Life/ Blended Family/ Abortion/ Social History/ Welfare/ Family Structure/ Surrogate Parenting/ Social Issues/ Social Change

0874 Moore, Kristin A.

(1979) Teenage Motherhood: Social and Economic Consequences. Lanham, MD: University Press of America. pp. 50. ISBN 0877662436.

Parenting/ Poverty/ Parent Child Relationships/ Teenage Mothers/ Marriage/ Education/ Family/ Women of Color*/ Labor Force Participation/ Welfare

0875 Morgan, L.

(1976) "A Re-examination of Widowhood and Morale." Journal of Gerontology 31:pp. 687-695.

Women of Color*/ Widows/ Images of Women/ Life Cycles/ Social Adjustment/ Home Life

0876 Mulroy, Elizabeth A.

(1988) Women as Single Parents: Confronting Institutional Barriers in the Courts, the Workplace, and the Housing Market. Dover, MA: Auburn House. pp. 300. ISBN

0865691762.

Women of Color*/ Family Structure/ Child Care/ Institutional Discrimination/ Single Mothers/ Single Parents/ Housing/ Employment/ Courts/ Court Decisions/ Welfare Reform/ Policymaking/ Nontraditional Family/ Female Headed Households/ Women Living in Poverty/ Single Parent Families/ Marriage and Family Law

0877　**National Association of Social Workers**
(1984) "Research on People of Color." National Association of Social Workers, Silver Spring, MD. pp. 45. ISBN 0871011255.

People of Color*/ Child Welfare/ Research Resources/ Research/ Social Issues/ Social Services/ Older Adults/ Social Work/ Juvenile Delinquency/ Teenage Pregnancy

0878　**Pope, Jacqueline**
(1988) "Women and Welfare Reform." Black Scholar 19:3:pp. 22-30.

Women of Color*/ Public Policy / Public Welfare/ Children Living in Poverty/ Welfare Reform/ Women Living in Poverty/ Public Assistance

0879　**Powell, Gloria Johnson**
(1982) "The Effects of Television on the Self-Concept of Minority-Group Children." in Television and the Minority-Group Child. C. Mitchel-Kennan and A. Morales. Boston, MA: Addison-Wesley Publishers.

Women of Color*/ Self Concept/ Children/ Image/ Roles/ Stereotyping/ Television/ Mass Media/ Norms/ Adolescents/ Race, Class and Gender Studies

0880　**Price, Dorothy Z.**
Wilhelm, Mari. (1988) Socioeconomic Stress in Rural Families. New York: Human Sciences Press. pp. 81. ISBN 0898854342.

People of Color*/ Rural Areas/ Poverty/ Family/ Rural Women/ Socioeconomic Conditions/ Unemployment/ Employment/ Stress/ Rural Living

0881　**Richardson, Laurel**
Taylor, Verta (eds.). (1989) Feminist Frontiers II: Rethinking Sex, Gender and Society. New York: Random House, Inc. pp. 512.

Women of Color*/ Male Female Relationships/ Socialization/ Health Care Services/ Gender Roles/ Discrimination/ Stereotypes/ Victimization/ Family Roles/ Feminism/ Wage Gap

0882　**Rodgers, Harrell R., Jr.**
(1986) Poor Women, Poor Families: The Economic Plight of America's Female Headed Households. Armonk, NY: M. E. Sharpe. pp. 167.

Women of Color*/ Disadvantaged/ Wage Gap/ Public Policy/ Economic Value of Women's Work/ Women Living in Poverty/ Economic Status/ Female Headed Households/ Family/ Families

0883　**Simon, Barbara Levy**
(1987) Never Married Women. Philadelphia: Temple University Press. pp. 198.

Women of Color*/ Life Styles/ Singles/ Spinsters/ Single Women/ Marital Status/ Images of Women/ Family Structure/ Home Life

0884　**Sullivan, Deborah A.**
Weitz, Rose. (1988) Labor Pains: Modern Midwives and Home Birth. New Haven, CT: Yale University Press. pp. 256. ISBN 0300040938.

Women of Color*/ Maternal and Infant Welfare/ Reproductive Health/ Home Birth/ Childbirth/ Birthing/ Health Care Services/ Midwifery/ Health Care Practitioners/ Pregnancy/ Health

0885 **U.S. Department of Commerce**
(1987) "Who's Minding the Kids?: Child Care Arrangement, Winter 1984-85." Current Population Report. Household and Economic Studies Series P-70, #9. Available: U.S. Government Printing Office, Washington, D.C.

Women of Color*/ Child Care/ Balancing Work and Family Life/ Employment/ Mothers Working Outside the Home/ Women Working Outside the Home/ 1980-1989

0886 **Whelehan, Patricia**
et al. (1988) <u>Women and Health: Cross Cultural Perspectives</u>. Granby, MA: Bergin and Garvey. pp. 304. ISBN 0897891392.

Women's Studies/ Anthropology/ Health Care Services/ Family Structure/ Politics/ Women of Color*/ Social Movements/ Cross Cultural Studies/ Stress/ Economics/ Comparative Studies

0887 **Zepeda, Marlene**
Espinosa, Michael. (1988) "Parental Knowledge of Children's Behavioral Capabilities: A Study of Low Income Parents." <u>Hispanic Journal of Behavioral Sciences</u> 10(June):2:pp. 149-159.

People of Color*/ Child Development/ Parent Child Relationships/ Comparative Studies/ Low Income Households/ Behavior/ Parenting/ Parental Attitudes

HEALTH

African American

0888 Allen, Larve Marie
(1986) "Perceptions of Problematic Behavior of Southern Female Black Fundamentalists and Mental Health Professionals." in Women, Health, and Culture. Phyllis Noerager Stern (ed.). New York: Hemisphere.

African American/ Religion/ Mental Health/ Women of Color/ South/ Fundamentalism/ Therapy/ Deviant Behavior/ Perceptual Bias

0889 Amaro, Hortensia D.
Beckman, L. J. et al. (1987) "A Comparison of Black and White Women Entering Alcoholism Treatment." Journal of the Studies of Alcohol 48:3:pp. 220-228.

Women of Color/ Comparative Studies/ African American/ Alcoholism/ Treatment/ Alcohol Treatment/ Alcohol Abuse/ Health/ European American

0890 Avery, Byllye
(1989) "Black Women's Health: A Conspiracy of Silence." Sojourner 14(January):5:pp. 15-16.

African American/ Teenage Pregnancy/ Women of Color/ Violence/ Health Care Services/ Prenatal Care/ Health Care Facilities/ Health Care Delivery/ Discrimination/ Disadvantaged/ Health Education

0891 Beardsley, Edward H.
(1987) A History of Neglect: Health Care for Blacks and Mill Workers in the Twentieth Century. Knoxville: University of Tennessee Press. pp. 383. ISBN 0870495232.

People of Color/ Health Care Services/ African Americans/ South/ Health Care/ Work Hazards/ Physicians/ 20th Century/ Poverty/ Diseases/ Health Care Delivery/ Factory Workers/ Textile Industry

0892 Brown, Diane Robinson
Gary, Lawrence E. (1987) "Stressful Life Events, Social Support Networks and the Physical and Mental Health of Urban Black Adults." Journal of Human Stress 13(Winter):4:pp. 165-174.

People of Color/ Support Systems/ African Americans/ Networks/ Urban Areas/ Physical Health/ Health/ Illness. Mental Health/ Stress/ Psychological Stress/ Coping Strategies

0893 Brown, Diane Robinson
(1988) "Employment and Health among Older Black Women: Implications for Their Employment Status." Available: Working Papers #177, Wellesley College Center For Research On Women, Wellesley, MA.

African American/ Health Care/ European American/ Women of Color/ Employment/ Status/ Middle Aged Adults/ Health/ Older Adults/ Employment Opportunity

0894 Brown, Diane Robinson
Thomas, Veronica G. et al. (1988) "Social Support and Depressive Symptoms among

Blacks." The Journal of Black Psychology 14(February):2:pp. 35-45.

Support Systems/ Networks/ Depression/ African Americans/ Health/ Illness/ Mental Health/ People of Color

0895 Brown, Diane Robinson
Gary, Lawrence E. (1988) "Unemployment and Psychological Distress among Black American Women." Sociological Focus 21(August):3:pp. 209-221.

Unemployment/ Illness/ Wellness/ Psychological Stress/ Mental Health/ Women of Color/ African American/ Stress

0896 Brown, Prudence
(1977) "Sex Role Attitudes and Psychological Outcomes for Black and White Women Experiencing Marital Dissolution." Journal of Marriage and the Family 39(August):pp. 549-562.

Women of Color/ African American/ Sex Role Behavior/ Mental Health/ Emotional Adjustment/ Separation/ Divorce/ Family Conflict/ European American/ Marriage

0897 Christmas, J. J.
(1984) "Black Women and Health Care in the 80's." Spelman Messenger 100(Spring):1:pp. 8-11.

Women of Color/ African American/ Physical Health/ Health Care Utilization/ Disadvantaged/ Health Care Delivery/ Race, Class and Gender Studies/ Mental Health

0898 Cope, Nancy R.
Mall, Howard. (1987) "Risk Factors Associated with the Health Status of Black Women in the U.S." in Health Care Issues in Black America. Woodrow Jones and Mitchell F. Rice (eds.). Westport, CT: Greenwood Press. pp. 272.

Women of Color/ Illness/ Wellness/ African American/ Health Care/ Health Hazards/ Community Health Services

0899 Covington, Jeanette
(1987) "Race, Crime and Feminism." Presented: American Sociological Association, Chicago, IL. August. Available: Department of Sociology, Rutgers University, New Brunswick, NJ.

African American/ Women of Color/ Heroin Addiction/ Feminism/ Life Styles/ Subculture/ Treatment/ Deviant Behavior/ Health

0900 Creighton-Zollar, Ann
Jude, Cynthia. (1987) "Race, Class and Infant Mortality in Richmond Virginia, 1979-1981." Proceedings of the Alpha Kappa Delta Research Symposium. Available: Dept. of Sociology and Anthropology, Virginia Commonwealth University, Richmond, VA.

People of Color/ 20th Century/ African Americans/ Living Conditions/ Race/ Poverty/ Social Inequality/ Social Class/ Social Indicators/ Infant Mortality/ Health/ Children/ South/ Virginia

0901 Day-Nawabi, Lumumba
(1986) "Dua Afe: Whole Women, Inc." Woman of Power (Fall):4:pp. 70-71.

Women of Color/ African American/ Midwifery/ Childbirth Training/ Natural Childbirth/ Folk Medicine/ South

0902 Dhooper, Sarijit S.
Dyars, Lauretta F. (1989) "Stress and Life Satisfaction of Black Social Workers." AFFILIA: Journal of Women and Social Work 4(Spring):1:pp. 70-78.

Social Workers/ Balancing Work and Family Life/ Stress/ Mental Health/ Satisfaction/ African American/ Women of Color/ Employment

0903 **Freeman, Anderson Clarke**
(1982) "Life Stress and Depression in Lower Socio-Economic Black Females."
Dissertation: Michigan State University, Lansing, MI.
African American/ Women of Color/ Mental Health/ Depression/ Stress/ Economic Factors/
Socioeconomic Status/ Low Income Households/ Women Living in Poverty/ Poverty/ Disadvantaged

0904 **Giele, Janet Zollinger**
Gilfus, Mary. (1988) "Race and Cohort Differences in Women's Life Patterns, 1934-
1982." Presented: American Sociological Association. August.
African American/ Family Roles/ European American/ Career Opportunities/ Higher Education/
Education/ Labor Force Participation/ Life Cycles/ Gender Roles/ Women of Color/ Socialization

0905 **Gilman, Sander L.**
(1985) "Black Bodies White Bodies: Toward an Iconography of Female Sexuality in
Late Nineteenth-Century Art, Medicine and Literature." Critical Inquiry
12(Autumn):1.
African American/ Women of Color/ Art Symbols/ Images of Women/ Sexuality/ Popular Culture/ Social
History/ 19th Century/ Literary Arts/ Medical Sciences/ Iconography

0906 **Jackson, Beryl Bernice H.**
(1982) "Life Satisfaction of Black Climacteric Women in Relation to Specific Life
Events." Dissertation: University of Pittsburgh, Pittsburgh, PA. DAI Vol.
43(10A)3440.
African American/ Middle Aged Adults/ Life Cycles/ Menopause/ Satisfaction/ Women of Color/ Home
Life

0907 **Jerrido, Margaret**
(1979) "Black Women Physicians: A Triple Burden." Alumnae News (The Medical
College of Pennsylvania) 30(Summer):1:pp. 4-5.
African American/ Women of Color/ Physicians/ Medical Sciences/ Health Care Occupations/ Male
Dominated Employment/ Race, Class and Gender Studies/ Professional Status/ Triple Jeopardy

0908 **Jerrido, Margaret**
(1981) "Early Black Women Physicians." Women and Health 5(Fall):3:pp. 1-3.
African American/ Women of Color/ History/ 19th Century/ Health Care Occupations/ Physicians/
Biographies/ Medical Sciences/ Professional Status/ Race, Class and Gender Studies/ Medical Education

0909 **Johnson, E. F.**
(1978) "Look at It this Way: Some Aspects of the Drug Mix-Up Problem among
Blacks, Poor, Aged and Female Patients." Journal of the National Medical
Association 70:11:pp. 745-747.
Women of Color/ African American/ Disadvantaged Persons/ Social Economic Conditions/ Aging/ Older
Adults/ Senior Citizens/ Drugs/ Health

0910 **Lightfoot, Sara Lawrence**
(1988) Balm in Gilead: Journey of a Healer. Reading, MA: Addison-Wesley.
African American/ Sex Discrimination/ Women of Color/ Career Aspirations/ Health Care/ Psychiatry/
Child Development/ Biographies

0911 **Malveaux, Julianne M.**
Englander, Susan. (1986) "Race and Class in Nursing Occupations." SAGE: A
Scholarly Journal on Black Women 3(Spring):1:pp. 41-45.
Women of Color/ African American/ Race, Class and Gender Studies/ Health Care Occupations/
Nursing/ Health Care Workers/ Community Health Services

0912   **Martin, Cortez Hezekiah**
(1984) "The Relationship between Level of Self-Concept and Drinking Patterns of Black Youths." Dissertation: Howard University, School of Social Work, Washington, D.C. pp. 130. DAI Vol. 46(02A)521.

African American/ Tennessee/ South/ Drinking/ Self Concept/ Teenagers/ Adolescents/ Self Esteem/ Women of Color/ Deviant Behavior/ Health

0913   **Mays, Vickie M.**
(1987) "Acquired Immune Deficiency and Black Americans: Special Considerations." Public Health Reports 102:2:pp. 224-231.

People of Color/ Sexually Transmitted Diseases/ African Americans/ Health Care/ Health/ Illness/ Diseases/ Acquired Immune Deficiency Syndrome/ Sexual Behavior

0914   **Mays, Vickie M.**
(1988) "The Interpretation of AIDS Risk and AIDS Risk Reduction by Black and Hispanic Women." American Psychologist 43:11.

Women of Color/ Acquired Immune Deficiency Syndrome/ Chicana/ Latina/ Sexually Transmitted Diseases/ African American/ Illness/ Health/ Health Education/ Diseases/ Health Seeking Behavior/ Sexual Behavior/ Intimacy

0915   **Mays, Vickie M.**
Cochran, S. D. (1988) "The Black Woman's Relationship Project: A National Survey of Black Lesbians." in A Sourcebook of Gay/ Lesbian Health Care. M. Shernoff (ed.). Washington, D.C.: National Gay and Lesbian Health Foundation.

Women of Color/ Relationships/ African American/ Health Care/ Lesbians/ Life Styles/ Lesbian Culture

0916   **Meleis, Afaf Ibrahim**
Sorrell, Leila. (1981) "Arab American Women and their Birth Experiences." The American Journal of Maternal Child Nursing 6(May/June):3:pp. 171.

African American/ Women of Color/ Arab/ Birthing/ Maternal and Infant Welfare/ Cultural Influences/ Health Care Delivery/ Family/ Families

0917   **Morse, D. W.**
(1976) "Aging in the Ghetto: Themes Expressed by Older Black Men and Women Living in a Northern Industrial City." Industrial Gerontology 3:pp. 1-10.

Women of Color/ Gerontology/ African American/ Urban Areas/ North/ Age/ Life Cycles/ Older Adults/ Ghettos/ Senior Citizens

0918   **National Black Women's Health Project**
(1985) "Health Fact Sheet on Black Women." SAGE: A Scholarly Journal on Black Women 2(Fall):2:pp. 76-77.

Women of Color/ Health Care/ Health Care Utilization/ Poverty/ Racial Factors/ Mental Health/ African American/ Economic Factors/ Disadvantaged/ Social Factors

0919   **Omolade, Barbara**
(1987) It's A Family Affair: The Real Lives of Black Single Mothers. Latham, NY: Kitchen Table Press (Freedom Organizing Pamphlet #4).

Women of Color/ Health Care/ African American/ Female Headed Households/ Single Parent Families/ Single Mothers/ Networks/ Kinship

0920   **Rogler, Lloyd H.**
(1981) "Unitas: Hispanic and Black Children in a Healing Community."

Monograph #6, Hispanic Research Center, Fordham University, Bronx, NY.

People of Color/ Community Care/ Latinos/ Community Health Services/ African Americans/ Comparative Studies/ Treatment/ Health Care

0921 **Snow, Loudell**
(1977) "Popular Medicine in a Black Neighborhood." in <u>Ethnic Medicine in the Southwest</u>. Edward H. Spicer (ed.) Tucson, AZ: University of Arizona Press.

Women of Color/ South West/ African American/ Help Seeking Behavior/ Health Care/ Medical Sciences/ Cultural Influences/ Neighborhoods/ Life Styles/ Folk Medicine/ Coping Strategies/ Home Remedies

0922 **Taylor, S. P.**
(1982) "Mental Health and Successful Coping among Aged Black Women." in <u>Minority Aging: Sociological and Social Psychological Issues</u>. R. C. Manuel (ed.). Westport, CT: Greenwood Press.

Women of Color/ African American/ Mental Health/ Aging/ Older Adults/ Coping Strategies

0923 **Wolf, Jacquelyn H.**
(1985) "Professionalizing Volunteer Work in a Black Neighborhood." <u>Social Science Review</u> 59(September):3:pp. 423-434.

African Americans/ People of Color/ Neighborhoods/ Physical Health/ Urban Areas/ Older Adults/ Aging/ Volunteers/ Volunteer Work/ Community

Asian American

0924 **Cabanilla, Gerardo**
(1982) "Health and Ethnomedicine: Implications of Alternative Health Care of Philipinos." Asian American Women Research Project, University of California-Los Angeles, Asian American Studies Center, Los Angeles, CA.

Asian/ Women of Color/ Philipinos/ Health Care Delivery/ Family/ Roles/ Health/ Illness/ Folk Medicine/ Health Seeking Behavior/ Cultural Influences

0925 **Calhoun, Mary Atchity**
(1986) "The Vietnamese Woman: Health/Illness Attitudes and Behaviors." in <u>Women, Health, and Culture</u>. Phyllis Noerager Stern. New York: Hemisphere.

Asian American/ Vietnamese/ Women of Color/ Illness/ Wellness/ Health Seeking Behavior/ Cultural Influences/ Attitudes/ Racial and Ethnic Differences

0926 **Cerroni-Long, E. L.**
(1982) "The Curative Use of Japanese 'New Religions' by Los Angeles Japanese Americans." Working Paper #7, University of California Los Angeles Asian American Studies Center, Los Angeles, CA.

Japanese American/ Family/ Asian American/ Folk Medicine/ Roles/ Women of Color/ Religions/ Health Care Delivery/ Health/ Illness

0927 **Fujii, S.**
(1980) "Elderly Pacific Island and Asian-American Women: A Frame-work for Understanding." in <u>Conference on the Educational and Occupational Needs of Asian-Pacific-American Women</u>. M. Timpane (ed.). Washington, D.C.: U.S. Government Printing Office.

Asian Pacific American/ Asian American/ Women of Color/ Pacific Islander/ Older Adults/ Aging/ Senior Citizens/ Elderly Care/ Health

0928   **Hauser, Vivian**
(1979) <u>Civil Rights Issues of Asian and Pacific Americans: Myths and Realities</u>.
Washington, D.C.: U.S. Government Printing Office.
Asian American/ Asian Pacific American/ Civil Rights/ Mental Health/ Health Care Delivery/ Racial
Equality/ Women of Color

0929   **Nelson, Claire Christopherson**
Hewitt, Margaret A. (1983) "An Indo Chinese Refugee Population in a Nurse-
Midwife Service." <u>Journal of Nurse-Midwifery</u> 28(September/October):5.
Women of Color/ Asian/ Midwifery/ Health Care Facilities/ Immigrants/ Refugees/ Maternal and
Infant Welfare/ Health Seeking Behavior

0930   **So, Alvin Y.**
Ito, Karen L. (1982) "The Perception of Gender and Ethnic Group Health Problems
by Asian American Doctors." Working paper #8. Health Care Alternatives of
Asian American Women Project, University of California Los Angeles Asian
American Studies Center, Los Angeles, CA.
Physical Health/ Mental Health/ Asian American/ Women of Color/ Physicians/ Ethnic Studies/
Gender/ Cultural Influences/ Health Care Delivery/ Health Care Providers

0931   **Takamura, Jeanette C.**
(1985) "Trouble and the Use of Informal Support Systems: A Case of the Japanese
Americans in Hawaii." Dissertation: Brandeis University, Heller Graduate School
for Advanced Studies in Social Welfare, Waltham, MA. DAI Vol. 46(03A)805.
Support Systems/ Japanese Americans/ Asian American/ Hawaii/ Pacific/ People of Color/ Coping
Strategies/ Networks/ Mental Health

0932   **Yanagida, E.**
Marsella, A. J. (1978) "The Relationship Between Depression and Self Concept
Discrepancy among Different Generations of Japanese-American Women." <u>Journal of
Clinical Psychology</u> 34:3:pp. 654-659.
Asian American/ Self Concept/ Women of Color/ Cultural Identity/ Japanese American/ Depression/
Mental Health/ Assimilation Patterns/ Emotional States

Latina

0933   **Alvarez, M.**
(1985) "Health Conditions of Mexican Women Immigrants: A Review of the
Literature." <u>Border Health</u> 1:3:pp. 48-52.
Women of Color/ Border Studies/ Latino/ Mexicans/ Immigrants/ Low Income Households/ Health Care
Costs/ Health Care Services/ Cultural Influences

0934   **Angel, Ronald J.**
Worobey, Jacqueline Lowe. (1988) "Single Motherhood and Children's Health."
<u>Journal of Health and Social Behavior</u> 29(March):1:pp. 38-52.
Women of Color/ Latina/ Marital Status/ Single Mothers/ Children/ Physical Health/ Health Seeking
Behavior/ Maternal and Infant Welfare/ Female Headed Households

0935   **Baezconde-Garbanati, Lourdes**
Salgado de Snyder, V. Nelly. (1987) "Mexican Immigrant Women: A Selected
Bibliography." <u>Hispanic Journal of Behavioral Sciences</u> 9(September):3:pp. 331-
358.
Women of Color/ Latina/ Mental Health/ Bibliographies/ Mexican/ Research Resources/ Immigrants

0936 Burgess, Norma J.
Howard, Don. (1988) "Alcohol and Substance Use among Native-Born Versus American-Born Mexican Origin Women in the U.S." Author: Dept. of Sociology and Anthropology, Mississippi State University, P. O. Drawer C, Mississippi State, MS 39762.

Alcoholism/ Chemical Dependency/ Alcohol Abuse/ Mexican/ Women of Color/ Substance Abuse/ Latina/ Chicana/ Women of Color/ Drug Addiction/ Comparative Studies/ Health

0937 Caetano, Raul
(1986) "Alternative Definitions of Hispanics: Consequences in an Alcohol Survey." Hispanic Journal of Behavioral Sciences 8:4:pp. 331-343.

Women of Color/ Health Care/ Latina/ Unemployment/ Alcohol Abuse/ Socioeconomic Status/ Lower Class

0938 Chavez, L. R.
Cornelius, W. and Jones, O. W. (1985) "Perinatal Care among Mexican Women in the U.S." Border Health 1:3:pp. 2-6.

Women of Color/ Family Planning/ Latina/ Mexican/ Health Seeking Behavior/ Prenatal Care/ Border Studies/ Health Care/ Maternal and Infant Welfare/ Immigrants/ Pregnancy

0939 Cosminsky, Sheila
(1978) "Midwifery and Medical Anthropology." in Modern Medicine and Medical Anthropology in the U. S.-Mexico Border Population. B. Velimirovic. Washington: Pan American Health Organization Scientific Publication #359.

Women of Color/ Border Studies/ Midwifery/ Midwives/ Childbirth/ Birthing/ Medical Anthropology/ Maternal and Infant Welfare/ Physical Health/ Chicana/ Latina/ Mexican/ Health Care Providers/ Folk Medicine

0940 Gilbert, M. Jean
(1987) "Alcohol Consumption Patterns in Immigrant and Later Generation Mexican-American Women." Hispanic Journal of Behavioral Sciences 9(September):3:pp. 299-314.

Women of Color/ Latina/ Chicana/ Alcohol Abuse/ Drug Rehabilitation/ Immigrants/ Comparative Studies/ Drinking/ Health

0941 Harwood, A.
(1981) "Puerto Rican Americans." in Ethnicity and Medical Care. A. Harwood. Cambridge: Harvard University Press.

Puerto Ricans/ Folk Medicine/ Latinos/ People of Color/ Health Seeking Behavior/ Nervousness/ Mental Health/ Health Care Providers/ Cultural Influences

0942 Lopez, Iris
(1987) "Extended Views: Social Coercion and Sterilization among Puerto Rican Women." SAGE: A Scholarly Journal on Black Women 8(August).

Women of Color/ Birth Control/ Latina/ Puerto Rican/ Health Care Costs/ Sterilization/ Migration/ Population Control/ Women Living in Poverty/ Demography

0943 Low, Setha M.
(1981) "The Meaning of Nervios." Culture, Medicine and Psychiatry 5:pp. 350-357.

Puerto Rican/ Latina/ Women of Color/ Nervousness/ Mental Health/ Physical Health/ Cultural Influences

0944   Low, Setha M.
(1984) "The Biomedical Response to Nervios." Author: Department of Landscape Architecture and Regional Planning, University of Pennsylvania, Philadelphia, PA 19104.

Puerto Rican/ Latina/ Women of Color/ Nervousness/ Mental Health/ Physical Health/ Cultural Influences/ Health Care Providers/ Medical Sciences

0945   Low, Setha M.
(1985) "Culturally Interpreted Symptoms or Culture-Bound Syndromes: A Cross-Cultural Review of Nerves." Social Science and Medicine 21:2:pp. 187-196.

Puerto Ricans/ Kentucky/ South/ Latinos/ People of Color/ Appalachia/ Poverty/ Nervousness/ Folk Medicine/ Lower Class/ Mental Health/ Physical Health/ Home Remedies/ Cultural Influences/ New York/ North East/ Health Seeking Behavior/ Comparative Studies

0946   Mays, Vickie M.
(1988) "The Interpretation of AIDS Risk and AIDS Risk Reduction by Black and Hispanic Women." American Psychologist 43:11.

Women of Color/ Acquired Immune Deficiency Syndrome/ Chicana/ Latina/ Sexually Transmitted Diseases/ African American/ Illness/ Diseases/ Health Seeking Behavior/ Sexual Behavior

0947   Perez, Robert G.
(1983) "Effects of Stress, Social Support and Coping Style on Adjustment to Pregnancy among Hispanic Women." Hispanic Journal of Behavioral Sciences 5:2:pp. 141-161.

Women of Color/ Health Care Services/ Latina/ Childbirth/ Childbearing/ Stress/ Support Systems/ Coping Strategies/ Pregnancy

0948   Rogler, Lloyd H.
(1981) "Unitas: Hispanic and Black Children in a Healing Community." Monograph #6, Hispanic Research Center, Fordham University, Bronx, NY.

People of Color/ Community Care/ Latinos/ Community Health Services/ African Americans/ Comparative Studies/ Treatment/ Health Care

0949   Rogler, Lloyd H.
Canino, Ian and Earley, Brian F. (1980) "The Puerto Rican Child in New York City: Stress and Mental Health." Monograph # 4,
Hispanic Research Center, Fordham University, Bronx, NY.

People of Color/ New York/ North East/ Latinos/ Puerto Ricans/ Coping Strategies/ Adolescents/ Mental Health/ Psychological Stress/ Children

0950   Salgado de Snyder, V. Nelly
(1987) "Factors Associated with Acculturative Stress and Depressive Symptomatology among Married Mexican Women." Psychology of Women Quarterly 11:4.

Women of Color/ Mental Health/ Latina/ Mexicans/ Wives/ Acculturation Process/ Stress/ Depression/ Immigration

0951   Sanchez, Carmen Delia
(1984) "Strengthening the Informal Support System of the Hispanic Elderly: Group Program for Caregivers and Potential Caregivers." Dissertation: City University of New York, New York, NY. pp. 285. DAI Vol. 45(07A)2258.

Support Systems/ Latinos/ Older Adults/ People of Color/ Coping Strategies/ Aging/ Caregivers/ Health

0952   **Shapiro, J.**
Tittle, K. (1986) "Psychosocial Adjustment of Poor Mexican Mothers of Disabled and Nondisabled Children." <u>American Journal of Orthopsychiatry</u> 56:2:pp. 289-302.

Women of Color/ Psychological Adjustment/ Latina/ Mexican/ Social Adjustment/ Support Systems/ Disabilities/ Children/ Coping Strategies/ Poverty/ Stress/ Mental Health

0953   **Shirley, Beatrice Zanger**
(1981) "A Study of Ego Strength: The Case of the Hispanic Immigrant Woman in the United States." Dissertation: Boston University School of Education, Boston, MA. pp. 192. DAI Vol. 42(06A)2583.

Immigrants/ Latina/ Women of Color/ Psychology/ Self Esteem/ Acculturation/ Mental Health

0954   **Vargas-Willis, Gloria**
Cervantes, Richard C. (1987) "Consideration of Psychosocial Stress in the Treatment of the Latina Immigrant." <u>Hispanic Journal of Behavioral Sciences</u> 9(September):3:pp. 315-330.

Women of Color/ Stress/ Latina/ Psychological Adjustment/ Immigrants/ Mental Health Treatment/ Psychological Stress/ Acculturation

0955   **Vega, W.**
Kolody, B. and Valle, J. (1986) "The Relationship of Marital Status Confidant Support and Depression among Mexican Immigrant Women." <u>Journal of Marriage and the Family</u> 48:3:pp. 597-605.

Women of Color/ Immigrants/ Latina/ Mexicans/ Mental Disorders/ Marital Status/ Support Systems/ Depression/ Mental Health

0956   **Vega, W.**
Kolody, B. et al. (1986) "Depressive Symptoms and Their Correlates among Immigrant Mexican Women in the U.S." <u>Social Science and Medicine</u> 22:6:pp. 645-652.

Women of Color/ Latina/ Mexicans/ Depression/ Mental Health/ Mental Disorders/ Immigrants

0957   **Williams, Mary Willson**
(1984) "Sex Role Orientation: A Cross Cultural Study of Sex Role Strain." Dissertation: University of New Mexico, Albuquerque, NM. DAI Vol. 45(08A)2075.

Latina/ Mental Health/ Sex Roles/ Sex Role Conflict/ Crosscultural Studies/ European American/ Women of Color/ Sex Role Development/ Cultural Influences

0958   **Zambrana, Ruth E.**
Merino, Rolando, and Santana, Sara (eds.). (1979) "Puerto Rican Elderly and Their Use of Health Services." in <u>Ethnicity and Aging</u>. D. Gelfand and A. Kutzik. New York: Springer. pp. 308-319.

Puerto Ricans/ Latinos/ People of Color/ Older Adults/ Health Care/ Health Services/ Health Seeking Behavior

0959   **Zambrana, Ruth E.**
Aquirre-Molina, Marilyn. (1987) "Alcohol Abuse Prevention among Latino Adolescents: A Strategy for Intervention." <u>Journal of Youth and Adolescence</u> 16:2:pp. 97-113.

Women of Color/ Latina/ Alcohol Abuse/ Treatment/ Drug Rehabilitation/ Adolescents/ Health

Native American

0960 **Begay, Shirley**
(1983) <u>Kinnaalda: A Navajo Puberty Ceremony</u>. Rough Rock, AZ: Navajo Curriculum Center.

Women of Color/ Native American/ Navajo/ Religious Practices/ Spiritualism/ Life Cycles/ Physical Development/ Cultural Heritage

0961 **Dillingham, Brint**
(1977) "Indian Women and IMS Sterilization Practices." <u>American Indian Journal</u> 3:1:pp. 27-28.

Women of Color/ Native American/ Fertility/ Sterilization/ Population Planning/ Contraception/ Reproductive Health/ Anthropology/ Rites/ Ceremonies/ Religious Acts/ Sex Roles

0962 **Jones, David E.**
(1987) <u>Sanapia: Comanche Medicine Women</u>. Prospect Heights, IL: Waveland. pp. 107.

Native American/ Comanche/ Women of Color/ Folk Medicine/ Folk Healer/ Medical Anthropology/ Health Care Providers/ Cultural Heritage/ Biographies/ Traditions/ Rites

0963 **Kunitz, Stephen J.**
Slocumb, John C. (1976) "The Use of Surgery to Avoid Childbearing among Navajo and Hopi Indians." <u>Human Biology</u> 48:pp. 9-21.

Women of Color/ Native American/ Navajo/ Fertility/ Sterilization/ Health/ Childbearing/ Surgery/ Contraception/ Medical Sciences/ Hopi

0964 **Larson, Janet Karsten**
(1977) "And then There Were None: Is Federal Policy Endangering the American Indian Species." <u>Christian Century</u> 94(January):26:pp. 61-63.

Women of Color/ Native American/ Fertility/ Sterilization/ Policies/ Population Planning/ Population Control/ Public Policy/ Reproductive Health

0965 **Mathes, Valerie Sherer**
(1982) "Susan La Flesche Picotte: Nebraska's Indian Physician, 1865-1950." <u>Nebraska History</u> 64(Winter):4:pp. 502-530.

Native American/ Physicians/ Biographies/ Women's History/ 19th Century/ Susan La Flesche Picotte/ Nebraska/ North Central/ Women of Color/ Health Care Providers/ Education

0966 **May, Philip**
(1983) "Epidemiology of Fetal Alcohol Syndrome among American Indians of the Southwest." <u>Social Biology</u> 30(Winter):pp. 374-387.

Native American/ Alcohol Abuse/ Fetal Alcohol Syndrome/ Childbirth/ Mothers/ South West/ Women of Color/ Maternal and Infant Welfare/ Epidemiology/ Health Care

0967 **Milligan, B. Carol**
(1984) "Nursing Care and Beliefs of Expectant Navajo Women, Parts I and II." <u>American Indian Quarterly</u> 7(Spring/ Summer):3-4:pp. 83.

Women of Color/ Acculturation Process/ Native American/ Navajo/ Assimilation Patterns/ Childbirth/ Maternal and Infant Welfare/ Health Care/ Cultural Influences/ Physical Health/ Pregnancy

0968 **Wright, Anne L.**
(1982) "An Ethnography of the Navajo Reproductive Cycle." <u>American Indian</u>

<u>Quarterly</u> 6(Spring/Summer):1-2:pp. 52-70.

Women of Color/ Acculturation/ Menstruation/ Menopause/ Fertility/ Ethnography/ Native American/ Navajo/ Reproductive Cycle/ Reproductive Health

Southern

0969   Allen, Larve Marie
(1986)   "Perceptions of Problematic Behavior of Southern Female Black Fundamentalists and Mental Health Professionals." in <u>Women, Health, and Culture</u>. Phyllis Noerager Stern. New York: Hemisphere.

African American/ Religion/ Mental Health/ Women of Color/ South/ Fundamentalism/ Therapy/ Deviant Behavior/ Perceptual Bias

0970   Beardsley, Edward H.
(1987)   <u>A History of Neglect: Health Care for Blacks and Mill Workers in the Twentieth Century</u>. Knoxville, TN: University of Tennessee Press. pp. 383. ISBN 0870495232.

People of Color/ Health Care Services/ African Americans/ South/ Health Care/ Work Hazards/ Physicians/ 20th Century/ Poverty/ Diseases/ Health Care Delivery/ Factory Workers/ Textile Industry

0971   Creighton-Zollar, Ann
Jude, Cynthia. (1987) "Race, Class and Infant Mortality in Richmond Virginia, 1979-1981."   Proceedings of the Alpha Kappa Delta Research Symposium. Available: Dept. of Sociology and Anthropology, Virginia Commonwealth University, Richmond, VA.

People of Color/ 20th Century/ African Americans/ Living Conditions/ Race/ Poverty/ Social Inequality/ Social Class/ Social Indicators/ Infant Mortality/ Health/ Children/ South/ Virginia

0972   Kenig, Sylvia
(1987) "Gaining Turf but Losing Ground: A Critique of Southern Nursing." <u>Frontiers: A Journal of Women Studies</u> 9:3:pp. 64-70.

Women of Color*/ Employment/ South/ Roles/ Female Intensive Occupations/ Nursing/ Health Care Providers/ Health Care Occupations

0973   Low, Setha M.
(1985) "Culturally Interpreted Symptoms or Culture-Bound Syndromes: A Cross-Cultural Review of Nerves." <u>Social Science and Medicine</u> 21:2:pp. 187-196.

Puerto Ricans/ Kentucky/ South/ Latinos/ People of Color/ Appalachia/ Poverty/ Nervousness/ Folk Medicine/ Lower Class/ Mental Health/ Physical Health/ Home Remedies/ Cultural Influences/ New York/ North East/ Health Seeking Behavior/ Comparative Studies

0974   Martin, Cortez Hezekiah
(1984) "The Relationship Between Level of Self-Concept and Drinking Patterns of Black Youths." Dissertation: Howard University, School of Social Work, Washington, D.C. pp. 130. DAI Vol. 46(02A)521.

African American/ Tennessee/ South/ Drinking/ Self Concept/ Teenagers/ Adolescents/ Self Esteem/ Women of Color/ Deviant Behavior/ Health

0975 **Meachen, Sarah**
Kelley, S. and Rond, P. (1988) "Barriers to Prenatal Care for Low-Income Women in Florida." Presented: Society for the Study of Social Problems, Annual Meeting, Atlanta, GA.
South/ Florida/ Prenatal Care/ Women of Color*/ Women's Studies/ Discrimination/ Childbearing/ Low Income Households/ Maternal and Infant Welfare/ Health Care Providers/ Health Care Delivery/ Poverty/ Disadvantaged

0976 **Roberts, Peggy**
(1988) "A Death in the Family." Southern Exposure 16(Winter):4:pp. 61-63.
South/ Health Care Services/ Alabama/ Prenatal Care/ Infant Mortality/ Maternal and Infant Welfare/ Death/ Medicaid/ Poverty/ Welfare

0977 **Tretter, Evelyn Kerr**
(1988) "Doctor Woman." The Tennessee Conservationist 54(Nov/Dec):6:pp. 18-22.
South/ Tennessee/ History/ 20th Century/ Health Care Providers/ Physicians/ Poverty/ Basic Human Needs/ Hospitals/ Health Care Facilities

0978 **Ward, Martha C.**
(1986) Poor Women, Powerful Men: America's Great Experiment in Family Planning. Boulder, CO: Westview Press. pp. 188. ISBN 0813303672.
Women of Color/ Health Education/ African American/ Childbirth/ South/ Infant Mortality/ Women Living in Poverty/ Family Planning/ Health Care Facilities/ Power/ Powerlessness/ Health Care Services

0979 **Weitzel, S. L.**
Blount, W. R. (1982) "Incarcerated Female Felons and Substance Abuse." Journal of Drug Issues 12(Summer):3:pp. 259-273.
Women of Color*/ South/ Prisoners/ Correctional Facilities/ Drug Abuse/ Substance Abuse/ Health

*Women of Color**

0980 **Baskin, David**
Nelson, M. (1980) "Clinical Diagnosis: New Light on Ethnic Differences." Presented: Annual Conference of the American Psychological Association, Montreal, Canada.
Women of Color*/ Mental Health Treatment/ Comparative Studies/ Diagnoses/ Race Bias/ Racial and Ethnic Differences

0981 **Chavkin, Wendy**
(1984) Double Exposure: Women's Health Hazards on the Job and at Home. New York: Monthly Review Press. pp. 288.
Race, Class and Gender Studies/ Workers/ Health Hazards/ Health/ Factory Conditions/ Electronics Industry/ Reproductive Hazards at Work/ Nursing/ Occupational Health/ Farms/ Employment/ Women of Color*

0982 **Chunn, Jay**
Dunston, Patricia and Ross-Sheriff, F. (eds.). (1988) Mental Health and People of Color: Curriculum Development and Change. Washington, D.C.: Howard University Press.
Mental Health/ People of Color*/ Curriculum Integration/ Education/ Change/ Teaching

0983 Dworkin, Rosalind J.
Poindexter, Alfred N. (1980) "Abortion Seeking Behavior Among Low-Income Women: Comparisons of Public Surveys and Group Behavior." Presented: Southwest Sociological Association Annual Meeting.

Low Income Families/ Help Seeking Behavior/ Abortion/ Health/ Medical Procedures/ Surveys/ Group Behavior/ South/ Texas/ Women of Color*

0984 Gibbs, Jewelle Taylor
(1986) "Psychosocial Correlates of Sexual Attitudes and Behaviors in Urban Early Adolescent Females: Implications for Intervention." Journal of Social Work and Human Sexuality 5(Fall/Winter):1:pp. 81-97.

Women of Color*/ Urban/ Adolescents/ Sexual Behavior/ Psychological Factors/ Counseling/ Health/ Sexuality

0985 Gibbs, Jewelle Taylor
(1982) "Psychosocial Factors Related to Substance Abuse among Delinquent Females: Implications for Prevention and Treatment." American Journal of Orthopsychiatry 52:2.

Women of Color*/ Substance Abuse/ Treatment/ Delinquent Behavior/ Crime Prevention/ Social Influences/ Psychological Factors/ Health

0986 Gibbs, Jewelle Taylor
(1985) "Psychosocial Factors Associated with Depression in Urban Adolescent Females." Journal of Youth and Adolescence 14:1.

Women of Color* / Social Influences/ Psychological Factors/ Depression/ Adolescents/ Urban/ Mental Health

0987 Heckler, M. M.
(1985) "Black and Minority Health: Report of the Secretary's Task Force." U.S. Department of Health and Human Services, Washington, D.C.

Women of Color*/ Health Care/ Health Care Utilization/ Mental Health/ Government Services/ Race, Class and Gender Studies/ Disadvantaged Persons/ Economic Status

0988 Ho, Man Keung
(1987) Family Therapy with Ethnic Minorities. Newbury Park: Sage Publication. pp. 320.

Therapy/ Diversity/ Cultural Influences/ Mental Health/ Treatment/ Family Relationships/ Women of Color*/ Racial and Ethnic Differences

0989 Jewell, Karen Sue
(1987) "Divorced Women's Use of Institutional and Noninstitutional Counseling Services: An Exploratory Study." Available: Ohio Department of Mental Health, Columbus, OH.

Women of Color*/ Drug Abuse/ Health/ Treatment/ Comparative Studies/ Counseling/ Conflict Resolution/ Divorce Rates/ Women Living in Poverty/ Delinquency/ Female Headed Households/ Alcoholism/ Support Systems

0990 Loring, Marti
Powell, Brian. (1988) "Gender, Race, and DSM III - A Study of the Objectivity of Psychiatric Diagnostic Behavior." Journal of Health and Social Behavior 29(March):1:pp. 1-22.

Women of Color*/ Diagnoses/ Stereotyping/ Gender Bias/ Race Bias/ Mental Health Treatment/ Racial Factors/ Objectivity/ Race, Class and Gender Studies/ Mental Health

0991 Manuel, R. C.
(1982) <u>Minority Aging: Sociological and Social Psychological Issues</u>. Westport, CT: Greenwood Press.

Health Care/ Women of Color*/ Older Adults/ Aging/ Cultural Influences/ Comparative Studies/ Life Cycles/ Self Concept/ Social Psychology

0992 Markides, Kyriakos S.
Mindel, Charles H. (1987) <u>Aging and Ethnicity</u>. Newbury Park, CA: Sage Publication.

People of Color*/ Life Cycles/ Cultural Influences/ Older Adults/ Aging/ Racial and Ethnic Differences/ Ethnicity/ Comparative Studies

0993 McLanahan, Sara
Garfinkel, Irwin. (1989) "Single Mothers, the Underclass, and Social Policy." <u>The Annuals</u> 501(Jan):pp. 92-104.

Female Headed Households/ Socioeconomic Status/ Single Mothers/ Race, Class and Gender Studies/ Women Living in Poverty/ Child Care/ Health/ Women of Color*/ Income Distribution/ Poverty/ Unemployment/ Social Policy/ Family/ Families/ Welfare Programs

0994 Meachen, Sarah
Kelley, S. and Rond, P. (1988) "Barriers to Perinatal Care for Low-Income Women in Florida." Presented: Society for the Study of Social Problems Annual Meeting.

South/ Florida/ Prenatal Care/ Women of Color*/ Women's Studies/ Discrimination/ Childbearing/ Low Income Households/ Maternal and Infant Welfare/ Health Care Providers/ Health Care Delivery/ Poverty/ Disadvantaged

0995 Nussbaum, Karen
(1984) "The 9 to 5 National Survey on Women and Stress." Available: 9 to 5 National Association of Working Women, 614 Superior Ave., NW, Cleveland, OH 44113. pp. 55.

Women of Color*/ Coping Strategies/ Support Systems/ Occupational Health/ Race, Class and Gender Studies/ Employment/ Comparative Studies/ Clerical Occupations/ Working Class/ Mental Health/ Stress

0996 Richardson, Laurel
Taylor, Verta (eds.). (1989) <u>Feminist Frontiers II: Rethinking Sex, Gender and Society</u>. New York: Random House, Inc. pp. 512.

Women of Color*/ Male Female Relationships/ Socialization/ Health Care Services/ Gender Roles/ Discrimination/ Stereotypes/ Victimization/ Family Roles/ Feminism/ Wage Gap

0997 Rix, Sara E.
(1988) <u>The American Woman 1988-89: A Status Report</u>. New York: W. Norton. (Edited for Women's Research and Education Institute)

Women of Color*/ Employment/ Social Trends/ Women's Roles/ Demography/ Educational Attainment/ Social Status/ Women in Politics/ Research Resources/ Health/ Illness/ Socioeconomic Indicators/ Occupational Segregation

0998 Rond, Philip C. III
Kelley, Susan D. M. and Meachen, S. (1988) "Prenatal Care Outreach for Low Income Women." Presented: Society for the Study of Social Problems Annual Meeting, Atlanta, GA.

Pregnancy/ Maternal and Infant Welfare/ Women's Studies/ Health Care Delivery/ Health Care Facilities/ Low Income Households/ Welfare/ Women of Color*/ Single Parents/ Mothers/ Prenatal Care

0999   Ruzek, Sheryl B.
(1986) "Integrating Minority Women's Health into the Curriculum." in Teaching Materials on Women, Health and Healing. Adele Clark et al. Women Health and Healing Project, University of California, San Francisco, CA. pp. 35-43.
Women of Color*/ Curriculum Integration/ Health/ Women's Health Movement/ Higher Education/ Teaching

1000   Ruzek, Sheryl B.
(1988) "Race, Class and Gender Issues in Reproductive Health." Presented: American Sociological Association Annual Meetings, Atlanta, GA.
Race, Class and Gender Studies/ Women of Color*/ Physical Health/ Reproductive Health/ Women's Health Movement

1001   Ruzek, Sheryl B.
(1988) "Women's Health: Sisterhood is Powerful, But So Are Race and Class." Presented: Southeastern Women's Studies Association Annual Meetings, Chapel Hill, NC. February.
Sisterhood/ Health/ Women of Color*/ Race, Class and Gender Studies

1002   Sullivan, Deborah A.
Weitz, Rose. (1988) Labor Pains: Modern Midwives and Home Birth. New Haven, CT: Yale University Press. pp. 256. ISBN 0300040938.
Women of Color*/ Maternal and Infant Welfare/ Reproductive Health/ Home Birth/ Childbirth/ Birthing/ Health Care Services/ Midwifery/ Health Care Practitioners/ Pregnancy/ Health

1003   Twin, Stephanie L.
(1986) Out of the Bleachers: Writings on Women and Sport. New York: Feminist Press. pp. 272.
Women of Color*/ Equal Opportunity/ Physical Health/ Women's Athletics/ Competitive Behavior/ Sports/ Education/ History/ Athletes

1004   U.S. Department of Health and Human Services
(1984) Minorities and Women in the Health Fields: Health Resources and Services Administration. Washington, D.C.: U.S. Government Printing Offices. pp. 191.
Women of Color*/ Health Care Professionals/ Employment/ Health Care Occupations/ 1980-1989/ Professional Status/ Health Care Workers/ Female Intensive Occupations

1005   U.S. Department of Health and Human Services
(1976) "Health Characteristics of Minority Groups, U.S 1976." U.S. Department of Health, Education and Welfare, Washington, D.C.
Health Care/ Comparative Studies/ Ethnicity/ Physical Health/ Mental Health/ Illness/ Wellness/ People of Color*

1006   Weick, Ann
Vandiver, Susan T. (eds.). (1982) Women, Power, and Change. Silver Spring, MD: National Association of Social Workers. pp. 214. ISBN 0871010925.
Women of Color*/ Change/ Living Conditions/ Counseling/ Social Services/ Mental Health/ Social Work/ Crisis Intervention/ Power

1007   Weitzel, S. L.
Blount, W. R. (1982) "Incarcerated Female Felons and Substance Abuse." Journal of Drug Issues 12(Summer):3:pp. 259-273.
Women of Color*/ South/ Prisoners/ Correctional Facilities/ Drug Abuse/ Substance Abuse/ Health

1008   **Whelehan, Patricia**
et al. (1988) <u>Women and Health: Cross Cultural Perspectives</u>. Granby, MA: Bergin and Garvey. pp. 304. ISBN 0897891392.
Women's Studies/ Anthropology/ Health Care Services/ Family Structure/ Politics/ Women of Color*/ Social Movements/ Cross Cultural Studies/ Stress/ Economics/ Comparative Studies

POLITICAL ACTIVISM/ SOCIAL MOVEMENTS

African American

1009   Anderson, Alan B.
Pickering, George W. (1987) <u>Confronting the Color Line: The Broken Promise of the Civil Rights Movement in Chicago</u>. Athens, GA: University of Georgia Press.
People of Color/ Illinois/ North Central/ Civil Rights Movement/ African Americans/ Racial Equality/ Segregation/ Racial Discrimination/ Social Change

1010   Aptheker, Herbert
(1987) "American Negro Slave Revolts: Fifty Years Gone." <u>Science and Society</u> 51(Spring):pp. 68-72.
Slaves/ Social History/ 19th Century/ Revolution/ African Americans/ People of Color/ Slavery/ Liberation Struggles

1011   Belknap, Michal R.
(1987) <u>Federal Law and Southern Order: Racial Violence and Constitutional Conflict in Post-Brown South</u>. Athens, GA: University of Georgia Press.
People of Color/ South/ African Americans/ History/ 1960-1969/ Violence/ Federal Legislation/ Race Relations/ Racial Discrimination/ Desegregation/ Social Movements

1012   Bell, Derrick
(1987) <u>And We Are Not Saved: The Elusive Quest for Racial Justice</u>. New York: Basic Books. pp. 288.
People of Color/ Racial Discrimination/ African Americans/ Civil Rights Movement/ Racial Equality/ Justice/ Economic Factors

1013   Berry, Mary Frances
Blassingame, John W. (1982) "Sex and Racism." in <u>Long Memory: The Black Experience in America</u>. Mary Frances Berry and John W. Blassingame. New York: Oxford University Press. pp. 114-141.
Women of Color/ Racial Discrimination/ SexDiscrimination/ African American/ Prejudice/ Bias/ Liberation Struggles

1014   Blumberg, Rhoda Lois
(1988) <u>Civil Rights: The 1960's Freedom Struggle</u>. Boston: Twayne Publishers. ISBN 0805797084.
Black Studies/ Civil Rights Movement/ People of Color/ Social History/ 1960-1969/ African Americans/ Social Movements/ Social Change

1015   Brady, Mary Dell
(1986) "Kansas Federation of Colored Women's Clubs, 1900-1930." <u>Kansas History</u> 9(Spring):pp. 19-30.
Women of Color/ Kansas/ African American/ North Central/ History/ 20th Century/ Social Movements/ Women's Organizations/ Women's Groups/ Voluntary Organizations/ Clubs

1016   Brewer, Rose M.
(1988) "The Women's Movement through the Prism of Gender, Race, and Class."
Presented: American Sociological Association Annual Meeting, Atlanta, GA.
August.

African American/ Feminist Theory/ Women of Color/ Inequality/ Feminism/ Race, Class and Gender
Studies/ Women's Movement

1017   Brown, Cynthia Stokes
(1986) <u>Ready from Within: Septima Clark and the Civil Rights Movement</u>.
Navarro, CA: Wild Trees Press. pp. 134.

Women of Color/ African American/ Civil Rights Movement/ Political Activism/ Social Change/ Social
Movements/ Biographies/ Resistance/ Septima Clark

1018   Bryan, Louis C.
(1986) "Modjeska A. Simkins: Profile of a Legend." <u>SAGE: A Scholarly Journal on
Black Women</u> 3(Spring):1:pp. 56-57.

Women of Color/ South/ African American/ Biographies/ Human Rights/ Modjeska Simkins/ Political
Activism/ Political Power/ Elected Officials

1019   Bryan, Violet Harrington
(1986) "Frances Joseph-Gaudet: Black Philanthropist." <u>SAGE: A Scholarly Journal
on Black Women</u> 3(Spring):1:pp. 46-49.

Women of Color/ African American/ Biographies/ History/ South/ Philanthropists/ Reformers/ Social
Movements/ Frances Joseph-Gaudet

1020   Bulkin, Elly
Pratt, Minnie Bruce and Smith, Barbara. (1984) <u>Yours In Struggle -- Three Feminist
Perspectives on Anti-Semitism and Racism</u>. Ithaca, NY: Firebrand Books. pp. 240.
ISBN 0932379532.

Women of Color/ Religious Factors/ African American/ Religion/ South/ Feminist Perspective/ Racial
Discrimination/ Liberation Struggles/ Jews

1021   Callahan, Nancy
(1987) <u>The Freedom Quilting Bee</u>. Tuscaloosa, AL: University of Alabama Press.
pp. 253.

Women of Color/ African American/ Women Living in Poverty/ South/ Alabama/ Rural Areas/
Biographies/ Quilting/ Craft Arts/ Civil Rights Movement/ Cooperatives/ Self Help/ Advocacy Groups

1022   Carby, Hazel V.
(1986) "It Jus Bes Dat Way Sometime: The Sexual Politics of Women's Blues."
<u>Radical America</u> 20:4:pp. 9-24.

African American/ Women of Color/ Music/ Blues/ Sexual Politics/ Activism

1023   Carter, Deborah
(1988) "The Local Labor Union as a Social Movement Organization: Local 282,
Furniture Division, IUE; 1943-1988." Dissertation: Vanderbilt University,
Nashville, TN.

African American/ Employee Benefits/ Women of Color/ Wage Gap/ Pay Equity/ South/ Labor Unions/
Labor Force/ Employment/ Labor History/ Economically Disadvantaged/ Social Movements/ Gender
Roles/ Furniture/ Manufacturing Industry

1024   Catlin, Robert A.
(1985) "Organizational Effectiveness and Black Political Participation: The Case

of Katie Hall." Phylon 46(Sept):pp. 179-192.

Organizing/ Power/ Influence/ Politics/ Political Participation/ Katie Hall/ Women of Color/ African
American/ Activism

1025 Chittenden, Elizabeth
(1975) "As We Climb: Mary Church Terrell." Negro History Bulletin
38(February/March):pp. 351-354.

Activists/ Women's History/ Biographies/ African American/ Leadership/ Women of Color/ Mary C.
Terrell

1026 Church, Roberta
(1989) "Mary Church Terrell." in Homespun Images: An Anthology of Black
Memphis Writers and Artists. Miriam DeCosta-Willis et al. (eds.). Memphis, TN:
LeMoyne-Owen College. pp. 46-48.

African American/ History/ 20th Century/ Women of Color/ Suffrage Movement/ Tennessee/ South/
Liberation Struggles/ Women's Groups/ Segregation/ Education/ Voluntary Organizations/ Equality/
Social Movements/ Biographies/ Mary C. Terrell

1027 Coalition for Publishers for Employment
(1987) Turning the World Upside Down: The Anti-Slavery Convention of American
Women Held in New York City, May 9-12, 1837. New York: The Feminist Press. pp.
32. ISBN 0935312781.

Interracial Relations/ Women of Color/ African American/ Slavery/ History/ 19th Century/ New York/
East/ Social Movements

1028 Colby, Ira C.
(1985) "The Freedmen's Bureau: From Social Welfare to Segregation." Phylon
46(September):pp. 219-230.

Social Welfare/ Social History/ 19th Century/ Segregation/ Freedmen/ South/ People of Color/ African
Americans/ Liberation Struggles

1029 Cruse, Harold Wright
(1980) Plural But Equal. New York: Quill Publishers (William Morrow and Co.).
pp. 420. ISBN 0688083315.

African American/ Civil Rights Movement/ South/ Social Movements/ 20th Century/ History/ Women
of Color/ Equality/ Racial Discrimination

1030 Davis, Angela Y.
(1983) Women, Race, and Class. New York: Vintage. pp. 271.

Women of Color/ Race, Class and Gender Studies/ Social Movements/ Bias/ Prejudice/ Social Change/
Discrimination/ African American/ Slavery/ Suffrage/ Women's Rights/ Women's History/ Voluntary
Organizations

1031 Dedman, Bill
(1988) "The Color of Money." Southern Exposure 16(Winter):4:pp. 56-59.

People of Color/ Housing/ Mortgages/ Economy/ Real Estate/ Neighborhoods/ Economic Power/ South/
Georgia/ Money/ Banks/ Redlining/ Discrimination/ African Americans/ Liberation Struggles

1032 Diggs, Irene
(1974) "Du Bois, and Women: A Short Story of Black Women, 1910-1934." A Current
Bibliography on African Affairs 7(Summer):3.

African American/ History/ 20th Century/ Women of Color/ Women's Rights/ Social Movements

1033   **Dorn, Edwin**
(1979) <u>Rules and Racial Equality</u>. New Haven, CT: Yale University Press.
Women of Color/ African American/ Education/ Employment/ Civil Rights/ Equality/ Inequality/ Discrimination/ Social Change

1034   **Engs, Robert Francis**
(1979) <u>Freedom's First Generation: Black Hampton, Virginia, 1861-1890</u>.
Philadelphia, PA: University of Pennsylvania Press.
Virginia/ South/ 19th Century/ History/ African American/ Women of Color/ Liberation Struggles

1035   **Fairclough, Adam**
(1987) <u>To Redeem the Soul of America: The Southern Christian Leadership Conference and Martin Luther King, Jr</u>. Athens, GA: University of Georgia Press.
People of Color/ Racial Discrimination/ African Americans/ Social Movements/ Civil Rights Movement/ Religion/ South/ Racial Equality/ Nonviolence/ Protest Actions

1036   **Fullinwider, Robert K.**
Mills, Claudia (eds.). (1986) <u>The Moral Foundations of Civil Rights</u>. Totowa, NJ: Rowman and Littlefield Publishers.
African American/ Social Movements/ Women of Color/ Civil Rights/ Social Change/ Ethic of Care/ Morality

1037   **Gilkes, Cheryl Townsend**
(1986) "The Role of Women in the Sanctified Church." <u>Journal of Religious Thought</u> 43:1.
African American/ Women of Color/ Religion/ Sex Role Behavior/ Churches/ Sex Roles/ Activism

1038   **Gilkes, Cheryl Townsend**
(1988) "Agency and Situation: Toward a Theoretical Perspective on Afro-American Woman and Social Change." Presented: Society for the Study of Social Problems Annual Meeting, Atlanta, GA.
African American/ Women of Color/ Social Change/ Activism/ Social Theory/ Feminist Theory/ Theories

1039   **Gilkes, Cheryl Townsend**
(1988) "Building in Many Places: Multiple Commitments and Ideologies in Black Women's Community Work" in <u>Women and the Politics of Empowerment: Perspectives from Communities and Workplaces</u>. Ann Bookman and Sandra Morgen. Philadelphia: Temple University Press.
African American/ Empowerment/ Activism/ Women of Color/ Community/ Time Management/ Organizing

1040   **Gordon, Vivian V.**
(1984) <u>Black Women, Feminism and Black Liberation: Which Way?</u> Chicago: Third World Press. pp. 59.
Women of Color/ African American/ Feminism/ Liberation Struggles/ Black Feminism/ Social Movements

1041   **Griffin, Jean Thomas**
(1986) "Black Women's Experience as Authority Figures in Groups." <u>Women's Studies Quarterly</u> 14(Spring/Summer):1-2:pp. 7-12.
Women of Color/ African American/ Authority/ Leadership/ Racial Discrimination/ Sex Discrimination/ Stereotypes/ Groups/ Activism

1042   Hamilton, Tullia Kay Brown
(1978) "The National Association of Colored Women, 1896 to 1920." Dissertation: Emory University, Atlanta, GA. DAI Vol. 40(01A)405.

African American/ Women's History/ Voluntary Organizations/ Women's Organizations/ 19th Century/ 20th Century/ Suffrage/ Women of Color/ Social Movements

1043   Harding, Vincent
(1988) The Other American Revolution. Los Angeles, CA: University of California Los Angeles Center for Afro-American Studies. pp. 261.

People of Color/ Racial Equality/ African Americans/ Race Relations/ Civil Rights Movement/ Oppression/ History/ Equal Rights/ Resistance/ Liberation Struggles/ Racial Discrimination

1044   Headley, Bernard D.
(1985) "Black Political Empowerment and Urban Crime." Phylon 46(September):pp. 193-204.

Politics/ Activism/ Crime/ Political Influence/ Urban Areas/ African Americans/ People of Color/ Empowerment

1045   Hill-Davidson, Leslie
(1987) "Black Women's Leadership: Challenges and Strategies." SIGNS: Journal of Women in Culture and Society 12(Winter):2:pp. 381-383. (Report on symposium held at the University of North Carolina, Spring, 1986.).

Women of Color/ Racial Discrimination/ African American/ Sex Discrimination/ Leadership/ Integration/ Feminism/ Social Movements

1046   Howard-Filler, Saralee R.
(1987) "A Place Called Safety: Detroit's Underground Railroad and the Museum of African American History." Michigan History 71(March/April):pp. 28-31.

Museums/ Liberation Struggles/ African Americans/ North Central/ Michigan/ Underground Railroad/ History/ 19th Century/ People of Color

1047   Hughes, C. Alvin
(1987) "We Demand Our Rights: The Southern Negro Youth Congress, 1937-1949." Phylon 48(March):pp. 38-50.

People of Color/ Racial Equality/ African Americans/ Liberation Struggles/ South/ 20th Century/ Equal Rights/ Civil Rights

1048   Humez, Jean McMahon
(1987) Gifts of Power: The Writings of Rebecca Jackson, Black Visionary, Shaker Eldress. Amherst, MA: University of Massachusetts Press. pp. 376. ISBN 0870235656.

Women of Color/ African American/ Power/ Activism/ Images of Women/ Religion/ 19th Century/ Women's History/ Rebecca Jackson

1049   Jackson, George F.
(1988) Black Women Makers of History: A Portrait. Available: National Women's History Project, Santa Rosa, CA 95402. pp. 202.

Women of Color/ Research Resources/ African American/ Women's History/ Slavery/ Living Conditions/ Biographies/ Social Movements

1050   Jacobs, Claude F.
(1988) "Benevolent Societies of New Orleans Blacks during the Late Nineteenth

and Early Twentieth Century." <u>Louisiana History</u> 29(Winter):pp. 21-33.

People of Color/ 20th Century/ African Americans/ Louisiana/ South/ Societies/ Organizations/ 19th Century/ History/ Voluntary Organizations/ Social Movements

1051 Jewell, Karen Sue
(1985) "Will the Real, Black, Afro-American, Mixed, Colored, Negro Please Stand Up." <u>Journal of Black Studies</u> 16(September):1:pp. 57-75.

Women of Color/ African American/ Social Movements/ Black Movement/ Institutional Racism/ Affirmative Action/ Cultural Identity/ Social Perception/ Images of Women/ Stereotypes/ Social Change

1052 Johnson, Mrs. A. E.
(1988) <u>Clarence and Corinne; or God's Way</u>. New York: Oxford University Press. pp. 240. ISBN 0195052641.

19th Century/ Novels/ Writers/ Social Problems/ Women of Color/ Alcoholism/ African American/ Family/ Women's Movement/ Social Reform

1053 Jones, Jacqueline
(1986) "The Uneasy Alliance of Feminism and Black Nationalism: Theoretical Considerations for Historians of Afro-American Women." Presented: Annual Meeting of Southern Historical Association, Charlotte, NC.

Women of Color/ Nationalist Movements/ African American/ Nationalism/ Feminism/ Women's Movement/ European American/ History/ 20th Century/ Social Change/ Black Feminism

1054 King, Deborah Karyn
(1988) "Multiple Jeopardy, Multiple Consciousness: The Context of a Black Feminist Ideology." <u>SIGNS: Journal of Women in Culture and Society</u> 14(Autumn):1:pp. 42-72.

Women of Color/ African American/ Feminist Theory/ Race, Class and Gender Studies/ Black Feminism/ Discrimination/ Double Bind/ Triple Jeopardy/ Socioeconomic Status/ Social Movements/ Political Activism

1055 King, Mary
(1988) <u>Freedom Song</u>. New York: Quill Publishers (William and Morrow Co.). pp. 592. ISBN 0688082513.

African Americans/ Class Differences/ History/ Civil Rights Movement/ 1960-1969/ Social History/ 20th Century/ South/ People of Color/ Discrimination/ Social Change/ European American

1056 Lang, Dwight
(1987) "Stratification and Prestige Hierarchies in Graduate and Professional Education." <u>Sociological Inquiry</u> 57(Winter):1:pp. 12-27.

Women of Color/ Stratification/ African American/ Status/ Prestige/ Race, Class and Gender Studies/ Civil Rights Movement/ Higher Education/ Financial Aid/ Graduate Degrees/ Academic Rank/ Academic Standards

1057 Litwack, Leon F.
Meier, August (eds.). (1988) <u>Black Leaders of the 19th Century</u>. Champaign, IL: University of Illinois Press.

Women of Color/ African American/ Biographies/ History/ 19th Century/ Essays/ Social Movements

1058 Lukas, J. Anthony
(1986) <u>Common Ground: A Turbulent Decade in the Lives of Three American Families</u>. New York: Random House. pp. 676. ISBN 0394746163.

Women of Color/ African American/ Class Differences/ Class Consciousness/ School Desegregation/ Desegregation Methods/ Busing/ Family/ Social Movements

1059   Mabee, Carleton
(1988) "Sojourner Truth, Bold Prophet: Why Did She Never Learn to Read." New York History 69(Jan):pp. 55-77.

Women of Color/ Slavery/ Slaves/ African American/ History/ 19th Century/ Orators/ Social Movements/ Women's History/ Liberation Struggles/ Biographies/ Sojourner Truth

1060   Manis, Andrew Michael
(1987) Southern Civil Religions in Conflict: Black and White Baptists and Civil Rights, 1947-1957. Athens, GA: University of Georgia Press.

People of Color/ Race Relations/ African Americans/ South/ 1950-1959/ Civil Rights Movement/ History/ 1940-1949/ Comparative Studies/ European Americans/ Social Conflict/ Religion/ Churches

1061   Mariam, A. G.
(1989) "The Declining Enrollment of Blacks in Higher Education." The Institute for Urban Research, Morgan State University "Research Notes" 5(Winter):1:pp. 5-6.

African Americans/ Inequality/ Higher Education/ Discrimination/ Colleges/ Universities/ People of Color/ Academic Achievement/ Racial Discrimination/ Civil Rights Movement

1062   Martin, Sandy
(1986) "Black Baptist Women and African Missionary Work, 1870-1925" SAGE: A Scholarly Journal on Black Women 3(Spring):1:pp. 16-19.

Women of Color/ Social Movements/ African American/ Social Influences/ History/ 19th Century/ Churches/ Religious Factors/ Missionary Societies/ Religion

1063   Mohr, Clarence L.
(1987) On the Threshold of Freedom: Masters and Slaves in Civil War Georgia. Athens, GA: University of Georgia Press.

People of Color/ South/ Georgia/ African Americans/ History/ 19th Century/ Slavery/ Slaves/ Civil War/ European Americans/ Relationships/ Liberation Struggles

1064   Neverdon-Morton, Cynthia
(1978) "The Black Woman's Struggle for Equality in the South." in The Afro-American Woman: Struggles and Images. Sharon Harley and Rosalyn Terborg-Penn. Port Washington, NY: Kennikat Press.

African American/ South/ Equality/ Women of Color/ Women's Movement/ Social Movements/ Liberation Struggles

1065   Neverdon-Morton, Cynthia
(1989) Afro-American Women of the South and the Advancement of the Race, 1985-1925. Knoxville, TN: University of Tennessee Press.

African American/ Liberation Struggles/ Women of Color/ Civil Rights/ South/ Human Rights/ Race Relations/ Social Movements/ Social History/ Teachers/ Racial Discrimination/ Professional Occupations

1066   O'Reilley, Kenneth
(1987) "The Roosevelt Administration and Black America: Federal Surveillance Policy and Civil Rights During the New Deal and World War II Years." Phylon 48(March):pp. 12-25.

People of Color/ Federal Government/ African Americans/ Roosevelt Administration/ Civil Rights Movement/ World War II/ History/ Freedom of Speech

1067   Okihiro, Gary Y.
(1986) In Resistance: Studies in African, Caribbean, and Afro-American History.

Amherst, MA: University of Massachusetts Press. pp. 240.

Women of Color/ African American/ Resistance/ Slavery/ History/ Oppression/ Caribbean/ Liberation Struggles

1068 Painter, Nell Irvin
(1987) "Race and Disenfranchisement." in <u>Standing at Armageddon: The United States, 1877-1919</u>. Nell Irvin Painter. New York: Norton. pp. 216-230. ISBN 0393024059.

Social Conditions/ African American/ Enfranchisement/ Women of Color/ Antilynching Campaign/ Violence/ Voluntary Organizations/ Club Women/ Women's Groups/ Civil Rights Movement

1069 Parish, Peter
(1988) <u>Slavery</u>. New York: Harper and Row. pp. 144. ISBN 0064370011.

Slavery/ Slaves/ Business/ Exploitation/ Life Styles/ History/ 19th Century/ African Americans/ People of Color/ Liberation Struggles

1070 Peebles-Wilkins, Wilma
(1989) "Black Women and American Social Welfare: Life of Fredericka Douglass Sprague Perry." <u>AFFILIA: Journal of Women and Social Work</u> 4(Spring):1:pp. 33-44.

African American/ Social Welfare/ Women of Color/ Fredericka Douglass Sprague Perry/ Social Change/ Social Movements

1071 Powers, Bernard Edward, Jr.
(1982) "Black Charleston: A Social History 1822-1885." Dissertation: Northwestern University, Evanston, IL. pp. 452. DAI Vol. 43(06A)2057.

African Americans/ People of Color/ South/ South Carolina/ Social History/ 19th Century/ Liberation Struggles

1072 Reed, Christopher Robert
(1988) "Organized Racial Reform in Chicago During the Progressive Era: The Chicago NAACP, 1910-1920." <u>Michigan Historical Review</u> 14(Spring):pp. 75-99.

People of Color/ African Americans/ Racial Equality/ Illinois/ North Central/ History/ 1910-1919/ Reforms/ Social Movements/ Advocacy Groups

1073 Richardson, Joe M.
(1987) <u>Christian Reconstruction: The American Missionary Association and Southern Blacks, 1861-1890</u>. Athens, GA: University of Georgia Press.

People of Color/ Civil War/ African Americans/ History/ 19th Century/ South/ Slavery/ Reconstruction/ Missionary Societies/ Social Movements

1074 Richardson, Marilyn
(1987) <u>Essays and Speeches: Maria W. Stewart, America's First Black Woman Political Writer</u>. Bloomington, IN: Indiana University Press. pp. 160.

Women of Color/ African American/ Writers/ Essays/ Speeches/ Politics/ Maria W. Stewart/ Social Movements

1075 Rogers, Kim Lacy
(1988) "Oral History and the History of the Civil Rights Movement." <u>The Journal of American History</u> 75(September):2:pp. 567-576.

People of Color/ Social Movements/ African Americans/ Political Activism/ Civil Rights Movement/ Oral History/ Narratives/ Testimonial Literature

1076   **Ross, B. Joyce**
(1975) "Mary McLeod Bethune and the National Youth Administration: A Case Study of Power Relationships in the Black Cabinet of Franklin D. Roosevelt." The Journal of Negro History (January).

African American/ Leadership/ Power/ Relationships/ History/ 20th Century/ 1930-1939/ 1940-1949/ Appointed Officials/ Women of Color/ Activists/ Mary McLeod Bethune

1077   **Salem, Dorothy C.**
(1986) "To Better Our World: Black Women in Organized Reform, 1890-1920." Dissertation: Kent State University, Kent, OH.

African American/ Women of Color/ History/ 1890-1899/ Reforms/ Reformers/ Social Movements

1078   **Schwarz, Philip J.**
(1988) Twice Condemned: Slaves and the Criminal Laws of Virginia, 1705-1865. Baton Rouge, LA: Louisiana State University Press.

People of Color/ South/ Virginia/ African Americans/ Slavery/ 18th Century/ Slaves/ 19th Century/ Rebellion/ Resistance/ Crime/ Laws/ Liberation Struggles

1079   **Sedgewick, Cathy**
Williams, Reba. (1976) "Black Women and the Equal Rights Amendment." Black Scholar 7(July-August):pp. 24-29.

African American/ Equal Rights Amendment/ Equality/ Social Movements/ Women of Color/ Black Feminism

1080   **Shakur, Assata**
(1987) Assata: An Autobiography. Chicago: Chicago Review. pp. 320.

African American/ Self Concept/ Correctional Rehabilitation/ Incarceration/ Women of Color/ Prisons/ Prisoners/ Criminal Justice/ Social Movements/ Political Activity/ Autobiographies/ Social Change

1081   **Sherman, Richard B.**
(1988) "'The Last Stand': The Fight for Racial Integrity in Virginia in the 1920's." Journal of Southern History 54(Feb): pp. 69-92.

People of Color/ Race Relations/ African Americans/ Racial Equality/ Virginia/ South/ History/ 1920-1929/ Integrity/ Social Reform/ Social Change/ Political Activism

1082   **Simson, Rennie Maria**
(1983) "The Afro-American Female: The Historical Content of the Construction of Sexual Identity." in The Power of Desire: The Politics of Sexuality. Ann Snitow, et al. New York: Monthly Review Press.

African American/ Sexual Politics/ Sex Identity/ Women of Color/ Sex Roles/ Social Movements

1083   **Smith, Amanda**
(1988) An Autobiography: The Story of the Lord's Dealings with Mrs. Amanda Smith the Colored Evangelist. New York: Oxford University Press. pp. 608.

Autobiographies/ Churches/ Women of Color/ Evangelists/ African American/ Evangelism/ Writers/ 19th Century/ Women Religious/ Religion/ Amanda Smith/ Religious Movements

1084   **Spelman, Elizabeth V.**
(1988) Inessential Women: Problems of Exclusion in Feminist Thought. Boston: Beacon Press. pp. 288.

African American/ Images of Women/ Women of Color/ Feminist Theory/ Lesbians/ Jewish/ Women's Movement/ Feminist Movement

1085   **Stewart, Maria W.**
Lee, Jarena and Foote, Julia A. J. et al. (1988) <u>Spiritual Narratives</u>. New York: Oxford University Press. pp. 496. ISBN 0195052668.
Women of Color/ Orators/ Autobiographies/ African American/ Public Speaking/ 19th Century/ Missionaries/ Religion/ Liberation Struggles/ Evangelists/ Christianity/ Women's History/ Personal Narratives

1086   **Terrell, Mary Church**
Baxter, Annette K. (ed.). (1980) <u>A Colored Woman in a White World</u>. Washington, D.C.: Ayer Co. ISBN 0405128614.
African American/ Social Movements/ Social Perception/ Women's History/ 20th Century/ Dominant Culture/ Women of Color/ Cultural Heritage

1087   **Washington, Patricia Lee**
(1978) "The Black Woman's Agenda: An Investigation into Strategies For Change." Dissertation: Arizona State University, Tempe, AZ. DAI Vol. 39(03A)1308.
African American/ Social Change/ Strategies/ Women of Color/ Social Movements

1088   **Wiggins, William H., Jr.**
(1988) <u>O Freedom! Afro-American Emancipation Celebrations</u>. Knoxville, TN: University of Tennessee Press. pp. 232. ISBN 0870495208.
People of Color/ History/ 19th Century/ African Americans/ Emancipation/ Slavery/ Festivals/ Celebrations/ Social Movements

1089   **Williams-Myers, A. J.**
(1988) "The African Presence in the Hudson River Valley: The Defining of Relationships between the Masters and the Slaves." <u>Afro-Americans in New York Life and History</u> 12(Jan):pp. 81-98.
People of Color/ African Americans/ Slavery/ Slaves/ Relationships/ New York/ North East/ History/ 19th Century/ Liberation Struggles

1090   **Wilson, Basil**
Green, Charles. (1988) "The Black Church and the Struggle for Community Empowerment in New York City." <u>Afro-Americans in New York Life and History</u> 12(Jan):pp. 51-79.
People of Color/ New York/ North East/ African Americans/ Power/ Churches/ Religion/ Community/ Empowerment/ Liberation Struggles

1091   **Winegarten, Ruthe**
Brewer, Rose, and Werden, Frieda. (1986) "A Documentary History of Black Texas Women." Author: Texas Women's History, Box 49084, Austin, TX 78765.
African American/ South West/ Texas/ Women of Color/ Employment/ Workers/ Women's History/ Documentaries/ Social Movements/ Social Change

1092   **Yancy, Dorothy Cowser**
(1986) "Dorothy Bolden, Organizer of Domestic Workers." <u>SAGE: A Scholarly Journal on Black Women</u> 3(Spring):1:pp. 53-55.
Women of Color/ African American/ History/ South/ Biographies/ Dorothy Bolden/ Domestic Services/ Household Labor/ Labor Unions/ Organizing/ Labor Movement/ Working Class

Asian American

1093 Chai, Alice Yun
(1981) "An Asian-American Woman's View of the Consciousness Raising Sessions."
Women's Studies Quarterly 9(Fall):3:p. 16.

Women of Color/ Women's Groups/ Asian American/ Educational Methods/ Consciousness Raising/ Feminist Movement

1094 Chan, Connie
(1986) "Teaching about Asian Women's Activism: The Poetry of Mila Aguilar."
Women's Studies Quarterly 14(Spring/ Summer):1-2:pp. 23-25.

Women of Color/ Asian American/ Poetry/ Literary Arts/ Political Activism/ Social Change/ Race, Class, and Gender Studies/ Sex Discrimination/ Labor Unions/ Factory Workers

1095 Chow, Esther N.
(1987) "The Development of Feminist Consciousness among Asian American Women." Gender & Society 1(September):3:pp. 284-300.

Women of Color/ Cultural Identity/ Asian American/ Consciousness Raising/ Feminist Movement/ Race, Class and Gender Studies/ Economic Factors

1096 Daniels, Roger
(1989) Asian America: Chinese and Japanese in the United States Since 1850.
Seattle: University of Washington Press. pp. 384.

People of Color/ History/ Bias/ Asian/ Chinese/ Japanese/ Social Construction of Reality/ Social History/ 19th Century/ 20th Century/ Objectivity/ Immigration/ Perception/ Asian American/ Social Movements/ Chinese American/ Japanese American

1097 Hart, Gail
(1986) "No Susie Wongs Here." Woman of Power 4(Fall):pp. 32.

Women of Color/ Racial Discrimination/ Asian American/ Prostitutes/ Images of Women/ Media Stereotyping/ Women's Movement

1098 Ho, Liang
(1982) "Asian-American Women: Identity and Role in the Women's Movement."
Heresies #15 4:3:pp. 60-61.

Asian American/ Feminism/ Women's Movement/ Stereotypes/ Identity/ Women's Roles/ Women of Color

1099 Loo, Chalsa
Ong, Paul. (1982) "Slaying Demons with a Sewing Needle: Feminist Issues for Chinatown's Women." Berkeley Journal of Sociology 27:pp. 77-88.

Women of Color/ Chinese American/ Feminism/ Feminist Perspectives/ Racial Discrimination/ Sex Discrimination/ Political Activism/ Asian American/ Textile Workers/ Employment/ Sewing/ Sewers

1100 Tsai, Shih-Shan Henry
(1986) The Chinese Experience in America. Bloomington, IN: Indiana University Press. pp. 223.

People of Color/ Political Activism/ Chinese Americans/ Demographic Factors/ Social History/ Immigrants/ Stereotypes/ Racial Discrimination/ Asian Americans

Latina

1101   Abalos, David T.
(1988) <u>Latinos in the United States: The Sacred and the Political</u>. Notre Dame, IN: University of Notre Dame Press. ISBN 0268012776.

Latinos/ People of Color/ Politics/ Activism/ Religion/ Political Participation/ Political Influence

1102   Castillo, Adelaida R. del
(1988) <u>Between Borders: Essays on Mexicana/Chicana History</u>. Encino, CA: Floricanto Press. pp. 300.

Mexican/ 19th Century/ Chicana/ Latina/ Women of Color/ Women's History/ Leadership/ Liberation Struggles

1103   Castillo, Adelaida R. del
Mora, Magdalena. (1980) "Sex, Nationality and Class: La Orbra Mexicana." in <u>Mexican Women in the United States: Struggles Past and Present</u>. Magdalena Mora and Adelaida R. del Castillo. Chicano Studies Research Center, University of California Los Angeles, Los Angeles, CA. pp. 1-4.

Latina/ Mexican/ Women of Color/ Women's History/ Race, Class and Gender Studies/ Discrimination/ Liberation Struggles

1104   Cecelski, David
(1988) "Flowers in the Desert Die." <u>Southern Exposure</u> 16(Winter):4:pp. 8-9.

South/ Migration/ Central America/ Latinos/ Immigration/ Public Policy/ People of Color/ Liberation Struggles

1105   Dubose, Louis
(1988) "Invisible City." <u>Southern Exposure</u> 16(Winter):4:pp. 24-26.

Salvadorans/ Central Americans/ Illegal Immigrants/ Latinos/ People of Color/ Demography/ Texas/ South West/ Networks/ Support Systems/ Refugees/ Immigrants/ Employment/ Activism

1106   Ferrer, Norma Valle
(1986) "Feminism and Its Influence on Women's Organizations in Puerto Rico." in <u>The Puerto Rican Woman</u>. Edna Acosta-Belen. New York: Praeger. pp. 38-50. ISBN 0030524660.

Puerto Rican/ Latina/ Feminism/ Women's Organizations/ Social Influences/ Women's Groups/ Women of Color/ Social Movements

1107   Garcia, F. Chris
(1988) <u>Latinos and the Political System</u>. Notre Dame, IN: University of Notre Dame Press. ISBN 0268012857.

Latinos/ Political Influence/ People of Color/ Political Factors/ Anthologies/ Politics/ Political Participation/ Political Power/ Activism

1108   Gelbspan, Ross
(1989) "The Death Squads in Houston." <u>Southern Exposure</u> 16(Winter):4:pp. 32-35.

Texas/ South West/ People of Color/ Salvadoran/ Latinos/ Central Americans/ Government/ Politics/ Activists/ International Relations/ Terrorism/ Death

1109   Hernandez, Isabel Pico De
(1986) "The History of Women's Struggle for Equality in Puerto Rico." in <u>The Puerto Rican Woman</u>. Edna Acosta-Belen. New York: Praeger. pp. 25-37. ISBN

0030524660.

Puerto Rican/ Latina/ Women's Movement/ Sexual Equality/ Social Change/ Women of Color

1110 Pottlitzer, Joanne
(1988) <u>Hispanic Theater in the United States and Puerto Rico</u>. New York: Ford Foundation. pp. 85. ISBN 091658433X.

Latinos/ Puerto Ricans/ Entertainment/ The Arts/ Theater/ Cultural Influences/ Poliltical Activism/ Political Influence/ People of Color

1111 Romero, Mary
"(1986) "Twice Protected? Assessing the Impact of Affirmative Action on Mexican American Women." <u>Ethnicity and Women</u> 5:pp. 135-156.

Latina/ Chicana/ Equal Opportunity/ Women of Color/ Affirmative Action/ Equal Rights/ Social Movements

1112 Ruiz, Vicki L.
(1985) "Obreras y Madres: Labor Activism among Mexican Women and Its Impact on the Family." in <u>La Mexicana/Chicana</u>, Renato Rosaldo Lecture Series Monograph, Vol. I. Tucson: University of AZ, Mexican American Studies and Research Center. pp. 19-38.

Latina/ Mexican/ Women of Color/ Family/ Employment/ Labor Movement/ Unions/ Activism/ Balancing Work and Family Life

1113 Salas, Elizabeth
(1985) "Chicanas in Mexican and U.S. History." Presented: Writing Women Back into History, Salt Lake City School District Conference. May.

Latina/ Mexican/ Women of Color/ Women's History/ Curriculum Integration/ Chicana/ Activism

1114 Salas, Elizabeth
(1985) "Latinas in American History." Presented: Hispanic Women's Conference, Salt Lake City, UT.

Latina/ Women of Color/ Women's History/ Curriculum Integration/ Activism

1115 San Miguel, Guadalupe, Jr.
(1987) <u>Let All of Them Take Heed: Americans and the Campaign for Equality in Texas, 1910-1981</u>. Austin, TX: University of Texas Press. pp. 278.

Women of Color/ Latina/ Chicana/ History/ 20th Century/ Equality/ Academic Freedom/ Social Movements/ Civil Rights/ Educational Equity

1116 Wells, Miriam
(1986) "Power Brokers and Ethnicity: The Rise of a Chicano Movement." <u>Aztlan</u> 17(Spring):pp. 47-77.

People of Color/ Chicanos/ Latinos/ Ethnicity/ Social Movements/ Power/ Consciousness Raising

1117 Winegarten, Ruthe
Brewer, Rose and Werden, Frieda. (1986) "A Documentary History of Black Texas Women." Author: Texas Women's History, Box 49084, Austin, TX 78765.

African American/ Chicana/ Latina/ South West/ Texas/ Women of Color/ Employment/ Workers/ Women's History/ Documentaries/ Social Movements/ Social Change

1118 Zamora, Emilio
(1980) "Sara Estela Ramirez: Una Rosa Roja en el Movimiento." in <u>Mexican Women in the US: Struggles Past and Present</u>. Magdalena Mora and Adelaida R. del

Castillo (eds.). Los Angeles: Chicano Studies Research Center, University of California Los Angeles. pp.163-169.

Latina/ Mexican/ Political Activity/ Women of Color/ Liberation Struggles/ Biographies/ Social Movements/ Sara Estela Ramirez

1119 **Zwerman, Gilda**
(1988) "Special Incapacitation: The Emergence of a New Correctional Facility for Women Political Prisoners." Social Justice 15:1:pp. 31-47.

Women of Color/ Human Rights Violations/ Latina/ Political Repression/ Reagan Administration/ Terrorism/ Legal Issues/ Freedom of Speech/ Prisons/ Civil Rights/ Political Prisoners/ Social Movements

Native American

1120 **Awiakta, Marilou**
(1988) "Rebirth of a Nation." Southern Style (Sept/Oct):pp. 12-13 Available: Whittle Publications, 505 Market St., Knoxville, TN 37902.

Native American/ Cherokee/ Women of Color/ Social Movements/ Oklahoma/ South West/ Leadership/ Cultural Heritage

1121 **Clifton, James A.**
(1987) "The Political Rhetoric of Indian History." Annals of Iowa 49(Summer/Fall):pp. 101-110.

People of Color/ Native Americans/ History/ Political Factors/ Politics/ Iowa/ North Central/ Social Movements

1122 **Gray, John S.**
(1986) "The Story of Mrs. Picotte-Galpin, A Sioux Heroine: Eagle Woman Becomes a Trader and Counsels for Peace." Montana 36(Summer):pp. 2-21.

Women of Color/ Native American/ Sioux/ Social Movements/ Women's Roles/ History/ Montana/ West/ Heroines/ Picotte-Galpin

1123 **La Duke, Winona**
(1986) "Interview with Roberta Blackgoat, Dine' Elder." Woman of Power (Fall):4:pp. 29-31.

Women of Color/ Social Change/ Native American/ Dine'/ Cultural Identity/ Leadership/ Cultural Influence/ Social Movements/ Relocation/ Protest Actions/ Roberta Blackgoat/ Social Action

1124 **Olguin, Rocky**
(1981) "Listening to Native American Women." Heresies #13 4:1:pp. 17-21.

Native American/ Protest Actions/ Feminism/ Lesbians/ Social Movements/ Women of Color/ Environmental Movement

1125 **Russell, Scott C.**
McDonald, Mark B. (1982) "The Economic Contributions of Women in a Rural Western Navajo Community." American Indian Quarterly 6(Fall/Winter):3-4:pp. 262-282.

Women of Color/ Race, Class and Gender Studies/ Native American/ Navajo/ Economic Value of Women's Work/ Economic Factors/ Arts and Crafts Movement/ Sex Roles/ Women's Roles/ Rural Areas/ West

1126 Seggerman, Victoria
(1986) "Navajo Women and the Resistance to Relocation." Off Our Backs 16(March):pp. 8-10.

Native American/ Navajo/ Resistance/ Politics/ History/ Relocation/ Women of Color/ Power/ Powerless/ Liberation Struggles

Southern

1127 Anderson, John Ryan
(1986) "American Women and Conservative Religion in Post-War Decades: Southern Baptist on Mormon Women's Magazines, 1945-1975." Dissertation: Washington State University, Pullman, WA.

South/ Religion/ History/ 1940-1949/ 1950-1959/ 1960-1969/ Print Media/ Women's Magazines/ Entertainment/ Social Movements

1128 Belknap, Michal R.
(1987) Federal Law and Southern Order: Racial Violence and Constitutional Conflict in Post-Brown South. Athens, GA: University of Georgia Press.

People of Color/ South/ African Americans/ History/ 1960-1969/ Violence/ Federal Legislation/ Race Relations/ Racial Discrimination/ Desegregation/ Social Movements

1129 Breen, William J.
(1978) "Southern Women in the War: The North Carolina Woman's Committee, 1917-1919." North Carolina Historical Review 55(July):3:pp. 251-281.

South/ World War I/ North Carolina/ Social Movements/ History/ 1910-1919/ Women's Roles

1130 Bryan, Louis C.
(1986) "Modjeska A. Simkins: Profile of a Legend." SAGE: A Scholarly Journal on Black Women 3(Spring):1:pp. 56-57.

Women of Color/ South/ African American/ Biographies/ Human Rights/ Modjeska Simkins/ Political Activism/ Political Power/ Elected Officials

1131 Bryan, Violet Harrington
(1986) "Frances Joseph-Gaudet: Black Philanthropist." SAGE: A Scholarly Journal on Black Women 3(Spring):1:pp. 46-49.

Women of Color/ African American/ Biographies/ History/ South/ Philanthropists/ Reformers/ Social Movements/ Frances Joseph-Gaudet

1132 Bulkin, Elly
Minnie Bruce Pratt and Barbara Smith. (1984) Yours In Struggle--Three Feminist Perspectives on Anti-Semitism and Racism. Ithaca, NY: Firebrand Books. pp. 240. ISBN 0932379532.

Women of Color/ Religious Factors/ African American/ Religion/ Southern/ Feminist Perspective/ Racial Discrimination/ Liberation Struggles/ Jews

1133 Callahan, Nancy
(1987) The Freedom Quilting Bee. Tuscaloosa, AL: University of Alabama Press. pp. 253.

Women of Color/ African American/ Women Living in Poverty/ South/ Alabama/ Rural Areas/ Biographies/ Quilting/ Craft Arts/ Civil Rights Movement/ Cooperatives/ Self Help/ Advocacy Groups

1134 Cameron, Cindia

(1988) "Issues and Strategies for Organizing in the Service Economy: Women Office Workers and 9 to 5 in the South." Presented: Society for the Study of Social Problems Annual Meeting, Atlanta, GA.

Labor Force Participation/ Organizing/ Unions/ Economy/ Social Movements/ Work Hours/ Employment Schedules/ Service Occupations/ South/ Office Work/ Employment

1135 Carter, Deborah

(1988) "The Local Labor Union as a Social Movement Organization: Local 282, Furniture Division, IUE; 1943-1988." Dissertation: Vanderbilt University, Nashville, TN.

African American/ Employee Benefits/ Women of Color/ Wage Gap/ Pay Equity/ South/ Labor Unions/ Labor Force/ Employment/ Labor History/ Economically Disadvantaged/ Social Movements/ Gender Roles/ Furniture/ Manufacturing Industry

1136 Cecelski, David

(1988) "Flowers in the Desert Die." Southern Exposure 16(Winter):4:pp. 8-9.

South/ Migration/ Central America/ Latinos/ Immigration/ Public Policy/ People of Color/ Liberation Struggles

1137 Clinton, Catherine

(1987) "Fanny Kemble's Journal: A Woman Confronts Slavery on a Georgia Plantation." Frontiers: A Journal of Women Studies 9:3:pp. 74-79.

Women of Color/ South/ Testimonial Literature/ Biographies/ Slavery/ Women's History/ 19th Century/ Plantations/ Georgia/ Social Movements

1138 Colby, Ira C.

(1985) "The Freedmen's Bureau: From Social Welfare to Segregation." Phylon 46(Sept):pp. 219-230.

Social Welfare/ Social History/ 19th Century/ Segregation/ Freedmen/ South/ People of Color/ African Americans/ Liberation Struggles

1139 Cornfield, Daniel B.

(1988) "Household, Work, and Labor Activism: Gender Differences in the Determinants of Union Membership Participation." Presented: American Sociological Association, Atlanta, GA.

World War II/ Domestic Labor/ South/ Tennessee/ Gender Differences/ Women's Movement/ Organizing/ Unions/ Labor Force Participation/ Employment/ Labor Unions/ Women's History/ Social Movements

1140 Dedman, Bill

(1988) "The Color of Money." Southern Exposure 16(Winter): 4:pp. 56-59.

People of Color/ Housing/ Mortgages/ Economy/ Real Estate/ Neighborhoods/ Economic Power/ South/ Georgia/ Money/ Banks/ Redlining/ Discrimination/ African Americans/ Liberation Struggles

1141 Fairclough, Adam

(1987) To Redeem the Soul of America: The Southern Christian Leadership Conference and Martin Luther King, Jr. Athens, GA: University of Georgia Press.

People of Color/ Racial Discrimination/ African Americans/ Social Movements/ Civil Rights Movement/ Religion/ South/ Racial Equality/ Nonviolence/ Protest Actions

1142 Friedman, Belinda Bundy

(1981) "Orie Latham Hatcher and the Southern Woman's Educational Alliance." Dissertation: Duke University, Durham, NC. DAI Vol. 42(11A)4702.

Southern/ Social Movements/ Educational Reform/ Leadership/ Change Agents/ Orie Latham Hatcher

1143   Hughes, C. Alvin
(1987) "We Demand Our Rights: The Southern Negro Youth Congress, 1937-1949.
Phylon 48(March):pp. 38-50.

People of Color/ Racial Equality/ African Americans/ Liberation Struggles/ South/ 20th Century/ Equal
Rights/ Civil Rights

1144   Jacobs, Claude F.
(1988) "Benevolent Societies of New Orleans Blacks during the Late Nineteenth
and Early Twentieth Century." Louisiana History 29(Winter):pp. 21-33.

People of Color/ 20th Century/ African Americans/ Louisiana/ South/ Societies/ Organizations/ 19th
Century/ History/ Voluntary Organizations/ Social Movements

1145   Jemison, Marie Stokes
(1979) "Ladies Become Voters: Pattie Ruffner Jacobs and Women's Suffrage in
Alabama." Southern Exposure 7:1:pp. 48-59.

Social History/ Alabama/ South/ Suffrage/ Social Movements/ Biographies/ Pattie Ruffner Jacobs/
Voting Behavior/ Women's History

1146   Kett, Joseph F.
(1985) "Women and the Progressive Impulse in Southern Education." in The Web of
Southern Social Relations: Women, Family and Education. Walter J. Fraser, Jr. et
al. (eds.). Athens, GA: University of Georgia Press. pp. 166-180.

South/ Education/ Reform Movement/ Educational Reform/ Technical Schools/ Social Structure/ Rural
Living

1147   King, Mary
(1988) Freedom Song. New York: Quill Publishers (William Morrow Co.). pp. 592.
ISBN 0688082513.

African Americans/ Class Differences/ History/ Civil Rights Movement/ 1960-1969/ Social History/
20th Century/ South/ People of Color/ Discrimination/ Social Change

1148   Manis, Andrew Michael
(1987) Southern Civil Religions in Conflict: Black and White Baptists and Civil
Rights, 1947-1957. Athens, GA: University of Georgia Press.

People of Color/ Race Relations/ African Americans/ South/ 1950-1959/ Civil Rights Movement/
History/ 1940-1949/ Comparative Studies/ European Americans/ Social Conflict/ Religion/ Churches

1149   Mohr, Clarence L.
(1987) On the Threshold of Freedom: Masters and Slaves in Civil War Georgia.
Athens, GA: University of Georgia Press.

People of Color/ South/ Georgia/ African Americans/ History/ 19th Century/ Slavery/ Slaves/ Civil
War/ European Americans/ Relationships/ Liberation Struggles

1150   Neverdon-Morton, Cynthia
(1978) "The Black Woman's Struggle for Equality in the South." in The Afro-
American Woman: Struggles and Images. Sharon Harley and Rosalyn Terborg-Penn.
Port Washington, NY: Kennikat Press.

African American/ South/ Equality/ Women of Color/ Women's Movement/ Social Movements/
Liberation Struggles

1151   Richardson, Joe M.
(1987) Christian Reconstruction: The American Missionary Association and

Southern Blacks, 1861-1890. Athens, GA: University of Georgia Press.

People of Color/ Civil War/ African Americans/ History/ 19th Century/ South/ Slavery/ Reconstruction/ Missionary Societies/ Social Movements

1152   **Roydhouse, Marion W.**
(1987) "Universal Sisterhood: Women and Reform in North Carolina, 1900-1940."
Author: Philadelphia College of Textile and Science, Department of Humanities and Social Science, School House Lane and Henry Avenue, Philadelphia, PA 19144.

Southern/ Sisterhood/ History/ 20th Century/ North Carolina

1153   **Sacks, Karen Brodkin**
(1988) <u>Caring by the Hour: Woman, Work, and Organizing at Duke Medical Center</u>. Urbana, IL: University of Illinois.Press pp. 239.

Women of Color/ Collective Bargaining/ African American/ Health Care Facilities/ South/ North Carolina/ Income/ Health Care Workers/ Employment/ Labor Unions/ Cultural Identity

1154   **Schwarz, Philip J.**
(1988) <u>Twice Condemned: Slaves and the Criminal Laws of Virginia, 1705-1865</u>. Baton Rouge, LA: Louisiana State University Press.

People of Color/ South/ Virginia/ African Americans/ Slavery/ 18th Century/ Slaves/ 19th Century/ Rebellion/ Resistance/ Crime/ Laws/ Liberation Struggles

1155   **Sherman, Richard B.**
(1988) "'The Last Stand': The Fight for Racial Integrity in Virginia in the 1920's." <u>Journal of Southern History</u> 54(Feb): pp. 69-92.

People of Color/ Race Relations/ African Americans/ Racial Equality/ Virginia/ South/ History/ 1920-1929/ Integrity/ Social Reform/ Social Change/ Political Activism

1156   **Taylor, A. Elizabeth**
(1987) <u>Citizens at Last! The Women Suffrage Movement in Texas</u>. Ellen C. Temple, Austin, TX. Distributed by: Texas Monthly, P.O. Box 1569, Austin, TX 78767.

Women's History/ Texas/ Suffrage Movement/ South West/ 20th Century/ Social Movements

1157   **Tobin, Gary A.**
(1987) <u>Divided Neighborhoods - Changing Patterns of Racial Segregation</u>. Newbury Park, CA: Sage Publications. pp. 288.

South/ Discrimination/ People of Color*/ Segregation/ Housing/ Segregated Housing/ Liberation Struggles

1158   **Williamson, Joel**
(1984) <u>The Crucible of Race: Black-White Relations in the American South Since Emancipation</u>. New York: Oxford University Press. pp. 561.

South/ Race Relations/ Social History/ 19th Century/ 20th Century/ Status/ Civil Rights/ Liberation Struggles/ Social Movements

1159   **Wolfe, Margaret Ripley**
(1987) "Twentieth-Century Feminism: Southern Styles." <u>Helicon Nine: Journal of Women's Arts and Letters</u> (Spring):17-18:pp. 148-157.

South/ Feminism/ Women's Movement/ Cultural Feminism/ Cultural Influences/ Women's History/ 20th Century

*Women of Color**

1160 **Ach, William K.**
(1987) "Sources for the Study of Civil Rights." <u>Microform Review</u> 16(Fall):pp. 316-328.

People of Color*/ Civil Rights Movement/ Bibliographies/ Research Resources

1161 **Andolsen, Barbara Hilkert**
Gudorf, Christine E. and Pellhauer, Mary. (1988) <u>Women's Consciousness, Women's Conscience: A Reader in Feminist Ethics</u>. New York: Harper and Row. pp. 336. ISBN 0062541021.

Women's Studies/ Women of Color*/ Religion/ Domestic Violence/ Feminist Ethics/ Economics/ Reproduction/ Social Values/ Social Movements

1162 **Bandarage, Asoka**
(1986) "Women of Color: Towards a Celebration of Power." <u>Woman of Power</u> (Fall):4:pp. 8-14.

Women of Color*/ Women's Movement/ Woman Power/ Women's History/ Political Power/ Federal Government/ Sex Discrimination/ Women Living in Poverty/ Racial Discrimination/ Sexual Exploitation/ Patriarchy

1163 **Boneparth, Ellen**
Stoper, Emily (eds.). (1988) <u>Women, Power, and Policy: Toward the Year 2000</u> (2nd Edition). Elmsford, NY: Pergamon Press. pp. 340.

Women of Color*/ Policy Making/ Power/ Social Policy/ Women's Rights/ Social Issues/ Reagan Administration/ Women's Movement/ Anthologies/ Work Experience/ Feminism/ Child Care/ Reproduction

1164 **Bullough, Vern L.**
Shelton, Brenda et al. (1988) <u>The Subordinated Sex: A History of Attitudes Toward Women</u>. Athens, GA: University of Georgia Press.

Women of Color*/ Inequality/ Women's History/ Oppression/ Attitudes/ Women's Roles/ Sex Discrimination/ Social Movements

1165 **Clark, Judith Freeman**
(1987) <u>Almanac of American Women in the 20th Century</u>. New York: Prentice Hall. pp. 274.

Women of Color*/ Women's History/ 20th Century/ Biographies/ Research Resources/ Social Movements

1166 **Ferrero, Pat**
Hedges, Elaine and Silber J. (1987) <u>Hearts and Hands: The Influence of Women and Quilts on American Society</u>. San Francisco: Quilt Digest Press. pp. 112.

Women of Color*/ Abolition/ Women's History/ 19th Century/ Women's Roles/ Craft Arts/ Women's Culture/ Social Movements/ Social Influences/ Suffrage Movement/ Civil War

1167 **Gardner, Tracey A.**
(1980) "Racism in Pornography and the Women's Movement." in <u>Take Back the Night: Women and Pornography</u>. Laura Lederer (ed.). New York: William Morrow. pp. 105-114.

Women of Color*/ Racial Discrimination/ Women's Movement/ Social Movements/ Pornography/ Images of Women

1168 Garland, Anne Witte
(1988) <u>Women Activists: Challenging the Abuse of Power</u>. New York: The Feminist Press. pp. 176. ISBN 093531279x.

Women of Color*/ Political Activists/ 20th Century/ History/ Social Movements/ Activism/ Reformers/ Abuse/ Power

1169 Gluck, Sherna Berger
(1985) <u>From Parlor to Prison: Five American Suffragists Talk About Their Lives</u>. New York: Monthly Review Press. pp. 320.

Women of Color*/ Women's History/ Social Movements/ Suffrage Movement/ Suffragists/ Oral History/ Political Activists

1170 Gornick, Vivian
Moran, Barbra K. (eds.). (1988) <u>Women in Sexist Society: Studies in Power and Powerlessness</u>. New York: Mentor. pp. 736. ISBN 0451624599

Women's Studies/ Education/ Feminist Scholarship/ Women's Movement/ Sex Discrimination/ Anthropology/ Discrimination/ Power/ Powerlessness/ Women of Color*

1171 Groneman, Carol
Norton, Mary Beth (eds.). (1986) <u>To Toil the Livelong Day: America's Women at Work, 1780-1980</u>. Ithaca, NY: Cornell University Press. pp. 320.

Women of Color*/ Labor History/ Women's History/ Employment/ Working Class/ Political Activism/ Sexual Division of Labor/ Domestic Services/ Tobacco Industry/ Farm Workers/ Slavery/ Industrial Revolution/ Race, Class and Gender Studies

1172 Hartmann, Betsy
(1988) <u>Reproductive Rights and Wrongs: The Global Politics of Population Control and Contraceptive Choice</u>. New York: Harper and Row. pp. 352. ISBN 0060550651.

Contraception/ Population Control/ Women of Color*/ Politics/ Reproductive Rights/ Social Movements

1173 Higginbotham, Elizabeth
(1986) "We Were Never on a Pedestal: Women of Color Continue to Struggle with Poverty, Racism and Sexism." in <u>For Crying Out Loud: Women and Poverty in the United States</u>. Ann Withorn and Rochelle Lefkowitz. New York: Pilgrim's Press. pp. 99-110.

Triple Jeopardy/ Economically Disadvantaged/ Women of Color*/ Images of Women/ Poverty/ Sex Discrimination/ Racial Discrimination/ Race, Class and Gender Studies/ Social Change/ Social Movements

1174 Johnson, Elisabeth
(1986) "We are Women of Color First." <u>Women's Studies Quarterly</u> 14(Spring/Summer):1-2:pp. 19-20.

Women of Color*/ Women Living in Poverty/ Feminist Movement/ Feminist Theory/ Socioeconomic Status/ Race, Class and Gender Studies/ Women's Studies/ Curriculum Integration/ Education

1175 Kirp, David L.
Yudof, Mark G. and Franks, Marlene S. (1986) <u>Gender Justice</u>. Chicago: University of Chicago Press. pp. 246. ISBN 0226437620.

Women of Color*/ Gender/ Justice/ Social Policy/ Policy Making/ Sexual Equality/ Inequality/ Social Movements/

1176 Lasser, Carol
Merrill, Marlene Deahl. (1987) <u>Friends and Sisters: Letters between Lucy Stone and Antoinette Brown Blackwell, 1846-1893</u>. Urbana, IL: University of Illinois Press.

pp. 278.

Women of Color*/ Women's Rights/ Sisterhood/ Friendship/ Women's Movement/ Women's History/ 19th Century/ Suffragists/ Feminists/ Abolition/ Letters/ Suffrage Movement/ Lucy Stone/ Antoinette Brown Blackwell

1177 Lorde, Audre
(1987) "Age, Race, Class and Sex: Women Redefining Difference." in Racism and Sexism. Paula S. Rothenberg. New York: St. Martin's Press.

Women of Color*/ Double Bind/ Race, Class and Gender Studies/ Triple Jeopardy/ Age Discrimination/ Sex Discrimination/ Racial Discrimination/ Comparative Studies/ Social Movements

1178 Lunardini, Christine A.
(1986) From Equal Suffrage to Equal Rights: Alice Paul and the National Woman's Party. New York: New York University Press. pp. 230.

Women of Color*/ Women's History/ Suffrage/ Suffragists/ Equal Rights/ Alice Paul/ Activists/ Suffrage Movement/ Women's Rights/ Feminism

1179 McCluskey, Audrey T.
(1985) Women of Color: Perspectives on Feminism and Identity. Bloomington, IN: Indiana University Press. pp. 177.

Women of Color*/ Feminism/ Gender Identity/ Cultural Identity/ Black Feminism/ Social Movements

1180 Naples, Nancy A.
(1987) "The Importance of Community for Women Workers in Anti-Poverty Programs, 1964-1984." Author: State University of New York, Division of Social Sciences, Purchase, NY 10577. Presented: American Sociological Association, Chicago, IL.

Women of Color*/ Community Organizers/ Poverty/ Race, Class and Gender Studies/ Networks/ Support Systems/ Low Income Households/ Advocacy Groups/ Social Movements

1181 Naples, Nancy A.
(1988) "The Political Participation of Female Community Workers From Low Income Communities." Presented: Society for the Study of Social Problems, Annual Meeting, Atlanta, GA.

Welfare/ Income/ Political Participation/ Low Income Households/ Political Activity/ Women of Color*/ Community/ Community Responsibility

1182 Peterson, Barbara Bennet
(1984) Notable Women of Hawaii. Honolulu, HI: University of Hawaii Press. pp. 427.

Women of Color*/ Hawaii/ Pacific/ Biographies/ Leadership/ Activists

1183 Rollins, Judith
(1986) "Part of a Whole: The Interdependence of the Civil Rights Movement with Other Social Movements." Phylon 47(March):1.

People of Color*/ Social Change/ Civil Rights Movement/ Protest Actions/ Social Movements/ Political Activity

AUTHOR INDEX

KEYWORD INDEX

Central American(s) - 127, 204, 530, 1104, 1105, 1108, 1136
Ceremonies - 153, 182, 961
Change - 168, 410, 683, 982, 1006
Change Agents - 312, 384, 390, 1142
Chicana - 25, 110, 111, 113, 115, 123, 125, 128, 133, 138, 139, 142, 342, 348, 351, 354, 355, 357, 361, 363, 365, 524, 526, 535, 547, 549, 550, 555, 557, 558, 559, 560, 561, 562, 563, 565, 566, 571, 573, 634, 802, 803, 810, 818. 914, 936, 939, 940, 946, 1102, 1111, 1113, 1115, 1117
Chicanos - 121, 141, 146, 795, 1116
Child Abuse - 33, 46, 715, 723, 864
Child Care - 414, 481, 631, 666, 680, 747, 858, 869, 876, 885, 993, 1163
Child Development - 173, 348, 724, 744, 760, 803, 887, 910
Child Rearing Practices - 167, 170, 343, 527, 699, 757, 787, 823, 826
Childbearing - 223, 424, 758, 790, 791, 807, 825, 865, 947, 963, 975, 994
Childbirth - 173, 791, 798, 803, 807, 827, 939, 966, 967, 978, 1002
Childbirth Training - 714, 901
Children - 218, 307, 337, 360, 520, 597, 752, 782, 788, 809,   811, 844, 879, 900, 934, 949, 952, 971
Chinese - 93, 100, 779, 1096
Chinese American - 95, 519, 1096, 1099, 1100
Churches - 15, 41, 190, 200, 236, 268, 696, 1037, 1060, 1062, 1083, 1090, 1148
Civil Rights - 277, 318, 355, 391, 494, 496, 928, 1033, 1036, 1047, 1065, 1115, 1119, 1143, 1158
Civil Rights Movement - 276, 301, 304, 1009, 1012, 1014, 1017, 1021, 1029, 1035, 1043, 1055, 1056, 1060, 1061, 1066, 1068, 1075, 1133, 1141, 1147, 1148, 1160, 1183
Civil War - 1, 228, 246, 477, 836, 841, 836, 841, 1063, 1073, 1149, 1151, 1166
Class - 27, 174, 193, 297, 474, 479
Class Consciousness - 303, 580, 1058
Class Differences - 4, 193, 303, 365, 399, 1055, 1058, 1147
Clerical Occupations - 669, 995
Club(s)- 96, 490, 1015, 1068
Coitus - 21, 82, 322
Collective Bargaining - 614, 1153
Colleges - 266, 273, 274, 299, 302, 304, 326, 421, 457, 1061
Colombian - 545, 802
Colorado - 116, 529, 561
Communication - 75, 84
Community - 5, 7, 41, 109, 117, 136, 149, 510, 595, 610, 662, 781, 815, 816, 819, 871, 923, 1039, 1090, 1180, 1181
Community Health Services - 482, 898, 911, 920, 948

Community Relations - 344, 528, 789
Competitive Behavior - 272, 431, 1003
Computer(s)- 300, 347, 518, 539, 581
Conflict Resolution - 216, 732, 852, 989
Consciousness Raising - 75, 146, 407, 697, 1093, 1095, 1116
Contraception - 543, 790, 800, 825, 961, 963, 1172
Cooperatives - 1021, 1133
Coping Strategies - 74, 132, 399, 415, 486, 545, 634, 669, 721, 743, 745, 751, 758, 802, 804, 807, 809, 811, 845, 892, 921, 922, 931, 947, 949, 951, 952, 995
Correctional Facilities - 25, 115, 219, 725, 813, 979, 1007
Correctional Rehabilitation - 775, 1080
Cost of Living - 843, 861
Counseling - 663, 683, 732, 872, 984, 989, 1006
Course Objectives - 270, 315, 434
Court(s) - 494, 665, 666, 759, 876
Craft Art - 94, 154, 179, 228, 426, 1133, 1166
Creoles - 210
Crime - 240, 345, 487, 629, 713, 985, 1044, 1078, 1154
Criminal Justice - 225, 399, 629, 775, 813, 1080
Criminals - 219, 240, 629, 725
Crisis Intervention - 683, 1006
Crosscultural Studies - 116, 148, 161, 168, 258, 529, 629, 801, 886, 957, 1008
Cuban(s) - 118, 567, 792
Cult of True Womanhood - 177, 208, 209
Cultural Groups - 83, 116, 222, 323, 529
Cultural Heritage - 12, 16, 31, 40, 50, 57, 71, 80, 84, 88, 89, 94, 95, 104, 111, 118, 123, 137, 145, 147, 152, 153, 154, 155, 157, 163, 166, 167, 177, 186, 188, 199, 208, 226, 229, 342, 365, 375, 792, 856, 925, 960, 962, 1086, 1120
Cultural Identity - 29, 40, 44, 55, 57, 71, 82, 86, 88, 93, 97, 98, 103, 104, 105, 110, 120, 127, 137, 155, 169, 186, 194, 195, 199, 215, 237, 244, 246, 250, 425, 526, 614, 657, 847, 932, 967, 973, 988, 991, 992, 1051, 1095, 1123, 1153, 1179
Cultural Influences - 2, 6, 8, 9, 14, 21, 25, 32, 36, 41, 42, 58, 62, 67, 74, 76, 84, 87, 90, 91, 100, 102, 107, 115, 117, 122, 128, 129, 130, 131, 134, 141, 148, 151, 159, 165, 168, 169, 173, 179, 184, 187, 210, 217, 233, 235, 238, 241, 243, 246, 248, 322, 339, 348, 386, 694, 695, 697, 779, 803, 823, 852, 863, 916,

921, 924, 925, 930, 933, 941, 943, 944, 945, 957, 967, 988, 991, 992, 1110, 1123, 1159
Culture Conflict - 33, 40, 97, 104, 155, 187, 199, 237, 715
Culture Heritage - 12, 16, 50, 92, 178, 179, 180, 181, 183, 375, 831
Curriculum Integration - 48, 49, 86, 215, 267, 268, 270, 290, 297, 306, 315, 319, 334, 335, 336, 354, 361, 367, 368, 370, 397, 398, 405, 409, 410, 411, 422, 423, 427, 428, 429, 434, 435, 442, 982, 999, 1113, 1114, 1174
Customs - 163, 178, 182, 183, 201, 211, 375, 386, 831

D

Dating - 22, 191
Death - 976, 1108
Decision Making - 317, 495
Delinquent Behavior - 345, 725, 781, 985
Demography - 20, 65, 86, 124, 215, 307, 424, 530, 540, 655, 659, 699, 750, 762, 795, 799, 848, 865, 870, 942, 997, 1105
Depression - 105, 894, 903, 932, 950, 955, 956, 986
Desegregation - 303, 404, 1011, 1058, 1128
Deviant Behavior - 219, 481, 629, 630, 836, 888, 899, 912, 969, 974
Diagnoses - 220, 980, 990
Diet(s) - 9, 168, 187
Dine' - 169, 1123
Disabilities - 165, 811, 823, 952
Disadvantaged - 218, 225, 264, 494, 664, 674, 735, 890, 897, 903, 909, 918, , 975, 987, 994
Discrimination - 111, 116, 121, 232, 264, 297, 304, 342, 346, 365, 399, 401, 402, 417, 418, 422, 470, 484, 529, 536, 600, 605, 651, 677, 853, 881, 889, 975, 994, 996, 1030, 1031, 1054, 1055, 1061, 1103, 1147, 1157, 1177
Diseases - 891, 913, 914, 970
Diversity - 224, 279, 405, 988
Division of Labor - 504, 518, 539, 597, 618, 665, 821, 844
Divorce - 701, 732, 866, 896, 989
Domestic Roles - 546, 716
Domestic Services - 449, 451, 503, 504, 511, 517, 557, 558, 560, 561, 562, 563, 591, 618, 648, 1092, 1171
Domestic Violence - 793, 1161
Dominance - 513, 716, 834, 835
Dominant Culture - 22, 80, 191, 259, 405, 686, 1086
Double Bind - 99, 233, 296, 400, 484, 801, 1054, 1177
Drinking - 912, 940, 974
Drug(s) - 25, 79, 115, 399, 909, 936, 940, 959, 979, 989, 1007

G

Gender - 102, 300, 347, 393, 394, 638, 645, 930, 1175
Gender Differences - 593, 1139
Gender Identity - 244, 1179
Gender Roles - 44, 87, 110, 120, 184, 200, 227, 236, 238, 245, 282, 397, 526, 562, 592, 608, 659, 697, 720, 850, 852, 870, 881, 904, 996, 1023, 1135
Georgia - 40, 199, 468, 582, 589, 599, 615, 753, 833, 846, 1031, 1063, 1137, 1140, 1149
Gerontology - 745, 917
Government - 632, 987, 1108
Graduate Degrees - 261, 301, 330, 354, 366, 1056
Graduate Education - 330, 354, 366, 415
Grandparents - 730, 738
Group(s) - 392, 430, 983, 1041

H

Hawaii - 513, 515, 520, 777, 782, 931, 1182
Heads of Household - 344, 464, 525, 528, 735, 786, 789
Health Care - 74, 173, 241, 255, 441, 744, 756, 827, 891, 893, 898, 910, 913, 915, 918, 919, 920, 921, 937, 938, 948, 958, 966, 967, 970, 987, 991, 1005
Health Care Costs - 107, 933, 942
Health Care Delivery - 67, 90, 102, 264, 776, 890, 891, 897, 916, 924, 926, 928, 930, 970, 975, 994, 998
Health Care Facilities - 264, 614, 890, 929, 977, 978, 998, 1153
Health Care Occupations - 292, 473, 482, 604. 681, 908, 911, 972, 1004
Health Care Professionals - 223, 681, 1004
Health Care Providers - 76, 102, 122, 130, 167, 212, 604, 930, 939, 941, 944, 962
Health Care Services - 107, 258, 264, 800, 807, 880, 884, 886, 891, 890, 933, 947, 970, 976, 978, 996, 1002, 1008
Health Care Utilization - 897, 918, 987
Health Care Workers - 482, 543, 607, 614, 681, 800, 911, 1004, 1153
Health Education - 264, 890, 914, 978
Health Hazards - 443, 583, 636, 898, 981
Health Seeking Behavior - 90, 91, 122, 131, 205, 785, 914, 924, 925, 929, 934, 938, 941, 945, 946, 958, 973
Help Seeking Behavior - 74, 237, 770, 921, 983
High Schools - 294, 298, 300, 347, 349, 388

Higher Education - 22, 191, 221, 234, 265, 266, 273, 274, 276, 277, 291, 293, 297, 299, 301, 302, 304, 311, 324, 326, 328, 330, 333, 336, 341, 346, 352, 354, 366, 381, 385, 387, 392, 395, 397, 398, 402, 405, 406, 409, 411, 415, 416, 419, 421, 422, 427, 429, 430, 435, 457, 495, 497, 505, 646, 720, 904, 999, 1056, 1061
Home Birth - 884, 1002
Home Life - 149, 356, 611, 663, 693, 713, 729, 731, 745, 761, 763, 764, 766, 812, 819, 832, 837, 849, 854, 872, 875, 883
Home Remedies - 74, 131, 205, 921, 945, 973
Household Division of Labor - 110, 256, 526, 608
Household Labor - 116, 511, 517, 562, 563, 582, 718, 833, 839, 1092
Household Workers - 449, 478, 503, 504, 516, 529, 546, 557, 558, 561, 562, 588, 618
Households - 662, 717, 753, 824, 846, 871
Housing - 66, 666, 700, 740, 876, 1031, 1140
Human Rights - 391, 433, 1018, 1065, 1119, 1130

I

Identity - 2, 32, 222, 246, 248, 254, 724, 1098
Illegal Immigrants - 132, 344, 528, 530, 635, 789, 804, 1105
Illinois - 247, 289, 308, 446, 703, 1009, 1072
Illness - 90, 91, 255, 776, 892, 894, 895, 898, 913, 914, 924, 925, 926, 946, 997, 1005
Images of Women - 10, 11, 18, 29, 32, 42, 43, 45, 53, 54, 55, 64, 73, 76, 77, 78, 81, 96, 98, 113, 117, 119, 125, 133, 175, 181, 194, 209, 213, 256, 270, 315, 449, 478, 501, 526, 548, 572, 581, 615, 617, 630, 661, 675, 684, 690, 716, 731, 817, 850, 875, 883, 905, 1048, 1051, 1084, 1097, 1167, 1173
Immigrants - 20, 92, 94, 95, 96, 97, 107, 108, 118, 124, 137, 252, 254, 257, 478, 513, 518, 530, 533, 534, 537, 538, 539, 543, 545, 546, 552, 567, 588, 637, 777, 779, 780, 784, 792, 794, 796, 797, 800, 802, 806, 834, 841, 929, 940, 933, 935, 938, 953, 954, 955, 956, 1100, 1105
Immigration _ 106, 124, 127, 204, 950, 1096, 1104, 1136
Incarceration - 775, 1080
Income - 225, 269, 450, 520, 582, 614, 625, 633, 644, 658, 735, 782, 833, 847, 857, 1153, 1181
Income Distribution - 300, 347, 472,

602, 869, 993
Indiana - 289
Industrial Revolution - 648, 1171
Industrialization - 471, 483, 601
Industries - 501, 613, 617, 647
Inequality - 89, 227, 304, 341, 365, 438, 472, 602, 621, 642, 651, 677, 1016, 1033, 1061, 1164, 1175
Infant Mortality - 444, 586, 900, 971, 976, 978
Inner City - 79, 739
Institutional Discrimination - 31, 439, 494, 666, 876
Institutional Racism - 54, 55, 297, 333, 1051
Institutional Sexism - 297, 333
Integration - 34, 250, 279, 1045
Interpersonal Relationships - 731
Interracial Relations - 56, 242, 415, 476, 503, 603, 1027
Iowa - 1121

J

Japanese - 776, 1096
Japanese American - 89, 93, 103, 104, 337, 516, 517, 926, 931, 932
Jazz - 13, 189
Jews - 448, 1020, 1132
Job Discrimination - 413, 433, 436, 464, 579, 620, 621, 640, 642, 652, 676, 677,682
Job Performance - 597, 844
Job Segregation - 656, 673
Job Training - 291, 318, 387, 496, 501, 615, 617, 656, 664
Juvenile Justice System - 345, 725, 781

K

Kansas - 1015
Kentucky - 131, 205, 597, 607, 844, 945, 973
Kinship - 154, 160, 183, 253, 344, 528, 574, 708, 711, 712, 722, 743, 756, 789, 821, 831, 845, 919
Korean - 92, 104, 513, 780

L

Labor Disputes - 436, 461, 490, 579, 580, 594, 607, 612
Labor Force - 414, 454, 456, 459, 464, 478, 500, 513, 520, 524, 531, 533, 535, 536, 544, 546, 550, 552, 553, 554, 555, 560, 565, 566, 588, 621, 626, 633, 641, 650, 653, 654, 661, 677, 782, 1023, 1135
Labor Force Participation - 282, 344, 416, 470, 474, 499, 528, 581, 585, 593, 595, 600, 613, 615, 620, 624, 635, 645, 646, 647, 661, 662, 684, 720, 789, 858, 859, 871, 874, 904. 1134, 1139
Labor Force Statistics - 475, 736
Labor History - 460, 471, 483, 500,

118, 164, 358, 584, 792, 1075, 1137

Texas - 5, 109, 196, 204, 385, 445, 530, 549, 570, 571, 588, 598, 635, 641, 843, 861, 983, 1091, 1105, 1108, 1117, 1156

Textile Industry - 94, 443, 531, 577, 583, 584, 610, 612, 891, 970

Theater - 18, 19, 134, 158, 1110

Therapy - 888, 969, 988

Time Management - 634, 1039

Tobacco Industry - 470, 471, 600, 601, 648, 1171

Trades - 501, 640, 658, 676

Traditional Family - 513, 537, 781, 796, 835

Traditional Roles - 597, 737, 844

Traditions - 16, 24, 57, 109, 150, 163, 166, 167, 178, 179, 182, 183, 192, 375, 831, 962

Treatment - 115, 889, 899, 920, 948, 959, 985, 988, 989

Triple Jeopardy - 297, 327, 473, 907, 1173, 1177

U

Unemployment - 615, 672, 675, 698, 869, 880, 895, 937, 993

Union Membership - 550, 551, 552, 612

Unions - 531, 535, 547, 585, 593, 670, 810, 1112, 1134, 1139

Universities - 263, 273, 302, 304, 311, 405, 457, 1061

Upper Class - 39, 198, 705, 752

Urban - 79, 92, 96, 160, 332, 421, 468, 472, 510, 512, 534, 558, 598, 99, 602, 615, 705, 708, 739, 740, 794, 822, 917, 923, 984, 986

V

Verbal Communication - 149, 433, 688, 819

Veterans - 622, 687

Victimizaion - 881, 996

Vietnamese - 91, 96, 925

Violence - 23, 240, 264, 1011, 1068, 1128

Violence Against Women - 713, 793

Virginia - 743, 759, 845, 900, 971, 1034, 1078, 1081, 1154, 1155

Vocational Education - 291, 332, 387, 512,

Voluntary Organizations - 552, 1015, 1030, 1042, 1050, 1068, 1144

Volunteer Work - 478, 510, 923

W

Wage Discrimination - 436, 447, 460, 461, 486, 579, 590, 594, 668, 751

Wage Earning Wives - 110, 475, 500, 526, 684, 736

Wage Gap - 269, 460, 508, 628, 637, 674, 678, 881, 882, 996, 1023, 1135

Wages - 269, 450, 452, 502, 580, 628, 678

Washington, DC - 263, 451, 591

Welfare - 326, 407, 664, 698, 853, 860, 867, 873, 874, 878, 976, 993, 998, 1028, 1070, 1138, 1181

Welfare Reform - 666, 876, 878

Wellness - 255, 895, 898, 925, 1005

West Virginia - 616

Widows - 486, 751, 764, 849, 875

Wisconsin - 855

Wives - 607, 633, 777, 950

Women in Transition - 149, 819

Women Living in Poverty - 58, 61, 203, 218, 272, 309, 423, 452, 487, 494, 616, 656, 666, 674, 765, 843, 861, 866, 867, 869, 876, 878, 882, 903, 942, 978, 989, 993, 1021, 1133, 1162, 1174

Women Owned Business - 447, 590

Women Working Outside the Home - 454, 624, 626, 662, 680, 684, 871, 885

Women's Groups - 281, 1015, 1026, 1068, 1093, 1106

Women's Language - 139, 149, 819

Women's Movement - 217, 418, 593, 631, 734, 1016, 1052, 1053, 1064, 1084, 1097, 1098, 1109, 1139, 1150, 1159, 1162, 1163, 1167, 1170, 1176

Women's Rights - 500, 631, 1030, 1031, 1163, 1176, 1178

Women's Roles - 42, 137, 150, 163, 171, 228, 329, 486, 501, 538, 546, 573, 574, 582, 592, 617, 627, 751, 772, 797, 818, 820, 833, 997, 1098, 1122, 1129, 1164, 1166

Work Attitudes - 332, 491, 512

Work Ethic - 332, 491, 507, 512

Work Experience - 325, 464, 468, 506, 544, 559, 599. 624, 626, 631, 661, 684, 1163

Working Class - 425, 463, 486, 490, 511, 517, 532, 563, 588, 595, 596, 608, 626, 648, 656, 664, 675, 726, 751, 834, 842, 995, 1092, 1171

World War I - 68, 453, 1129

World War II - 89, 103, 337, 501, 593, 617, 647, 1066, 1139

Writers - 1, 11, 12, 17, 19, 37, 50, 78, 98, 101, 188, 202, 212, 316, 338, 437, 734

Writing - 11, 12, 37, 77, 78, 98, 123, 188, 202, 212, 1052

Wyoming - 181

Y

Young Adults - 317, 495